RESHAPING GLOBAL VALUE CHAINS IN LIGHT OF COVID-19

RESHAPING GLOBAL VALUE CHAINS IN LIGHT OF COVID-19

Implications for Trade and Poverty Reduction in Developing Countries

Paul Brenton
Michael J. Ferrantino
Maryla Maliszewska

WORLD BANK GROUP

Contents

Foreword   *xi*
Acknowledgments   *xv*
About the Authors   *xvii*
Abbreviations   *xix*

Main Messages   1

Lessons from the COVID-19 pandemic for global value chains   1

Measures for managing a crisis and the recovery   2

Main policy messages   4

References   6

Chapter 1: Introduction and Overview   7

Experience from historical shocks   9

Scope and depth of the COVID-19 shock   9

Econometric evidence   11

Responses of firms and governments to supply chain shocks   12

Measures to maintain and enhance trade   13

Emerging climate change policies   14

Integration into the global economy and GVC participation remain key   15

Note   15

References   15

Chapter 2: Lessons from Historical Shocks to GVCs   17

Key messages   17

Introduction   18

GVCs and the impact of shocks on trade   19

Impacts at the intensive and the extensive margins   19

Export survival   21

Network analysis   23

Conclusions   26

Notes   28

References   28

Chapter 3: The COVID-19 Crisis and Trade Outcomes: A Review and Analysis of Major Trade Trends   31

Key messages   31

Introduction   32

Trends in trade and GDP   32

Short-term trade and GVC effects of the pandemic   52

Annex 3A Empirical strategy used to assess the short-term impact of COVID-19 on trade and GVCs   61

Notes   62

References   63

Chapter 4: Responses of Firms and Governments to Supply Chain Shocks Surrounding COVID-19   65

Key messages   65

Introduction   66

Traditional supply chain management and its limitations   66

Issues revealed by COVID-19   70

Firm-level adaptations in 2020   72

Private sector views of the transition   75

Government responses to supply chain issues during COVID-19   78

Issues with the recovery: Containers, semiconductors, and overlapping shocks   81

Notes   84

References   85

Chapter 5: The Key to COVID-19 Recovery and Poverty Alleviation: Globalization, Not Localization   89

Key messages   89

Introduction   90

Methodological framework and scenarios: Using data and tools to find answers   93

Scenarios: COVID-19, climate change, and protectionist shocks to GVCs   93

The risks of GVC reshoring   96

The distributional impacts of reshoring   102

Climate change mitigation policies: Reshaping the comparative advantages of countries   106

Annex 5A Regional and sectoral aggregations in computable general equilibrium analysis   119

Notes   120

References   121

Chapter 6: COVID-19 and the Reshaping of GVCs: Policy Messages for Resilient
Trade-Driven Development   125

Key messages   125

Introduction   126

Appropriate trade policy responses during a global crisis and in the recovery   126

Reviewing trade policies for better management of future shocks   129

Trade and development in a more uncertain world   136

Notes   140

References   141

Boxes

3.1   Vietnam's trade experience during the pandemic   46

3.2   Impact of the COVID-19 shock on the export performance of Cambodian firms   47

4.1   Global supply chain disruption in 2021: Causes, consequences, and solutions   83

6.1   Dos and don'ts of trade policy responses to a global crisis: The COVID-19
pandemic   127

Figures

1.1   Trade and poverty reduction in low- and middle-income countries, 1990–2017   8

1.2   Effects of COVID-19 lockdown policies on global value chains   10

3.1   Volume and type of trade and GDP, 2005–20   33

3.2   Monthly year-over-year change in the value of goods and services trade, 2019–21   34

3.3   Share of borders closed, by region, May 2020–February 2021   35

3.4   Number of commercial flights, by month, 2019–21   36

3.5   Value, volume, and price of merchandise trade   37

3.6   Merchandise trade of major trading countries, 2020 vs. 2019   39

3.7   Imports of China, EU-27, Japan, and the United States,
January 2019–February 2021   40

3.8   Contribution of the intensive and extensive margins to the year-over-year change in
global trade, 2019 and 2020   41

3.9   Contribution of the intensive and extensive margins to the year-over-year change in
global trade of low-income countries, 2019 and 2020   42

3.10   Propensity for lost and new trade flows at the extensive margin, 2019 and 2020   43

3.11   Propensity for lost imports of inputs from China and other countries, by country
income level, 2019 and 2020   45

B3.2.1 Average firm survival rate in Cambodia, by type and size of firm,
2016 Q1 to 2020 Q3   48

3.12   China's share of global merchandise exports, 2002–20   49

3.13   China's share of global exports, by product group, 2002–19   49

3.14   Change in the share of global exports, by country or region and sector, 2011–19   50

3.15   Shares of mirror exports to four economies (China, EU-27, Japan, and the
United States), by country and product group, 2019–20   51

3.16   Change in IPI and work mobility in exporting countries, February to June 2020   53

3.17   Change in IPI and export growth in exporting countries, February to June 2020   54

3.18   Change in IPI and import growth in partner countries, February to June 2020   55

3.19   A simplified framework of bilateral trade growth   56

3.20   Impact of demand, supply, and third-country COVID-19
         shocks on bilateral export growth   57

3.21   The impact of COVID-19 shocks on bilateral exports across sectors, 2020   58

3.22   The impact of COVID-19 shocks on bilateral exports through global
         value chain channels   60

5.1   Computable general equilibrium modeling scenarios   94

5.2   Change in real income in 2030 relative to 2019, by region and scenario   96

5.3   Real exports and real imports in 2030 relative to 2019, by region and scenario   97

5.4   Real income compared with COVID-19 L-shape recovery, by region and
         scenario, 2030   99

5.5   Distributional impacts, by region and scenario, 2010–30   104

5.6   Reduction in extreme poverty in the GVC-friendly liberalization and TF imports
         scenario relative to pre-COVID-19 conditions, by region   105

5.7   Change in income of the bottom 40 percent and top 60 percent of the income
         distribution relative to the COVID-19 L-shape recovery, by scenario and region   107

5.8   Wages for unskilled females relative to rest of wages, 2030, by
         scenario and region   108

5.9   Change in CO_2 emissions in 2030 relative to the pre-COVID-19 baseline:
         Impact of the COVID-19 pandemic and NDC targets, by region   109

5.10   Change in exports and imports due to the implementation of NDC policies, 2030
         relative to the post-COVID-19 baseline, by region   111

5.11   Impacts of the CBAM on total exports by EU trading partners and carbon intensity
         of exports to the EU: 2030 relative to the EU Green Deal implementation scenario,
         by region   112

5.12   Impacts of the EU Green Deal and CBAM on output in the EU: 2030 relative to the
         scenario with NDCs, by sector   113

5.13   Impacts of the EU Green Deal and CBAM on EU imports, 2030 relative to scenario
         with NDCs, by sector   114

5.14   Impacts of CBAM on Europe and Central Asia, 2030   116

5.15   Impacts of climate mitigation policies on GVC participation: 2030 relative to the
         the post-COVID-19 baseline and GVC participation rate, by country and region   117

5.16   Impacts of climate mitigation policies on GVC participation: 2030 relative to the the
         post-COVID-19 baseline, by sector   118

5.17   Impacts of the CBAM on GVC participation for the electronics sector, by
         country and region   119

Maps

3.1   COVID-19-related travel restrictions, February 2021   35

6.1   Implementation status of COVID-19-related export curbs in the medical sector   130

Tables

3.1   Growth of exports and imports, by region and income group, 2020 vs. 2019   37

3.2   Share of exiting trade flows that did not reappear by the end of the year,
         2019 and 2020   43

3A.1   Short-term impact of COVID-19 on trade: Regression coefficients for different
         samples of countries   62

4.1 Top concerns of Chamber of Commerce members in Europe, 2019 and 2020   68

5.1 Real income, real exports, and real imports compared with a COVID-19 L-shape recovery, by region and scenario, 2030   100

5.2 Top-three increases in export sectors for the reshoring leading economies scenario: Change in the value of exports compared with the COVID-19 L-shape scenario, by region   101

5.3 Top-three increases in import sectors for the reshoring leading economies scenario: Change in the value of imports compared with the COVID-19 L-shape scenario, by region   103

5.4 Number of people lifted from extreme poverty and joining the global middle class, by region and scenario   106

5.5 Changes in output following NDC implementation, by sector and region   110

5.6 Impacts of the EU Green Deal and CBAM on selected sectors of EU trading partners relative to the scenario with NDCs, by region   114

5A.1 Regional and sectoral aggressions in computable general equilibrium analysis   119

Foreword

Global value chains (GVCs) have been at the heart of trade-driven poverty reduction in low- and middle-income countries for the past 30 years. As GVCs expanded, the production of many manufactured products was split into distinct activities that were spread across the globe. This division of production brought gains in efficiency and economies of scale for each activity and enabled many low- and middle-income countries to increase their participation in global trade. Think about a car: the engine might be assembled in the United States from parts made in Europe or Japan, Mexico or Brazil.

The COVID-19 (coronavirus) pandemic dealt an unprecedented blow to the world economy and highlighted the vulnerability of supply chains. Lockdowns and border closures reverberated across borders, disrupting production, transportation, and demand. The poor in low- and middle-income countries were hit hardest. A collapse in travel battered tourism-dependent economies from the Caribbean to Southeast Asia. Critical transport and logistics hubs struggled to cope first with lockdowns and then with the surge in demand for containerized trade. Low- and middle-income countries whose exports are highly concentrated in a few products and whose firms are not deeply integrated into GVCs can be very vulnerable in a global downturn. Garment factories in Bangladesh, Vietnam, and elsewhere shut down as retailers based in the European Union and United States canceled orders. Small-scale merchants in Africa could no longer sell fruits and vegetables across borders. All told, an estimated 100 million people fell into extreme poverty.

The pandemic added to growing skepticism about the benefits of globalization in rich and poor countries alike. Even before the pandemic, some countries that depend on a narrow range of commodity exports were being left behind. The poor, women, and other marginalized groups often lack the resources to take advantage of the opportunities that trade can offer. Concern about unfair trade practices and the outsourcing of jobs contributed to the recent trade war between China and the United States. Trade also can contribute to global warming, to which poor nations are the most vulnerable. In wealthier nations, pandemic-induced shortages of critical supplies, from surgical masks to semiconductors, reinforced calls for reshoring of production and economic self-sufficiency.

Yet, by the second half of 2020, trade had rebounded quickly and has since helped to boost the recovery from the global recession. Trade has provided sustained foreign demand for exports and ensured the availability of imported intermediate products and services. The pandemic has highlighted the need to keep critical goods flowing through borders but also the risks that arise for low- and middle-income countries when the production of key products, such as medicines and vaccines, is concentrated in a few countries and there are limited restraints on using export restrictions to curtail access.

However, the recovery from the global recession has been uneven. Countries such as those in East Asia that are deeply integrated into GVCs have recovered more quickly, especially those whose trading partners were also recovering rapidly and where COVID-19 infection rates were lower. In contrast, countries and regions that are less integrated in the global economy have lagged behind, and many low- and middle-income countries are not expected to return to their 2019 levels of gross domestic product per capita until 2023.

This report analyzes both the short-term impacts of the COVID-19 crisis on trade and the factors that are reshaping GVCs in the medium to longer terms, including climate change and the policy responses to global warming. It focuses on the implications for low- and middle-income countries and discusses the role that GVCs will play as a driver of development in the decades to come.

The analysis in this report shows that, although participation in GVCs increases exporters' vulnerability to foreign shocks, it also reduces their exposure to domestic shocks. GVCs act both as a propagator and as an absorber of shocks. GVCs ensure that, in a global recession, a recovery in any part of the world is transmitted to other regions through the value chain. Further, the report documents how GVCs are a source of resilience. The costs of establishing relationships with new suppliers led some firms to maintain trade links during the crisis, paving the way for trade to drive the recovery.

Hence, well-operating GVCs are a source of resilience far more than they are a source of vulnerability. Improving border procedures and easing impediments to trade flows are an appropriate approach to a supply chain crisis. With the support of institutions such as the World Bank Group, low- and middle-income countries can take important steps to diversify their exports and deepen their integration into GVCs. Steps include reducing trade costs by streamlining border procedures and removing logistical constraints. Firms could also benefit from information that helps them to make better matches with overseas buyers, for example, information on firms with robust corporate social responsibility. Improving the framework for contract enforcement to support firms in low- and middle-income countries is also vital.

A key conclusion from the modeling in this report is that steps to maintain and enhance trade contribute to managing a crisis and the recovery, whereas addressing supply chain fragility through measures to reshore production makes all countries worse off, including those that implement them. A shift toward global reshoring to high-income countries and China could drive an additional 52 million people into extreme poverty, most of them in Sub-Saharan Africa. Although there is no sign yet that this shift is occurring and it may be too early to draw firm conclusions, it is clear that widespread retrenchment from globalization would be folly.

As we strive to emerge from the economic crisis, we have an opportunity: we can reshape the global economy into a greener, more resilient, and inclusive system, one that is better equipped for a changing world. Trade is a powerful tool for achieving these goals. Policy measures to increase the price of carbon, including carbon border adjustment mechanisms, so as to meet climate change commitments will contribute to a shift in demand and trade away from fossil fuels and heavily carbon-intensive products. New export opportunities will arise in the greening of GVCs, as countries innovate with cleaner production techniques and greener products. The World Bank Group is ready to support low- and middle-income countries in putting in place the right policy framework and ensuring that they have the tools and capacity to exploit new areas in which they can be competitive in a low-carbon world.

Mari Pangestu
Managing Director of Development Policy and Partnerships
World Bank

Acknowledgments

The authors are indebted to the following colleagues from the World Bank's Trade and Regional Integration Unit (ETIRI) for their contributions to the substance of this report: Cristina Constantinescu (economist), Alvaro Espitia (consultant), Niels Junker Jacobsen (senior trade specialist), Lin Zhang Jones (senior economist, seconded from the United States International Trade Commission), Emine Elcin Koten (consultant), Karen Muramatsu (consultant), Mila Malavoloneke (consultant), Nadia Rocha (senior economist), Michele Ruta (lead economist), Maria Filipa Seara e Pereira (consultant), and Deborah Winkler (senior consultant). The authors are also very grateful to the anonymous senior staff of manufacturers, service providers, and consultancies around the world who participated in our focused interviews. Caroline Freund (former global director, Trade, Investment, and Competitiveness Unit [ETIDR], World Bank, now dean, School of Global Policy and Strategy, University of California at San Diego), Mona Haddad (global director, ETIDR), and Antonio Nucifora (practice manager, ETIRI) provided valuable guidance throughout.

Many colleagues, inside and outside the World Bank Group, provided useful comments, suggestions, and inputs at various drafting stages with special thanks going to Jakob Engel (economist, ETIRI), Mary Hallward-Driemeier (senior economic adviser, ETIDR), Bernard Hoekman (European University Institute), Bert Hofman (National University of Singapore), Sébastien Miroudot (Organisation for Economic Co-operation and Development), Alberto Portugal (senior economist, ETIRI), Bob Rijkers (senior economist, Trade and International Integration Unit [DECTI], World Bank), and Daria Taglioni (research manager, DECTI).

The team also deeply thanks Erik Churchill (vice president of Public Affairs, United Parcel Service, United States), Mohini Datt (consultant, ETIRI), and Pratyush Dubey (consultant, ETIRI) for their inputs and suggestions. Tanya Cubbins, Victoria L. Fofanah, Aidara Janulaityte, and Flavia Nahmias da Silva Gomes (all ETIRI) provided invaluable administrative support.

The authors are deeply grateful to Anna Brown, Elizabeth Reed Forsyth, and Bill Shaw, who edited the text. Amy Lynn Grossman and Patricia Katayama expertly led the publishing process. Sergio Moreno Tellez created the cover and interior design. Elizabeth Price and Nandita Roy provided excellent guidance on the communications strategy.

This report is an output of the Trade and Regional Integration Unit of the World Bank. Funding support was received from the Umbrella Trust Fund for Trade, which is supported by the UK Foreign, Commonwealth & Development Office; the State Secretariat for Economic Affairs of Switzerland; the Ministry of Foreign Affairs of Norway; the Ministry of Foreign Affairs of the Netherlands; and the Swedish International Development Cooperation Agency.

About the Authors

Paul Brenton is lead economist in the Macroeconomics, Trade, and Investment Global Practice at the World Bank. He focuses on analytical and operation work on trade and regional integration. He is currently working on issues such as small-scale cross-border trade in Africa, trade and climate change, and regional integration in the Horn of Africa. Brenton co-authored the World Bank report *The Trade and Climate Change Nexus* and the joint World Bank–World Trade Organization report *The Role of Trade in Ending Poverty*. He is coeditor of the books *De-Fragmenting Africa: Deepening Regional Trade Integration in Goods and Services* and *Africa Can Help Feed Africa*. A collection of his work has been published in *International Trade, Distribution, and Development: Empirical Studies of Trade Policies*. Many of his research and policy papers are available at http://ideas.repec.org/f/pbr273.html. He joined the Bank in 2002; previously, he was a senior research fellow and head of the Trade Policy Unit at the Centre for European Policy Studies in Brussels. Before that, he lectured in economics at the University of Birmingham in the United Kingdom. He holds a PhD in economics from the University of East Anglia. A collection of his work has been published in the volume *International Trade, Distribution, and Development: Empirical Studies of Trade Policies* (https://www.worldscientific.com/worldsci-books/10.1142/9172). Many of his research and policy papers are available at http://ideas.repec.org/f/pbr273.html.

Michael J. Ferrantino is lead economist for trade policy in the Macroeconomics, Trade, and Investment Global Practice at the World Bank. Before joining the Bank, he was lead international economist at the United States International Trade Commission, where he served from 1994 to 2013. Most recently, Ferrantino was a core team member on *World Development Report 2020: Trading for Development in the Age of Global Value Chains* and on *Breaking Out of Fragility: A Country Economic Memorandum for Diversification and Growth in Iraq* (2020). He is also the editor of COVID-19 Trade Watch, a monthly publication that has monitored fluctuations in goods and services trade and logistics capacity since April 2020. His published research spans a wide array of topics relating to international trade, including nontariff measures and trade facilitation; global value chains; the relationship of trade to the environment, innovation, and productivity; and US-China trade. He has taught at Southern Methodist, Youngstown State, Georgetown, American, and George Washington Universities and partnered on research projects with Asia-Pacific Economic Cooperation, Organisation for Economic Co-operation and Development, World Trade Organization, and World Economic Forum. He holds a BA from Northwestern University and a PhD from Yale University.

Maryla Maliszewska is a senior economist in the Macroeconomics, Trade, and Investment Global Practice at the World Bank. She covers various aspects of trade policy and regional integration with a special focus on the impacts of trade on poverty and income distribution. Her area of expertise covers global analyses of structural and demographic change, pandemics, climate change mitigation policies, and trade policy using computable general equilibrium models. Maliszewska contributed analyses underlying several World Bank publications, including *China 2030: Building a Modern, Harmonious, and Creative Society* and the annual publications *Global Monitoring Report*, *Global Development Horizons*, and *Global Economic Prospects*, and has published articles in peer-refereed journals. She recently co-authored *The African Continental Free Trade Area: Economic and Distributional Effects* and *The Distributional Impacts of Trade: Empirical Innovations, Analytical Tools, and Policy Responses*. She joined the World Bank in 2010. Previously, she was a research fellow at the Center for Social and Economic Research in Warsaw and an adviser to the National Bank of Romania. She holds master's degrees in international economics from Sussex, United Kingdom, and Warsaw University, Poland, and a PhD from the University of Sussex in Brighton, United Kingdom.

Abbreviations

AMIS	agricultural market information system
ASEAN	Association of Southeast Asian Nations
CBAM	carbon border adjustment mechanism
CES	constant-elasticity-of-substitution (function)
CGE	computable general equilibrium
CO_2	carbon dioxide
ETS	emissions trading scheme
EU	European Union
FDI	foreign direct investment
fintech	financial technology
GDP	gross domestic product
GIDD	Global Income Distribution Dynamics
GRID	green, resilient, and inclusive development
GSP	Generalized System of Preferences
GTAP	Global Trade Analysis Project
GVC	global value chain
HS	Harmonized System
IPI	industrial production index
ISIC	International Standard Industrial Classification of All Economic Activities
MNE	multinational enterprise
MPO	Macro and Poverty Outlook (World Bank)
MRIO	multiregional input-output
NDC	Nationally Determined Contribution
PPE	personal protective equipment
SCOR	Supply-Chain Operations Reference
SKU	stock-keeping unit
SSP	Shared Socioeconomic Pathways (database)
WTO	World Trade Organization

For a list of the 3-letter country codes used by the World Bank, please go to https://datahelpdesk.worldbank.org/knowledgebase/articles/906519-world-bank-country-and-lending-groups.

Main Messages

In previous decades, global value chains (GVCs) drove dramatic expansions in trade, productivity, and economic growth, boosting development by raising productivity and incomes. Between 1990 and 2017, the growth of GVCs contributed to an increase in the share of low- and middle-income countries in global exports, from 16 percent to 30 percent, and a fall in the proportion of the world's population living in extreme poverty, from 36 percent to 9 percent.

GVCs also enabled an international division of labor whereby activities that used to be undertaken in a single location were dispersed among many countries, with gains in efficiency and economies of scale in the execution of each task. Firms in low- and middle-income countries now can supply intermediate inputs (both goods and services) to global production networks, taking advantage of the industrial bases of other states; they no longer need to wait for an in-country industrial base to emerge. This spatial fragmentation of production allows firms to export at lower cost, to benefit from specialization in niche tasks, and to gain access to larger markets for their output. Through imports, firms are also able to access cheaper and better inputs, productivity-enhancing technologies, and improved management practices developed elsewhere. This ability enables them to grow faster, contributing to the creation of better, higher-paying jobs (World Bank 2020).

Lessons from the COVID-19 pandemic for global value chains

However, tensions and skepticism over the impact of GVCs rose during the COVID-19 (coronavirus) crisis, as the pandemic severely disrupted global trade. In 2020 global trade fell by 8 percent, comparable to the contraction of the Great Recession of 2008–09. This disruption compounded increasing uncertainty over the role of GVCs arising from other developments, such as the evolving role of China in the global economy and emerging policy responses to global warming. At the same time, there is greater awareness that, in the absence of accompanying policies, not all will gain from trade (Engel et al. 2021). During the pandemic, concerns were raised about the propensity for GVCs to transmit shocks from one country to another. For example, a scarcity of microprocessors had knock-on effects in sectors such as motor vehicle production. When firms in high-income countries abruptly canceled clothing orders following lockdowns, garment-producing factories in countries such as Bangladesh had to close, laying off thousands of relatively poor workers. In poorer countries, the infeasibility of remote work constrained a mechanism that mitigated, to an extent, the negative effects of reduced worker mobility on export growth in richer countries. For example, the negative impact of COVID-19 on Hungary's exports of pulp, paper, and paperboard, for which less than one-third of occupations can be performed remotely, is found to be 19 percentage points larger than the impact on Japan's exports of electric motors, generators, and transformers, for which more than two-thirds of production can be done remotely.

The COVID-19 crisis highlighted the risks to low- and middle-income countries reliant on trade for access to essential items such as medicine and food. Opportunistic actions by trade partners, especially the use of export restrictions, exacerbated those risks. Worldwide, as of January 2021, 140 of 142 export measures announced to the International Trade Centre were restrictive, whereas 163 of the 264 import measures announced were liberalizing. The vast majority of these measures covered medical supplies and food. The gains from trade through specialization mean that production of certain essential products may become concentrated in a small number of countries. During the COVID-19 crisis, access to essential personal protective equipment, medicine, and vaccines demonstrated the challenges that can arise. The current challenges echo the experience of previous crises, during which, in the face of episodes of uncertainty, producing nations too easily resorted to limits on exports of food at the expense of consumers around the world. Rich countries restricted exports, which limited the access of low- and middle-income countries to essential medical items, and this practice bred skepticism about the fairness of trade. Concentrated GVCs are especially vulnerable when shocks affect key nodes in the network and opportunities to find alternative suppliers or buyers are limited.

The pandemic also demonstrated that GVCs can maintain trade relationships during a crisis, paving the way for a strong trade-led recovery. When the costs of establishing a network of suppliers are significant, lead firms tend to maintain, rather than end, relationships during a crisis. During the COVID-19 lockdowns, some lead firms provided their suppliers with financial and technical assistance in order to preserve their investments in network relationships and reputations. This assistance included support of multinational corporations for their affiliates and support of affiliates for local suppliers. GVCs ensure that, in a global recession, recovery in any part of the world is transmitted through the value chain. Indeed, trade has been the engine driving global growth as the world recovers from the pandemic, rebounding faster and stronger than any other component of global output. This growth has occurred in many goods sectors, especially those related to new patterns of demand from home working. Services trade was hit harder and has been slower to recover, although various types of services have performed differently. COVID-19 restrictions have affected travel and tourism severely, whereas business services have remained resilient, as they did in previous global downturns. The fall and subsequent rapid rise of the value of transport services reflect the unusual circumstances surrounding container shipping.

Measures for managing a crisis and the recovery

This report finds that measures to maintain and enhance trade contribute to managing a crisis and the recovery. By contrast, efforts to reshore production reduce trade and increase poverty in low- and middle-income countries. The economic modeling in this report demonstrates how steps to support trade will strengthen the recovery from the COVID-19 pandemic, whereas measures to restrict trade and promote reshoring will weaken it. Both high-income countries and low- and middle-income countries are better off in a globalized world during and after a crisis. Steps toward creating a more "hostile" environment for GVCs, with a shift toward global reshoring to high-income countries and China, could drive an additional 52 million people into extreme poverty, 80 percent of whom would be in Sub-Saharan Africa. Although there is no sign yet that this shift is occurring, it may be too early to draw firm conclusions. Nevertheless, the results from the economic modeling in this report show that attempting to deal with supply chain fragility through measures to reshore production would make all countries worse off, including those that implement them. In contrast, measures to reduce trade barriers, streamline trade procedures, and facilitate trade at borders contribute to the response to a crisis by expediting the movement, release, and clearance of goods, including goods in transit, and by enabling the exchange of services, paving the way for greater resilience to future shocks. Such measures support integration into GVCs, boost incomes, and could lift almost 22 million additional people out of poverty by 2030. They also would improve the incomes of the bottom 40 percent.

Some measures can enhance the resilience of GVCs in low-income countries and protect low- and middle-income countries from export restrictions on critical products. First, policies can address the heightened risk to small exporters posed by the sudden cancellation of contracts, especially the risk to firms not deeply embedded in trade networks. This situation is more likely to happen in countries where contracts are poorly specified and contract enforcement is weak. Governments can address factors such as failures in the market for information, weak contracts, and limited access to trade finance. Doing so can lead to better and more resilient relationships with overseas buyers and sellers. Development partners can promote corporate social responsibility among buyers and lead firms in GVCs and help companies with corporate social responsibility commitments to honor contracts during periods of crisis. Second, governments can invest in collecting and sharing information to support effective monitoring of conditions in the markets for strategic goods. Such investments can reduce the likelihood that countries will resort to the use of costly ad hoc export restrictions on key products, to the detriment of low-income countries, and allow importers to prepare for the possibility that such restrictions will emerge. This effort needs to be combined with more effective global discipline on the use of export restrictions in concert with the opening of import markets that provide greater certainty of market access.

Climate change is already affecting the trade of low- and middle-income countries and could have a far greater impact on GVCs than recent shocks to global trade. The increasing prevalence and greater violence of extreme weather events as well as rising temperatures and changing precipitation are altering traditional comparative advantages. Low- and middle-income countries continue to be the most affected by climate change and are also the least able to afford its consequences. Fighting climate change and its consequences is an imperative for spurring development and fighting poverty. More extreme weather events are creating greater uncertainty and the need for greater resilience of trade in low- and middle-income countries. Moreover, the longer-term adaptation to the changing climate and the shift to a lower-carbon growth trajectory will be key challenges for countries with the fewest resources and weakest capacity to adjust to a changing climate.

Exporters in low- and middle-income countries will also be affected by emerging policy responses to climate change. Measures to achieve Nationally Determined

Commitments (NDCs) under the Paris Agreement, including carbon border adjustment mechanisms (CBAMs), will prompt a shift in demand away from fossil fuels and carbon-intensive products in major markets. Under the European Union (EU) Green Deal, for example, imports of coal could be reduced by almost two-thirds. Most heavily affected will be fossil fuel exporters and countries that are heavily involved in carbon-intensive GVCs, such as chemicals. Hence, the prevalence of policies to support climate mitigation objectives, including through CBAMs, will increase the importance of export and output diversification in countries highly reliant on exports of fossil fuels and carbon-intensive manufactures.

The shift away from carbon-intensive GVCs will entail new opportunities in GVCs that are less carbon intensive. As trade in carbon-intensive manufactures declines, suppliers in GVC-intensive sectors, such as electronics, motor vehicles and parts, and other light manufacturing, will see higher demand for their goods, resulting in even stronger GVC links across countries. As a result, key exporters of these products, such as Malaysia and Vietnam, can strengthen their integration into GVCs following carbon border adjustment measures. Thus, climate mitigation policies not only will lead to the decarbonization of the economy but also will stimulate higher integration into the GVCs of low-carbon-intensive commodities. Countries that are already heavily involved in these GVCs or have the potential to participate in them will see new opportunities for trade.

Main policy messages

This report finds that integration into the global trading system helps build resilience and so trade can play a key role in achieving green, resilient, and inclusive development (GRID) in the recovery from the COVID-19 pandemic. Diversifying exports, increasing access to overseas markets through new trade agreements, and continuing integration into GVCs can all build resilience to future shocks.

The following summarizes the report's main policy messages for strengthening the resilience of trade in low- and middle-income countries in a world where multiple shocks and policy trends are framing the global trading environment.

Trade policies

Policies to maintain trade flows during a global crisis are crucial. A crisis is generally a bad time to raise trade barriers, because the need for imports may increase and exports are an important stabilizer and source of jobs and incomes. Trade in both goods and services plays a key role in overcoming global shocks and limiting their impact in the following ways:

- Providing access to essential goods (including material inputs for their production) and services

- Ensuring access to food throughout the world

- Providing farmers with necessary inputs (seeds, fertilizers, equipment) for the next harvest

- Supporting jobs and maintaining economic activity in the face of a global recession

Trade policies are also essential for managing a global crisis. Trade policy reforms, such as tariff reductions, contribute in the following ways:

- Reducing the cost and improving the availability of essential goods and services, such as medical equipment, pharmaceuticals, and food
- Reducing tax and administrative burdens on importers and exporters
- Reducing the cost of products heavily consumed by the poor
- Supporting the eventual economic recovery and building resilience through greater diversification of imports and exports

Measures to streamline trade procedures and facilitate trade

Measures to streamline trade procedures and facilitate trade can contribute to the response to a crisis. Expediting the movement, release, and clearance of goods, including goods in transit, and enabling exchange of services can play a key role in responding to and recovering from a crisis. During COVID-19, for example, reforms were designed to reduce the need for close contact between traders, transporters, and border officials so as to protect stakeholders and limit the spread of the virus, while ensuring revenue, health, and security. Interventions to sustain and enhance the efficiency of logistics operations can also be critical in avoiding the substantial disruption of both distribution networks and regional and global value chains.

Measures to maintain access to finance and enforce contracts

Access to finance is important for the most vulnerable traders, as is stronger contract enforcement. Small exporters not deeply embedded in networks with lead firms can be subject to a heightened risk of contract cancellation during a crisis. When there is no support from the network, the financial system and government are the remaining backup. In the poorest countries, governments and financial systems may not have the strength to provide such a function. For this reason, international development institutions could consider offering some form of insurance for exposed firms in low-income countries. Reforms to contract enforcement that clearly spell out how risk is to be distributed in an unforeseen situation would also help.

Measures to improve supply chain mapping

Improved supply chain mapping is a critical element of an appropriate response to a supply chain disruption. Many of the costs of GVC disruptions arise simply from not knowing how GVCs are constructed and where lower-tier suppliers of major products are located. Better information within firms, aided by improved managerial techniques, can help. Governments, for their part, should become more aware of the interlinkages within their own economy and with economies in the rest of the world. Such awareness includes information about key stockpiles of medical and food supplies.

Measures to improve coordination and discipline

Countries and the international community can take steps to protect low-income countries in future crises. One of the biggest international policy challenges in the COVID-19 crisis has been how to avoid having countries with production capacity in medical products, vaccines, and staple food products apply export restrictions that limit the access of other countries to these essential products. Economists agree that export restrictions and precautionary purchases of essential goods by a small number of key countries can lead to rapid rises in global prices and severe shortages in other countries. Hence, such measures need better coordination and discipline, in particular,

- Investing in collecting and sharing information to support effective monitoring of conditions in the markets for strategic goods, and

- Exercising more effective global discipline on the use of export restrictions in concert with opening import markets that provide greater certainty of market access.

Support for adjustment to trade measures that address climate change

Low- and middle-income countries need support to adjust to trade measures that are being introduced to meet climate change objectives. Measures to reduce carbon emissions will increasingly affect the trade of low- and middle-income countries. This situation brings not only challenges, especially for exporters of carbon-intensive products, but also opportunities to diversify into new products driven by access to low-carbon technologies. Aid-for-trade programs can be recalibrated and enhanced to support the technical assistance and capacity building that countries will require to identify and exploit areas of carbon competitiveness effectively.

References

Engel, Jakob, Deeksha Kokas, Gladys Lopez-Acevedo, and Maryla Maliszewska. 2021. *The Distributional Impacts of Trade: Empirical Innovations, Analytical Tools, and Policy Responses*. Washington, DC: World Bank.

World Bank. 2020. *World Development Report 2020: Trading for Development in the Age of Global Value Chains*. Washington, DC: World Bank.

1

Introduction and Overview

COVID-19 (coronavirus) has dealt an unprecedented setback to the global economy, impairing worldwide efforts to reduce extreme poverty and inequality. In 2020 the pandemic caused a global contraction in gross domestic product (GDP) of 3.3 percent, the deepest economic recession since the Second World War. An estimated 100 million people fell into extreme poverty (World Bank 2020). Global trade contracted sharply, as lockdown, quarantine, and social distancing measures, along with travel restrictions and border closures (an important part of the initial policy response to the pandemic), disrupted freight transport, business travel, and the supply of services that rely on the presence of individuals abroad (WTO 2020). The use and threat of export restrictions on essential items during the crisis bolstered skepticism of an open trading system by limiting access in many low- and middle-income countries and raising prices.

International trade and global value chains (GVCs) have been essential to development and poverty reduction over the past three decades. From 1990 to 2017, the share of low- and middle-income countries in global exports rose from 16 percent to more than 30 percent, and the proportion of the world's population living in extreme poverty fell from 36 percent to 9 percent (figure 1.1). Many countries, especially in East Asia, have used trade to create jobs, integrate into global and regional value chains, and reduce poverty.

However, it has become increasingly apparent that globalization has left some behind and that the benefits are not always distributed equitably. The poor face numerous constraints on their capacity to benefit from trade, including lack of instruments (insurance, social security) to mitigate the greater risks they face in specializing in trade-related activities and limited mobility to take advantage of new, but distant, opportunities (Engel et al. 2021; World Bank and WTO 2015, 2018). Measures that reduce the costs of labor mobility and reforms that deepen the links between tradable and nontradable sectors can help to maximize the benefits of trade and minimize the costs of adjustment (Engel et al. 2021). Recent analysis also shows that a broad range of policies is necessary to ensure that women benefit from trading opportunities to the same extent as men (World Bank and WTO 2020). Such policies include increasing

FIGURE 1.1 Trade and poverty reduction in low- and middle-income countries, 1990–2017

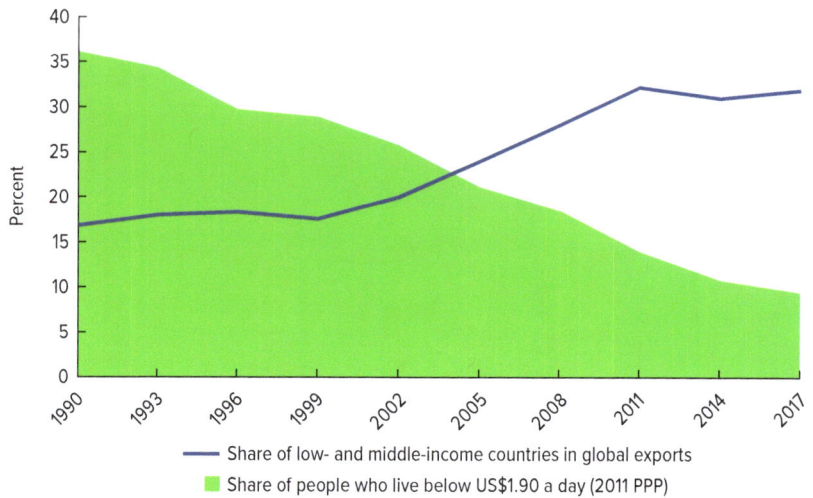

Source: World Bank, World Development Indicators data.
Note: PPP = purchasing power parity.

women's access to higher education, digital technology, finance, information, and transport infrastructure.

Trade also intersects with other factors that are shaping outcomes for the poor, such as climate change. Trade-driven growth helps to eliminate extreme poverty, but it also risks driving higher emissions of greenhouse gases. The poor are especially vulnerable to the negative impacts of climate change, and trade is an essential part of the solution, enhancing both mitigation and adaptation (Brenton and Chemutai 2021). It also serves as a conduit for disseminating low-carbon technologies, which can provide new routes out of poverty. Coordinating climate change, development, and trade policies will allow trade to drive the low-carbon transition and achieve poverty-reducing and inclusive growth.

In light of rising awareness of the need for complementary policies to ensure that the poor benefit from trade reforms and increasing uncertainty over policies affecting trade, can GVCs continue to be a driver of trade and development in the coming decades? Do countries need to adjust their trade strategies now that COVID-19 has shone a light on the risks that GVCs may bring? This assessment is taking place during a period when the evolving role of China in the global economy, increasing trade restrictions, and the policy responses to global warming are exacerbating uncertainty over the role of GVCs.

To address these questions, this report first reviews the impacts of previous crises and what they say about the resilience of GVC firms to shocks. It provides a platform by which (a) to interpret the observed impact of COVID-19 on trade using the available data for 2020 and early 2021 and (b) to analyze the outcomes of discussions with GVC firms on how they have been affected by and are responding to the COVID-19 shock. To go beyond the tentative conclusions that are possible from the data and firms' responses during the initial period of the crisis, which will be updated as the pandemic continues to affect economic activity around the world, the report explores simulations from a global model to enhance understanding of the potential longer-term impacts on low- and middle-income countries of COVID-19 and other key factors shaping the global economy, including the policy responses by countries.

This chapter summarizes the outcomes of each of the related steps of the report that underpin these messages, starting with (a) a review of historical experiences, followed by (b) the interpretation and analysis of high-frequency data on the impact of COVID-19 on trade; (c) insights from the responses of firms and governments to the supply chain shocks surrounding COVID-19; (d) the structural modeling of COVID-19 impacts and how possible trade policy responses, such as reshoring in rich countries, will affect the recovery; and (e) scenarios regarding possible measures to address climate change that will affect trade.

Experience from historical shocks

Experience from historical shocks shows that trade flows contracted, but trading relationships were not broken to a greater degree than usual, paving the way for recovery. Studies of historical episodes of both global and specific shocks to global trade yield important evidence about the way supply chains respond under stress. Analyses of episodes such as the 2008–09 Great Trade Collapse, the 2011 earthquake-tsunami in Japan, and the 2011 floods in Thailand show that, in most cases, contractions in trade took place on the intensive margin (reductions in existing trade flows) rather than on the extensive margin (disappearances of trade in particular products between particular countries). Trade in intermediate goods has been relatively resilient to shocks, as has intrafirm trade between related parties in multinational firms, although the evidence for the latter is mixed. Very few studies have looked at the impacts of such shocks on low- and middle-income countries, the focus of this report.

Firms involved in trade networks are at risk of disruption following a shock, especially when the network is dominated by a few large buyers or suppliers of critical inputs. Indeed, firms in a trade network that cannot substitute quickly and easily away from critical suppliers or buyers are affected most negatively. Following the Japanese earthquake, affiliates of Japanese firms in the United States were adversely affected because they were unable to substitute away from specialized inputs from Japan. However, after Hurricane Sandy, firms in international networks had more opportunities to substitute away from inputs produced by afflicted firms.

Scope and depth of the COVID-19 shock

The shock to GVCs induced by the COVID-19 pandemic was unique in scope and depth. The Great Trade Collapse of 2008–09 was global in scope, but primarily a demand shock induced by a financial crisis. The Fukushima tsunami, earthquake, and core meltdown of 2011 were a supply shock targeted to a narrow geography, as were the floods in Thailand. By contrast, the chain reaction effect of global lockdowns imposed to contain COVID-19 had adverse effects on demand, supply, and transport networks in every country in the world. Figure 1.2 maps the ways in which lockdowns affected all aspects of the economy.

The output and trade contractions of 2020 were of historic magnitude, comparable to those in the Great Recession of 2008–09. Real GDP fell by 3.5 percent, and nominal

FIGURE 1.2 Effects of COVID-19 lockdown policies on global value chains

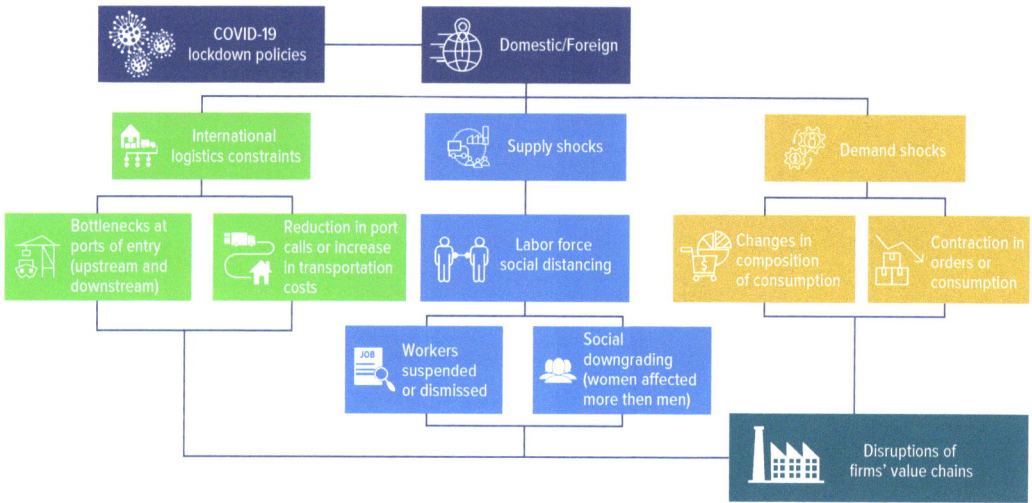

COVID-19 lockdown policies → Domestic/Foreign

International logistics constraints

Supply shocks

Demand shocks

Bottlenecks at ports of entry (upstream and downstream)

Reduction in port calls or increase in transportation costs

Labor force social distancing

Changes in composition of consumption

Contraction in orders or consumption

Workers suspended or dismissed

Social downgrading (women affected more then men)

Disruptions of firms' value chains

Source: World Bank staff.

goods trade fell by 8.3 percent in 2020 relative to 2019. Services trade contracted by 15 percent, more rapidly than goods trade. The figures for the full year include very sharp contractions concentrated in the second quarter of 2020, followed by a rapid recovery in many countries. Multiple layers of uncertainty affected foreign direct investment perhaps even more than trade. During 2020, the value of global foreign direct investment declined by an estimated 42 percent, reaching levels not seen since 2005.

The tourism and travel sector was affected the most negatively as a result of border closures, travel restrictions, and the cancellation of many commercial flights. In February 2021, 32 percent of international borders remained closed, and almost all countries maintained some form of restrictions on travel. Commercial passenger flights, which had collapsed by 80 percent in April 2020, have recovered partly. However, much of the tourist ecosystem is based on small and medium enterprises and simply went bankrupt, making consolidation among larger players likely.

The poor in low- and middle-income countries were affected the most adversely. The incomes of small-scale cross-border traders in Africa, who earn the smallest of margins, declined as a result of border closures. Workers in these countries have far fewer opportunities for remote working and therefore fewer options to maintain their income than their counterparts in richer countries. In certain value chains such as apparel, major brands and retailers based in the European Union (EU) and the United States canceled or postponed orders, including for goods already produced by suppliers in low- and middle-income countries. This situation led to factory closures in countries such as Bangladesh, Myanmar, and Vietnam and the loss of jobs, mostly for female workers.

Like COVID-19 itself, which spread around the world in waves, trade has recovered unevenly, with countries that are well integrated in GVCs experiencing the most dramatic recoveries. This situation is most apparent in East Asia and above all in China. Most high-income economies were able to adapt as well, despite start-and-stop lockdowns. But trade in the Middle East and North Africa, South Asia, and

Sub-Saharan Africa was slower to recover, with volumes at the end of 2020 well below those of the previous year.

The composition of merchandise trade underwent substantial shifts in response to changing consumer demand. In value terms, trade in medical supplies and food increased, whereas trade in minerals and fuels, motor vehicles, and footwear contracted. This shift was accompanied by a substantial increase in demand in richer countries toward goods and services consumed at home for both work and leisure purposes, for example, goods related to work from home and to exercise. Some of these changes reflect the transitory impacts of the pandemic, but some may become entrenched if preferences are adjusted.

Contractions in trade during 2020 largely took the form of reductions in volume rather than the disappearance of country- and product-specific trade flows (extensive margin). However, the extensive margin was more fragile for low-income exporters. Aside from an increasing role of East Asian countries in the area of light manufacturing, there is little evidence that global trade pivoted away from China in 2020; if anything, the opposite occurred.

Econometric evidence

Experience from the first six months of the crisis shows how GVCs both propagated and mitigated the impact of COVID-19 lockdowns. Countries relying heavily on imports of intermediate goods were more likely to experience negative effects from COVID-19 lockdowns in countries from which they sourced imports as well as from lockdowns in export markets. However, countries with greater involvement in GVCs also experienced milder effects on trade from their own domestic lockdowns, indicating that the ability both to buy and to sell internationally provided economic resilience. These results suggest that GVCs also played an important role in the rapid recovery of trade observed in the second half of 2020.

Policies designed to limit the spread of COVID-19 affected economic activity and international trade. Attempts to prevent the movement of persons across international borders led to bottlenecks of trucking in Africa and Europe. The activities of seaports in many countries were limited, as restrictions on the movement of truckers prevented ships from being unloaded. Physical lockdowns within countries often left factories closed, especially if they were deemed "nonessential" or workers could not travel to work.

The largest impacts were in sectors heavily reliant on imported intermediate goods, as industrial production of intermediate goods declined in source countries. Similarly, domestic lockdowns restricted the physical mobility of workers, contributing to slower export growth on average. Lower demand in destination markets, as measured by declines in retail mobility, also had an impact on export growth. By contrast, the reduction in competition from third countries tended to boost bilateral growth of exports.

The trade effects of the pandemic were smaller in industries where the possibility of working remotely was greater, which limited the adverse effects in higher-income countries. However, in low- and middle-income countries the scope for remote working was smaller because of limited availability of the services and equipment required for remote working, lack of prior experience with remote working, and dominance of sectors such as agriculture and tourism that require a physical presence.

Responses of firms and governments to supply chain shocks

Although firms have made significant investments in new data-driven methods of supply chain management (Supply Chain 4.0), these methods were not fully diffused at the beginning of 2020, even among large firms. Many firms were caught off guard when COVID-19 struck. For example, firms did not always know whether they had suppliers in Hubei Province, China, particularly tier 2 and tier 3 suppliers.[1] The key principle of Supply Chain 4.0 is end-to-end visibility of the supply chain, which can allow firms to identify and address vulnerabilities along their supply chains and hence increase resilience to future shocks. Analysis of an entire supply chain with big data analytics can lead to superior optimization of everything, including inventories, production, which product varieties to offer at a particular retail location, and whether marketing ought to be done by store displays, advertisements, or e-commerce platforms.

The COVID-19 shock took place against a background of preexisting trends associated with a reshaping of trade. These trends included an outbreak of trade conflicts among major trading partners beginning in 2018, an increase in automation that caused some production to return to high-income countries, and an increase in production costs in China. The pandemic accelerated preexisting mega trends, including e-commerce and working from home. In the face of the COVID-19 shock and ongoing trends, firms responded by reducing the variety of products, increasing the flexibility in factory procedures and labor scheduling, and seeking alternate suppliers.

Support from the top can have positive spillover effects: support of parent firms for affiliates and affiliates for suppliers was widespread, but not universal, during the crisis. The most common types of support provided were new technology or managerial guidance to help with operations, followed by financial support, managerial guidance to help with product differentiation, and new technology for supply chain mapping and management. Large GVC firms were more likely to provide support than medium and small firms.

Some producers experienced sudden cutoffs in payments for goods already produced, highlighting the importance of strong network relationships. In the face of sudden declines in demand, some importers refused to take possession of goods already in transit, forcing losses on exporters. These firms were then compelled to rely on the leniency of banks or on government support programs. Buyers with stronger network relationships, by contrast, often were more generous in dealing with suppliers.

Although widely discussed, near-shoring, reshoring, or international decoupling were apparently limited. Interviews with private sector stakeholders indicate that most foreign investors that had been considering relocating from China before 2020 because of labor costs or trade tensions have already done so. Business surveys of European and US firms with investments in China indicate that relatively few firms plan to reduce their presence in China going forward.

Government trade policy responses to COVID-19 proliferated worldwide, including both restrictive and liberalizing measures. Export controls on medical goods and food dominated the restrictive measures. As of January 25, 2021, 140 of 142 export measures announced to the International Trade Centre were restrictive, whereas 163 of the 264 import measures announced were liberalizing.

The rapid but uneven recovery from COVID-19 brought new types of problems for supply chains. As trade and production began to recover in the second half of 2020 and into 2021, different activities returned at different speeds. Although this unevenness happens in any recovery, the abruptness of the current episode was particularly striking. Demand for motor vehicles and electronics recovered sharply, whereas demand for services continued to lag. The variable-speed recovery caused bottlenecks in both transportation and production, as economic activity was constrained by activities whose recovery lagged in relative terms or by the inability of firms to forecast the pace of recovery accurately. Unprecedented shortages of shipping containers and semiconductors were emblematic of this problem.

Measures to maintain and enhance trade

Attempting to deal with supply chain fragility by reshoring would make all countries worse off. Although there is no sign yet of policy measures to promote reshoring, it may be too early to make firm conclusions. But, as in previous crises, there has been much discussion about using more restrictive trade policies to lower the risks associated with global shocks. However, previous experience shows that such steps do not tend to stabilize domestic output, especially if pursued by multiple countries. Moreover, such measures tend to have substantial adverse impacts on trade-dependent low- and middle-income countries. The simulations in this report suggest that, if major trading countries (high-income countries plus China) attempt to reshore production by limiting trade and subsidizing domestic production, global income would drop by 1.5 percent, with losses in all regions. If low- and middle-income countries pursue similar policies, global income would drop by 2.2 percent, with higher losses in many regions. However, if low- and middle-income countries respond by developing "GVC-friendly policies," including eliminating tariffs on intermediate inputs and pursuing a vigorous program of trade facilitation, they would experience gains large enough to overcome the collateral damage from any program of reshoring on the part of major trading countries.

Trade would grow more rapidly in a globalized world than in a world where reshoring policies are prevalent. In a globalized world, global trade could grow by 25 percent over 2019–30. In a world where countries reshore their production, global trade would decline by as much as 22 percent by 2030. A "hostile" environment for GVCs, with a shift toward global reshoring, could drive an additional 52 million people into extreme poverty by 2030. About 80 percent of the new poor would be in Sub-Saharan Africa, with most of the rest in the Middle East and North Africa and South Asia.

In contrast, if low- and middle-income countries implement trade-enhancing measures, they would experience substantial gains even if other countries choose to reshore. Measures such as eliminating tariffs on intermediate inputs and pursuing a vigorous program of trade facilitation would lead to an overall increase in real income in low- and middle-income countries of about 10 percentage points by 2030 and could lift almost 22 million additional people out of poverty by raising the incomes of the bottom 40 percent. Exports of several sectors deeply integrated into GVCs would expand in this scenario. These sectors include motor vehicles and transport equipment and textiles and apparel in Sub-Saharan Africa or computer, electronic, and optical products, other manufacturing, chemical products, motor vehicles, crops, and textiles in South Asia. A policy environment that enhances trade also would boost resilience to future supply shocks by broadening access to goods and services in short supply and diversifying the economies of low- and middle-income countries.

Emerging climate change policies

Climate change policies could fundamentally alter GVCs to a far greater extent than transitory shocks such as the COVID-19 pandemic or unique events such as the 2011 Japan tsunami. Climate change has already contributed to shifts in global supply chains as firms shore up vulnerabilities in production centers and as governments adjust climate policies to reach their commitments under the Paris Climate Agreement. Each region and sector will be affected differently as countries strive to reach their Nationally Determined Contributions (NDCs) targets, with the greatest adjustments in countries heavily reliant on coal.

The impact that climate change mitigation in high-income economies will have on GVCs will depend on how policies are designed and implemented, but such policies will result in reshaping of GVCs away from carbon-intensive activities. Simulations done for this report based on stylized modeling of NDCs, the EU Green Deal, and carbon border adjustment mechanisms (CBAMs) show that climate policies would affect different countries differently, depending on the importance of carbon-intensive sectors in the economy, with countries in Central Asia and Europe potentially the most vulnerable. The design and implementation of carbon border adjustment schemes will be critical in determining their impact on trade and income in low- and middle-income countries.

By raising the implicit price of carbon by more than the Paris commitments, the EU Green Deal will have an impact on trade. Under the EU Green Deal, EU countries would reduce their imports of fossil fuels and other carbon-intensive products as EU-wide demand falls. The impact of EU climate policies on other countries will depend on the degree of carbon intensity of their exports and links with the EU in general.

As part of the EU Green Deal, a CBAM would likely lead to greater integration in archetypal GVCs such as electronics, motor vehicles, and apparel. CBAMs that target carbon-intensive sectors with relatively higher participation in GVCs, such as wood and paper products, chemicals, nonmetallic minerals, and metals, could reduce trade in those products significantly. However, computers and electronics, motor vehicles and parts, and other light manufacturing could become integrated even more deeply into GVCs. In the absence of policy responses by low- and middle-income countries, the greatest potential reductions in production and trade outside the EU are likely to be in Europe and Central Asia.

Countries can mitigate the potential negative impacts of climate policies on selected sectors by initiating their own policy responses. By pursuing more ambitious climate mitigation policies themselves, low- and middle-income countries could transform potential income losses into long-term income gains by supporting the use of more efficient and cleaner technologies, which would facilitate a green transition. In addition, countries would gain from the environmental and health benefits of more stringent climate action. Under ambitious climate mitigation scenarios, even energy exporters—a group of countries that would be hit hard by implementation of the EU Green Deal—would improve their welfare by transitioning from a traditional to a proactive diversification of assets (with increasing investments in research and development), as shown by Peszko et al. (2020).

Integration into the global economy and GVC participation remain key

The report concludes by discussing the main policy messages from the analysis and the findings that maintaining trade flows in a global crisis is essential and that well-operating GVCs can be a source of resilience. First, as the prevalence of risks from pandemics, extreme weather events, and other shocks increases, trade becomes more important as a stabilizer, requiring stable and predictable trade policies. Reducing impediments to trade flows can contribute to an effective response to a supply chain crisis. During the COVID-19 pandemic, many countries restricted the movement of critical food and medical supplies, including vaccines, showing that there is substantial scope for improved policies. Second, better sharing of information can help support more-informed policy decisions and build improved resilience. This includes information on the supply of medical products and food as well as information that enhances the operation of value chains such as between logistics providers. Third, improving access to finance is crucial for small firms and the most vulnerable traders who are especially susceptible to the risk of contracts being canceled and to the disruption of trade routes. Finally, policies to promote trade diversification and integration into a broader set of GVCs remain important for low-income countries to limit the impact of, and speed the recovery from, more frequent shocks.

Note

1. Tier 1 suppliers are suppliers of major components and assemblies for complex goods (for example, drive trains for automobiles). Tier 2 suppliers provide subassemblies for tier 1 suppliers (for example, pistons), and tier 3 suppliers (for example, piston rings) sell to tier 2 suppliers.

References

Brenton, Paul, and Vicky Chemutai. 2021. *Trade and Climate Change Nexus: The Urgency and Opportunities for Developing Countries.* Washington, DC: World Bank.

Engel, Jakob, Deeksha Kokas, Gladys Lopez-Acevedo, and Maryla Maliszewska. 2021. *The Distributional Impacts of Trade: Empirical Innovations, Analytical Tools, and Policy Responses.* Washington, DC: World Bank.

Peszko, Grzegorz, Dominique van der Mensbrugghe, Alexander Golub, John Ward, Dimitri Zenghelis, Cor Marijs, Anne Schopp, John A. Rogers, and Amelia Midgley. 2020. *Diversification and Cooperation in a Decarbonizing World: Climate Strategies for Fossil Fuel–Dependent Countries.* Washington, DC: World Bank.

World Bank. 2020. "Projected Poverty Impacts of COVID-19 (Coronavirus)." World Bank, Washington, DC. https://thedocs.worldbank.org/en/doc/461601591649316722-0090022020/original/ProjectedpovertyimpactsofCOVID19.pdf.

World Bank and WTO (World Trade Organization). 2015. *The Role of Trade in Ending Poverty.* Washington, DC: World Bank Group. http://documents.worldbank.org/curated/en/726971467989468997/The-role-of-trade-in-ending-poverty.

World Bank and WTO (World Trade Organization). 2018. *Trade and Poverty Reduction: New Evidence of Impacts in Developing Countries*. Washington, DC: World Bank Group. http://documents.worldbank.org/curated/en/968461544478747599/Trade-and-Poverty-Reduction-New-Evidence-of-Impacts-in-Developing-Countries.

World Bank and WTO (World Trade Organization). 2020. *Women and Trade: The Role of Trade in Promoting Gender Equality*. Washington, DC: World Bank.

WTO (World Trade Organization). 2020. "Trade in Services in the Context of COVID-19." Information Note, WTO, Geneva. https://www.wto.org/english/tratop_e/covid19_e/services_report_e.pdf.

2

Lessons from Historical Shocks to GVCs

Key messages

- Studies of historical episodes of supply shocks, such as the 2008–09 Great Trade Collapse, the 2011 earthquake-tsunami in Japan, and the 2011 floods in Thailand, yield important evidence about the ways in which supply chains respond under stress.

- In part reflecting the impact of global value chains (GVCs), contractions in trade have taken place mainly on the intensive margin (reductions in existing trade flows) rather than on the extensive margin (disappearances of trade in particular products between particular countries).

- Trade associated with GVCs or multinational firms appears to be more resilient than arms' length trade between unrelated parties.

- The ability to substitute alternative inputs for inputs affected by a disaster is a key factor in the international propagation of shocks. A negative impact can be reduced significantly through connections to foreign firms.

- The effect of government measures to enhance the resilience of supply chains can spread beyond the direct recipients to other firms in the value chain.

- The structure of trade networks matters in determining the impact of shocks. There is greater propagation of a shock when the partners of a damaged firm are densely connected with one another.

- Newer research applies network analysis tools to trade flow data to identify and rank the fragility of individual traded goods. Parts for computers, aircraft and motor vehicles, mechanical appliances, and medical equipment are ranked highest in terms of risk.

Introduction

Analyses of previous shocks to trade can contribute to an understanding of how and where to look for the main impacts of the COVID-19 (coronavirus) shock—the second major shock in the past 15 years, following the global financial crisis of 2008–09. The 2008–09 crisis led to what some call the Great Trade Collapse (for example, Baldwin 2009) because the shock to demand was followed by a very large, sharp, and synchronized decline in imports and exports across the world. An important feature of this crisis is that the decline in the real value of world trade exceeded that of the fall in real gross domestic product (GDP) by a factor of roughly four. The crisis had other features as well, noted by Bems, Johnson, and Yi (2013); but the dominant feature was asymmetry across sectors. First, trade in goods declined by much more than trade in some services; for example, business, professional, and technical services increased throughout the crisis. Second, trade in durable goods declined much more than trade in nondurable goods. Third, there is some evidence that trade in intermediates fell faster and recovered more quickly than trade in final goods. In addition, financial factors played a limited role (for example, see Lanz and Miroudot 2011), trade protectionism played no role, and the trade collapse was driven by adjustments in the volume of trade rather than by changes in the price of traded goods. The prices of commodities fell, but the prices of noncommodity and differentiated goods, which make up the majority of trade, remained broadly unchanged.

In addition to analyses of global crises, studies of recent shocks caused by weather-related and natural disasters also shed light on important trade adjustments. The two main events that have been explored are the Japanese earthquake and the floods in Thailand, both occurring in 2011. These studies assess how the impact of local events can spread, with aggregate and global implications as a result of trade and supply chain links. They are also important for understanding the effects of COVID-19 because they examine how supply-side shocks affect trade. The general conclusion from analysis of the 2008–09 financial crisis is that the contraction in demand was primarily responsible for the decline in trade. The COVID-19 pandemic affected trade as a result of both supply constraints, as workplaces closed following lockdowns to constrain the spread of the virus, and substantial declines in demand, as lost jobs and incomes and heightened uncertainty reduced consumption expenditures.

An important issue is the role of supply chains and specifically GVCs in propagating the initial shock over a wider area and magnifying the impact on trade relative to output and GDP. A range of empirical studies addresses questions of whether trade in GVCs is more resilient to shocks than other trade. Are firms in GVCs less or more affected?

This chapter first looks at research that seeks to understand the nature of trade shocks by decomposing changes in trade that are explained by the intensive margin (changes in the volume of existing flows) and changes that are explained by the extensive margin (changes in the number of flows). The former is linked to resilience with regard to the ability to recover quickly from the crisis. The latter is linked to robustness with regard to the ability to sustain flows during the crisis: in the presence of fixed costs of exporting, it is expected that trade flows that cease during the crisis will not be able to resume quickly, if at all, afterward. Another strain of the relevant literature seeks to understand the pattern of survival of exporting firms or export flows following shocks to trade. Several studies explore the intensive and extensive margins and export survival to identify differences for firms involved in GVCs and for the type of products or sectors that are traded heavily within these networks. Finally, the chapter explores emerging approaches to network analysis that are of relevance for understanding the implications of extensive interconnectivity in the global economy.

GVCs and the impact of shocks on trade

Trade within GVCs may respond differently to shocks than arm's length trade. A key argument revolves around the role of inventories. Because a firm faces more uncertainty and risk the farther it is from the final consumer, upstream firms tend to hold more inventories. When a demand shock to downstream firms forces them to reduce orders, the impact will be magnified the farther it reaches up the value chain. Hence, trade within GVCs may decline faster and farther than trade in final goods. In addition, because these value chains extend over many countries, the impact of the shock will spread more widely and quickly through the GVC channel than if trade were more concentrated in final goods whose inputs are sourced within the exporting country.[1]

Several studies have identified ways in which GVCs may induce more resilience and stability in trade following shocks. Establishing a GVC entails substantial costs that cannot be recovered easily, if at all. These costs may include the costs of searching for appropriate partners in foreign markets, capital investments that require knowledge of all local regulations, and costs associated with workforce training. These sunk costs create an incentive to spread adjustments following a shock throughout the chain rather than to disrupt the whole chain by removing particular suppliers (Altomonte and Ottaviano 2009). In addition, given the presence of large multinational firms within these value chains, liquidity challenges in times of crisis may be less binding on value chain participants. Trade flows within an established value chain may depend less on trade credit from financial institutions. From a trade perspective, adjustments will appear primarily at the intensive margin, via changes in the volume of imports and exports within a GVC, and less so at the extensive margin, in the form of changes in the number of trade flows. This adjustment will be enhanced if building trust between value chain participants has value and if longer-term contractual relationships are costly to break in the short-run response to a shock.

Impacts at the intensive and the extensive margins

The literature strongly suggests that adjustment to shocks is driven by changes primarily in the intensive margin rather than the extensive margin, likely reflecting the influence of GVCs. The intensive margin captures the extent to which adjustments take place with regard to variation in the volume of existing firm-product-country trade flows. The extensive margin is driven by changes in the number of firm-product-country trade flows as a result of firms entering or exiting particular product-country markets, firms exiting entirely, or new firms entering. A large number of studies finds that adjustments at the intensive margin tend to be more muted for multinational firms and GVCs relative to other types of trade. The available studies are based on trade in goods, with little information about trade in services, reflecting data limitations to some extent.

Analyses using firm-level data

Studies using firm-level data on exports and imports find mixed results for the impact of GVC participation on trade flows. Studies of rich countries indicate either that trade within GVCs is a source of stability during crises or that, although trade between affiliated firms declines more than arm's length trade, it also recovers more rapidly. There is, however, very little information on the response of trading firms in low- and middle-income countries. The following summarizes the results from some of the key studies in this area.

Bernard et al. (2009) find that, following the Asian financial crisis of 1997, the decline in exports was greater for "arm's length" trade than for "related-party"[2] trade akin to multinational firms. They also find that the majority of the changes in US imports and exports with Asia at the level of the firm were accounted for by the intensive margin. Their findings suggest that GVC links may have dampened the negative impact on trade at the product level and that GVC links for each product are important in explaining the impact of the 2008–09 financial crisis. Two GVC measures are used: a simple dummy variable for intermediate goods and a more sophisticated variable that reflects the degree of vertical integration for each product. The latter is measured as the average amount of each product required as an input to produce US$1 of all products. These measures are included in regression equations that explain the decline in trade during the crisis and the subsequent recovery.

Lanz and Miroudot (2011) find that the decline in domestic demand is the main factor behind the collapse in trade during the global financial crisis. Nevertheless, after controlling for this demand shock, there is no evidence that products with a high degree of intrafirm trade or with strong downward links saw greater declines in imports. However, intermediate goods saw significantly larger declines than final goods. Positive coefficients on interaction terms between intrafirm trade and measures of GVCs suggest, first, that trade actually increased for products with a high degree of intrafirm trade and strong backward links and, second, that the trade collapse for intermediate inputs was weaker for products that were traded intrafirm. This finding suggests that intrafirm trade can be a force for stability when GVCs are disrupted by demand shocks.

Altomonte et al. (2012) exploit a data set for France that matches transaction-level trade data with information on intrafirm links to identify affiliated firms where trade is internalized and firms where trade takes place at arm's length through separate supply contracts. They find that the decline in trade during a crisis is driven by trade in intermediate products but also that trade in intermediates expands more quickly than trade in other products once recovery is under way. They also present evidence suggesting that these impacts are greater for trade between affiliated firms than for arm's length trade. In turn, they propose that the decline and recovery in intermediates reflect the superior management of inventory and value chain information within multinational groups.

Analyses using bilateral trade data

Studies using cross-country data on trade flows provide evidence that trade within GVCs tends to be as stable as, or more stable than, trade in final goods and that the intensive margin tends to dominate the trade response to shocks more than the extensive margin. The following are some of the key studies.

Wang and Whalley (2010) explore the impact of the global financial crisis on the trade of Asian countries using a broad decomposition of monthly data by product and type of trade. They find considerable variation in trade performance across countries and by product group but little change in the share of processing versus nonprocessing trade in China's exports and imports. This finding suggests that GVC-related trade was not affected differently than other types of trade. In the recovery after 2009, the rebound was greatest for trade between Association of Southeast Asian Nations (ASEAN) members and China, which may indicate that geography plays a role in the recovery of trade from global shocks.

Haddad, Harrison, and Hausman (2010), following Bernard et al. (2009), apply a decomposition that identifies separately changes at the intensive and extensive margins but then breaks down the changes at the intensive margin into price and quantity effects. They apply this decomposition to monthly import data at the six-digit level of the Harmonized System (HS) for all partners of Brazil, Indonesia, the United States, and each European Union (EU) country for 2007 to 2009. The main findings are that changes in trade at the intensive margin (adjustments in existing trade flows) dominated those at the extensive margin (the appearance and disappearance of bilateral product flows). Within the intensive margin, quantities declined and prices fell, consistent with a demand-driven shock. However, there are enormous differences across types of products, with commodities responsible for the overall decline in prices. For manufactures, whereas quantities fell, prices often rose, which is more suggestive of supply-side constraints; there is some evidence that price increases were more pronounced in sectors typically seen as being dependent on access to external financing.

Ando and Kimura (2012) apply this decomposition approach to Japanese exports during the global financial crisis and focus on changes for machinery parts and components relative to final machinery products. They find that the extent of exit of product-market flows for machinery and parts, which is taken to be representative of the international movement of goods within GVCs, was much smaller than that of product-market flows for final machinery products.

Export survival

The limited role of the extensive margin in explaining trade responses to shocks implies that shocks should not have a substantial impact on export survival rates. Studies of export survival measure the rate at which exporting firms exit international markets or, where firm-level data are not used, the extent to which the number of product-market import or export flows contracts during a crisis relative to periods before and after. Few, if any, studies look specifically at the impacts of a crisis on survival in low- and middle-income countries and whether links with value chains enhance or reduce hazards.[3]

Nevertheless, some studies using trade flow data find evidence that trade relationships are more stable for intermediate goods, in which GVCs are heavily represented, than for final goods. Much of the limited analysis that has looked for links between the survival of trade flows and participation in GVCs has used product-level trade data rather than firm-level information and has focused on the machinery sector, given the ability to identify parts and components for this sector easily in the trade classification. The following are the key studies in this area.

Obashi (2010), one of the first of these studies, explores whether the survival characteristics of trade in intermediate goods (defined as parts and components) differ from those of final goods using data on product-country flows (at the six-digit level of the HS) for intra-Asian trade in machinery products between 1993 and 2006.

The results suggest that trade relationships in intermediate goods are, on average, more stable and of longer duration than trade in final goods.

Okubo, Kimura, and Teshima (2014) use much more detailed trade data for Japan (nine-digit level) for machinery products and parts and components to explore the impacts of the global financial crisis on the pattern of entry and exit into exporting. Estimates of the determinants of the hazard rate during the crisis suggest that export flows to larger markets and to geographically closer markets are less likely to cease. The longer the trade relationship has existed, the lower the hazard rate. Coefficients on dummy variables for trade with Asian countries and for both parts and components are found to be negative and significant, implying that these factors lower the risk that a product-market flow will cease during the crisis. The study also finds that these factors have a similar impact on the probability of reentry of products that exited the market during the crisis.

Córcoles, Díaz-Mora, and Gandoy (2015) explore product-market data at the six-digit level of the HS for Spanish exports over the period 1996–2010, again comparing survival rates for flows classified as parts and components relative to final products within the machinery sector. They find higher survival rates for flows of parts and components than for flows of final goods, which they conclude indicates the greater stability of trade within global production networks. Estimation of a discrete-time survival model, controlling for unobservable heterogeneity across flows, finds that the following factors increase the probability of survival of a Spanish product-market export flow: the initial size of the export flow, geographic diversification (number of markets in which the specific product is sold), product diversification (number of products sold in the specific market), geographic and linguistic proximity, and common membership in the European Union. This finding is consistent with a range of previous studies that have looked at the survival of trade more broadly, although the impact of these factors on the survival of exports of parts and components is found to be significantly greater than for exports of final goods. They conclude that many of these factors reflect the presence of fixed entry costs and the benefits of trust and reliability and that these factors tend to be more important in global value chains, which in turn leads to less churning of suppliers in these networks.

Türkcan (2016) explores highly disaggregated data on machinery exports at the product, but not the firm, level for Turkey over the period 1998–2013. The analysis suggests that the likelihood of the survival of exports varies widely across types of products (total machinery products, finished machinery products, and machinery parts and components) and types of trade (horizontally differentiated products and vertically differentiated products). Based on discrete-time duration models, the empirical results demonstrate that vertical differentiation and product and market diversification are associated with a higher export survival rate, particularly for parts and components linked with global production networks. The evidence supports the hypothesis that global production-sharing activities greatly increase the chances of survival in export markets.

A few analyses use firm-level data to explore the survival patterns of firms integrated into GVCs but face the challenge of precisely identifying such firms relative to other firms. The standard approach has been to treat firms that both import and export as being part of GVCs. This approach is problematic for several reasons. For example, in countries that restrict access to foreign exchange, firms may export products, which they may or may not produce themselves, to obtain the foreign exchange they need to be able to import. Further, firms may simply be trading companies that both import and export without, at least initially, producing anything.[4] The following are the key studies in this area.

Córcoles, Díaz-Mora, and Gandoy (2019) use a more rigorous definition of firms involved in global production networks: firms that import components, export, and are involved in international production through inward or outward foreign direct investment (FDI). Using data from a regular survey of manufacturing firms in Spain and controlling for a variety of firm characteristics, they find that, over the period 2000–13, firms participating in this "complex internationalization" have a lower probability of exiting exporting than other exporting firms. There is no evidence of any increase in exiting from exporting for any type of firms during the financial crisis of 2008–09. Further, using a dynamic panel data model of export values, they find that being involved in more complex internationalization is associated with a smaller negative impact of the global crisis and a stronger subsequent recovery. They conclude that firms that are embedded in global production networks are better able to address uncertainty over foreign market conditions and global shocks, have a lower probability of exiting from exporting, and have higher export values than other firms.

Kostevc and Kejžar (2020) use transaction-level trade data with financial information on all Slovenian firms and data on cross-border financial flows for the period 2002–11. They identify firms in production networks through foreign ownership or the ownership of foreign affiliates and link this information to bilateral trade flows. They estimate a discrete-time hazard function for product-market export spells and find that variables reflecting foreign ownership from the destination market and ownership of foreign affiliates in the destination market reduce the hazard rate. This positive effect of bilateral FDI on the likelihood that an export flow will survive is greatest for intermediate goods, which likely captures the finding that survival rates are higher for GVC-related trade flows. Finally, the study finds that hazard rates were significantly higher during the financial crisis of 2008–09 and that the crisis lowered the beneficial impact of foreign ownership on export survival. This finding suggests greater adjustment in GVC trade during the crisis.

Network analysis

Another approach is to use network analysis to identify dependencies between nodes within the overall trade network and how these dependencies may propagate a shock to the rest of the network. The structure of a particular trade or production network can explain whether and how a particular shock spreads more widely throughout the economy and has impacts considerably larger than those of the initial shock itself. Most of the analysis explores how location-specific shocks such as earthquakes and floods can have impacts beyond the area specifically affected, including aggregate country and even global impacts.

One of the key areas for network analysis has been the impact of the Japanese earthquake of 2011 on supply chains. The main studies show that the structure of networks, particularly the presence of a large, central node affected by the shock and the degree of substitution possible for affected products, has an important impact on the degree to which shocks are propagated.

Todo, Nakajima, and Matous (2015) combine detailed data from surveys of Japanese firms to identify firms affected by the earthquake and to explore information, from before the disaster, on the number of suppliers and clients of each firm. The postdisaster survey also provides information from each firm on how long after the earthquake its access to materials and intermediates from suppliers was affected. They find that, after controlling for firm characteristics, such as size and productivity, and for the level of damage, the number of days before production was resumed after the earthquake was lower, the more extensive the network with firms outside of the affected area. This finding likely reflects the ability of firms to continue to source supplies from or to satisfy the demands of firms that were not damaged during the crisis or to substitute away from suppliers or clients that were adversely affected. The positive impact of direct networks on recovery time is enhanced the larger the indirect network—that is, the number of suppliers of direct suppliers and clients of direct clients. Although firms with strong networks within the affected area did not resume activities more quickly, their sales recovered more quickly in the medium term. The authors conclude that, following a major shock, the positive effects of being in a supply chain typically exceed the negative effects for a firm.

Carvalho et al. (2021) quantify the extent to which the presence of direct and indirect input-output links to firms in the Japanese earthquake-hit areas had an impact on the performance of firms outside the directly affected area in the year after the disaster. They derive a production network for Japanese firms that captures supply chain links and then compare the growth rates in the year after the earthquake of firms with different downstream and upstream network distance to disaster-area firms with the growth rates of firms in a control group: firms that were more distant in the supply chain network. They find that, after the earthquake, the growth rate of firms with disaster-hit suppliers declined 3.6 percentage points and that of firms with disaster-hit customers declined 2.9 percentage points relative to the growth rate of firms farther away in the network. There was also evidence of wider impacts on the growth of customers' customers and suppliers' suppliers and so on. Hence, they conclude that there is strong evidence that the shock spread beyond the firm directly affected in the disaster area through supply chain links.

Inoue and Todo (2017) simulate outcomes from the Japanese earthquake using data on the actual supply chain network in Japan compared with randomly generated network structures. Damages as a result of both the direct effects on firms affected by the disaster and the indirect effects on their suppliers and clients and the suppliers and clients of these firms were substantially larger in the actual network than in the random networks. This finding shows the importance of network structure in propagating shocks through supply chains. A key difference between the actual network and the randomly generated networks is the degree distribution (number of connections a node has to other nodes),[5] with the former being highly right-skewed, meaning that most nodes have a low degree distribution, but a few nodes—"hubs"—have a large number of connections. In addition, the average length of the actual supply chain network—the number of steps between two arbitrary nodes in a network—is much shorter than that in random networks, which means that shocks spread faster in networks such as those among firms in Japan. Another important finding from the simulations is that the more difficult it is to substitute suppliers, the faster an adverse shock is propagated through the network.

Whereas there is substantial evidence that supply links amplify the impact of shocks within countries, the evidence of propagation across countries within the networks of global supply chains is less extensive and clear. Boehm, Flaaen, and Pandalai-Nayar (2019) examine the impact of the Japanese earthquake on the production of US affiliates of Japanese multinationals. Using detailed monthly data on trade transactions for firms operating in the United States and after identifying intermediate goods in firm-level import transactions, they derive the inputs imported from Japan as a share of the total cost of inputs as a measure of a firm's exposure to the earthquake in Japan. They find that exposure to the shock is highly concentrated among affiliates of Japanese multinationals relative to non-Japanese firms. For these exposed firms, a proxy for output falls by almost the same proportion as the decline in imported intermediate inputs from Japan, and this reduction is driven by changes in the quantity of imports rather than by changes in dollar-denominated prices.

The ability to substitute alternative inputs for those affected by a disaster is a key factor in the international propagation of shocks. Following the Japanese earthquake, affiliates of Japanese firms in the United States were unable to substitute alternative inputs quickly in the short run. Indeed, the application of a standard production function approach finds that the short-run elasticity of substitution between inputs is close to zero. The low degree of substitution between inputs is therefore found to be an important factor in determining the transmission of shocks between firms.[6] The performance of Japanese affiliates in the United States also suggests that inventories played an insignificant role in mitigating the impact of the shock, despite the fact that, with low substitutability between inputs, firms would be expected to hold large inventories.

Connections to foreign firms may be an important way of accessing substitute inputs or alternative buyers for those affected by a crisis. Using data on supply chain links among major firms, Kashiwagi, Matous, and Todo (2018) find propagation from firms damaged by Hurricane Sandy to upstream and downstream suppliers and customers within the United States, but not to overseas firms. This finding remains after controlling for distance between firms. Their results also suggest that the negative impact on suppliers and customers of damaged firms is significantly lower if they are also connected to foreign firms and have a large number of workers. This finding is interpreted as suggesting that large firms and firms with links to GVCs have greater opportunities to substitute away from suppliers and customers negatively affected by economic shocks because they face lower search costs relative to sales than firms that are smaller or not connected internationally. Finally, this study shows that the structure of the network matters; there is greater propagation of a shock when a damaged firm's partners are densely connected with each other through supply chains.[7]

Positive shocks are also contagious. For example, the effect of government measures to enhance the resilience of supply chains can spread beyond the direct recipients to other firms in the value chain. Kashiwagi and Todo (2020) investigate the impact of subsidies provided to small and medium enterprises in Japan to support the repair and reinstallation of capital goods and facilities damaged in the earthquake. The subsidies not only had a direct positive effect on the sales and employment of the recipients after the disaster but also had an indirect benefit for other firms in disaster-affected areas that were linked through supply chains but did not receive any subsidy. It would be interesting to see whether government interventions targeting national firms had some benefit for linked firms in other countries.

Newer research applies network analysis to trade flow data to identify and rank the fragility of individual traded goods. Korniyenko, Pinat, and Dew (2017) use information at the six-digit level of the HS for 223 countries to derive three measures of fragility for each traded good. First, with regard to the degree distribution, they identify the presence of influential exporting nodes in terms of the standard deviation of weighted out-degree centrality.[8] This figure captures the extent to which the network of each product has a small number of central exporters, which, in turn, can propagate supply shocks internationally. Second is the density of the network or degree of clustering. For each good, the weighted average local clustering coefficient is used to capture the extent to which the trade partners of a particular country are also trading that good among each other.[9] This figure is then multiplied by the diameter of the network for each product, which is the length of the shortest path between the most distant nodes. A third and final factor is the availability of close substitutes for products traded internationally. Ideally this factor would be captured by estimated elasticities of substitution, but there is little consensus because the value depends on the data and approach to estimation. In this case, a very simple proxy is used: the distribution of human capital across exporting countries. The idea is that the more similar countries are in terms of human capital, the easier it is to find substitutes for the product from an afflicted country. Cluster analysis is then used to identify the riskiest products in the global economy.

Perhaps not surprising, parts for computers, aircraft and motor vehicles, mechanical appliances, medical equipment, and some pharmaceuticals are ranked highest in terms of risk. Countries are then ranked by the share of these risky products in their imports and exports: the higher the share, the greater the vulnerability to supply shocks. In terms of imports, the most vulnerable countries are those producing minerals (Chad, the Republic of Congo, Equatorial Guinea, Gabon, and Turkmenistan) and, more generally, those with low economic diversification. A second group of vulnerable importing countries consists of those integrated into global and regional value chains, including Canada, the Czech Republic, Germany, Hungary, Mexico, and Romania. China, Japan, and the Republic of Korea have below-average import vulnerability. Exports of risky products are concentrated in a few suppliers: China, Germany, Japan, and the United States, followed by several middle-income countries. Most countries export few, if any, risky products. However, in a model of export growth, the share of risky imports from partners suffering a localized supply shock in the previous period, such as the Japanese earthquake or Thai floods, is estimated to be only weakly significant.

Conclusions

GVCs can propagate shocks across countries and enhance resilience to a crisis. The analysis of the impact of previous shocks on trade highlights a range of mechanisms by which GVCs may amplify shocks across countries, but GVCs also have characteristics that lend themselves to greater stability. The weight of evidence from a variety of methodological and empirical approaches suggests that, in previous shocks such as the Asian financial crisis, the global financial shock of 2008–09, and the Japanese earthquake, the latter may dominate.

Using both firm-level data and detailed trade data, most studies find that adjustments at the intensive margin tend to dominate the response to shocks. When the response is primarily at the intensive margin of trade, with firms reducing their average sales rather than exiting from markets, this response is likely to be associated with a faster recovery (greater resilience) than in the case of adjustments on the extensive margin. It is suggested that firms within GVCs have incentives to preserve the structure of the chain and to avoid the sunk costs of finding new partners. In the context of the COVID-19 shock, there are reasons to believe that search costs increased because of the inability to travel to verify new suppliers, for example. Robustness (ability to keep operating) is then linked to resilience (capacity to resume normal operations quickly), such that trade within GVCs recovers more quickly than other types of trade.

The structure of trade networks matters in determining the impacts of shocks. Studies using information from detailed firm-level surveys on the connections between firms both as customers and suppliers and as the customers of customers and suppliers of suppliers are able to map the structure of the resulting network. The structure of a network is important for the propagation of shocks. For example, the presence of large central nodes makes it more likely that shocks will spread through the network if something happens to the node. The lack of close substitutes for a particular product (network node) may also promote fragility of the whole network. These network characteristics tend to vary with different types of products. Initial empirical evidence suggests that network characteristics associated with parts and components of machinery, such as vehicles and electronics, are particularly likely to promote propagation of shocks in GVCs.

The available literature has several important gaps that can be addressed in the analysis of the impact of the COVID-19 pandemic. Most notable is the very small number of studies that have looked explicitly at the impact of shocks, and adjustments within GVCs, on firms in, and the trade of, low- and middle-income countries. Are suppliers in these countries more likely to be included in adjustments at the intensive margin or to be part of the extensive margin and, at least temporarily, excluded from the network? There is some evidence that the latter may be the case for certain value chains such as apparel, where major brands and retailers based in the European Union and the United States canceled or postponed orders during the pandemic, including orders for goods already produced by suppliers in low- and middle-income countries. This practice led to factory closures in countries such as Bangladesh, Myanmar, and Vietnam. Pasquali and Godfrey (2020) find initial evidence from the apparel sector in Eswatini that smaller indirect suppliers that have arm's length relationships with global design houses were hit harder than direct suppliers of South African retailers. It is important to assess whether firms in low- and middle-income countries that participate in production networks based on regional demand and supply networks were affected less negatively than firms serving buyers in richer countries.

Little is known about whether firms in low- and middle-income countries that participate in GVCs face lower substitution elasticities and hence higher risks of being affected by supply chain contagion than firms in richer countries. This situation would likely arise if firms in low- and middle-income countries face higher search costs in finding alternative suppliers or customers.

With regard to the extensive margin, much attention has been focused on survival rates and how they may be higher for GVC-related trade. Less attention has been paid to how crises may affect entry rates. While it is important to understand the robustness and resilience of existing flows that contribute to a quick recovery of actual trade, it is also important to understand how dampening the entry rates of new firms or flows will affect long-term export growth and diversification.

There is little knowledge about how trade shocks affect workers and their households in low- and middle-income countries. If the adjustment is primarily through a decline in the volume of trade, are workers affected through reductions in wages or reductions in the number of people employed?

Finally, little notable work has been conducted on the impact of shocks on trade in services, reflecting the lack of detailed data. This subject is important because services trade, especially tourism and transportation, was hit especially hard during the pandemic. However, some services trade actually increased, such as information technology–related services, and the pandemic is putting increasing focus on the opportunities for e-trade.

Notes

1. Similar effects will also emanate from a supply shock in which GVCs amplify the direct supply shock as suppliers of intermediates along the chain find it increasingly harder to obtain the imported industrial inputs they require from the initially hit countries and then from each other.

2. Related-party trade is defined as trade in which the firms involved in a US export transaction own 10 percent or more of the other party. For a US import transaction, the criterion is 6 percent or more.

3. A few studies have looked at the survival of exports from low- and middle-income countries but have not explored the impact of global, regional, or country-specific shocks. See, for example, Brenton, Saborowski, and von Uexkull (2010).

4. For example, Sutton and Kellow (2010) find that in Ethiopia import-export trading activities provide a crucial base from which manufacturing firms subsequently emerge.

5. In directed networks, such as trade networks, the degree of a node is the sum of the in-degree, which is the total number of connections onto that node from other nodes (import connections), and the out-degree, which is the total number of connections coming from that node (export connections).

6. Barrot and Sauvagnat (2016) find that, for the United States, measures of input specificity are a major determinant of the propagation of shocks among firms in the economy. Suppliers are typically unable to find alternative buyers for their products after their customer is affected by a shock.

7. The density of a network can be measured by the local clustering coefficient: the actual number of links between a node's partners divided by the total number of all possible links between the partners.

8. For each product, the weighted out-degree centrality is measured as the sum of ties that a node directs outward to other nodes as a share of the total number of other nodes, weighted by the value of the flows to each node. Negative spillovers from an adverse supply shock are more likely in networks with a small number of countries with a high intensity of exports to many partners.

9. For node i, this coefficient is calculated as the number of connections between i's neighbor relative to the number of possible connections for that neighbor.

References

Altomonte, Carlo, Filippo Di Mauro, Gianmarco I. P. Ottaviano, Armando Rungi, and Vincent Vicard. 2012. "Global Value Chains during the Great Trade Collapse: A Bullwhip Effect?" CEP Discussion Paper dp1131, Centre for Economic Performance, London School of Economics. http://cep.lse.ac.uk/pubs/download/dp1131.pdf.

Altomonte, Carlo, and Gianmarco Ottaviano. 2009. "Resilient to the Crisis? Global Supply Chains and Trade Flows." *VOX.EU/CEPR* (blog), November 27, 2009. https://voxeu.org/article/resilient-crisis-global-supply-chains-and-trade-flows.

Ando, Mitsuyo, and Fukunari Kimura. 2012. "How Did the Japanese Exports Respond to Two Crises in the International Production Networks? The Global Financial Crisis and the Great East Japan Earthquake." *Asian Economic Journal* 26 (3): 261–87. https://www.tandfonline.com/doi/full/10.1080/1540496X.2020.1785426.

Baldwin, Richard, ed. 2009. *The Great Trade Collapse: Causes, Consequences, and Prospects.* Washington, DC: Center for Economic and Policy Research.

Barrot, Jean-Noel, and Julien Sauvagnat. 2016. "Input Specificity and the Propagation of Idiosyncratic Shocks in Production Networks." *Quarterly Journal of Economics* 131 (3): 1543–92. https://papers.ssrn.com/sol3/papers.cfm?abstract_id=2427421.

Bems, Rudolfs, Robert Johnson, and Kei-Mu Yi. 2013. "The Great Trade Collapse." *Annual Review of Economics* 5 (1): 375–400.

Bernard Andrew, J. Bradford Jensen, Stephen Redding, and Peter Schott. 2009. "The Margins of US Trade." *American Economic Review* 99 (2): 487–93.

Boehm, Christoph E., Aaron Flaaen, and Nitya Pandalai-Nayar. 2019. "Input Links and the Transmission of Shocks: Firm-Level Evidence from the 2011 Tōhoku Earthquake." *Review of Economics and Statistics* 101 (1): 60–75. https://www.mitpressjournals.org/doi /abs/10.1162/rest_a_00750.

Brenton, Paul, Christian Saborowski, and Erik von Uexkull. 2010. "What Explains the Low Survival Rate of Developing Country Export Flows?" *The World Bank Economic Review* 24 (3): 474–99.

Carvalho, Vasco M., Makoto Nirei, Yukiko U. Saito, and Alireza Tahbaz-Salehi. 2021. "Supply Chain Disruptions: Evidence from the Great East Japan Earthquake." *Quarterly Journal of Economics* 136 (2): 1255–321. http://vasco-m-carvalho.github.io/pdfs/JapanEQ.pdf.

Córcoles, David, Carmen Díaz-Mora, and Rosario Gandoy. 2015. "Export Survival in Global Production Chains." *The World Economy* 38 (10): 1526–54. https://www.aeefi.com/RePEc /pdf/defi12-03.pdf.

Córcoles, David, Carmen Díaz-Mora, and Rosario Gandoy. 2019. "Complex Internationalization Strategies and Firm Export Performance during the Great Trade Collapse." *Journal of Economic Studies* 46 (2): 246–65. https://ruidera.uclm.es/xmlui /bitstream/handle/10578/19853/Preprint%20Complex%20internationalization%20 and%20firm%20export%20dynamics-Journal%20of%20Economic%20Studies .pdf?sequence=1&isAllowed=y.

Haddad, Mona, Ann Harrison, and Catherine Hausman. 2010. "Decomposing the Great Trade Collapse: Products, Prices, and Quantities in the 2008–2009 Crisis." NBER Working Paper 16253, National Bureau of Economic Research, Cambridge, MA.

Inoue, Hiroyasu, and Yasuyuki Todo. 2017. "Propagation of Negative Shocks through Firm Networks: Evidence from Simulation on Comprehensive Supply-Chain Data." RIETI Discussion Paper 17-E-044, Research Institute of Economy, Trade, and Industry, University of Hyogo. https://www.rieti.go.jp/jp/publications/dp/17e044.pdf.

Kashiwagi, Yuzuka, Petr Matous, and Yasuyuki Todo. 2018. "International Propagation of Economic Shocks through Global Supply Chains." WINPEC Working Paper Series E1810, Waseda Institute of Political Economy, Waseda University, Tokyo. https://www.waseda.jp /fpse/winpec/assets/uploads/2018/11/No.E1810.pdf.

Kashiwagi, Yuzuka, and Yasuyuki Todo. 2020. "Propagation of Positive Effects of Post-Disaster Policies through Supply Chains: Evidence from the Great East Japan Earthquake and Tsunami." ADB Economics Working Paper 604, Asia Development Bank, Metro Manila.

Korniyenko, Yevgeniya, Magali Pinat, and Brian Dew. 2017. "Assessing the Fragility of Global Trade: The Impact of Localized Supply Shocks Using Network Analysis." IMF Working Paper WP/17/30, International Monetary Fund, Washington, DC.

Kostevc, Črt, and Katja Zajc Kejžar. 2020. "Firm-Level Export Duration: The Importance of Market-Specific Ownership Links." *The World Economy* 43 (5): 1277–308. https://onlinelibrary .wiley.com/doi/full/10.1111/twec.12939.

Lanz, Rainer, and Sébastien Miroudot. 2011. "Intra-Firm Trade: Patterns, Determinants, and Policy Implications." OECD Trade Policy Paper 114, OECD Publishing, Paris. http:// dx.doi.org/10.1787/5kg9p39lrwnn-en.

Obashi, Ayako. 2010. "Stability of Production Networks in East Asia: Duration and Survival of Trade." *Japan and the World Economy* 22 (1): 21–30.

Okubo, Toshihiro, Fukunari Kimura, and Nozomu Teshima. 2014. "Asian Fragmentation in the Global Financial Crisis." *International Review of Economics & Finance* 31 (C): 114–27. https://www.sciencedirect.com/science/article/pii/S1059056014000021.

Pasquali, Giovanni, and Shane Godfrey. 2020. "Apparel Regional Value Chains and COVID-19: Insights from Eswatini." Research Briefing, University of Manchester Global Development

Institute. https://www.research.manchester.ac.uk/portal/files/177957615/Research_Briefing _Eswatini_Regional_value_chains_Covid19.pdf.

Sutton, John, and Nebil Kellow. 2010. "An Enterprise Map of Ethiopia." International Growth Centre, London. https://www.theigc.org/publication/an-enterprise-map-of -ethiopia-by-john-sutton/.

Todo, Yasuyuki, Kentaro Nakajima, and Petr Matous. 2015. "How Do Supply Chain Networks Affect the Resilience of Firms to Natural Disasters? Evidence from the Great East Japan Earthquake." *Journal of Regional Science* 55 (2): 209–29. https://onlinelibrary.wiley.com /doi/full/10.1111/jors.12119.

Türkcan, Kemal. 2016. "On the Role of Vertical Differentiation in Enhancing Survival of Export Flows: Evidence from a Developing Country." MPRA Paper 71023, University Library of Munich, Germany. https://mpra.ub.uni-muenchen.de/71023/1/MPRA_paper_71023.pdf.

Wang, Jing, and John Whalley. 2010. "The Trade Performance of Asian Economies during and following the 2008 Financial Crisis." NBER Working Paper 16142, National Bureau of Economic Research, Cambridge, MA.

3

The COVID-19 Crisis and Trade Outcomes: A Review and Analysis of Major Trade Trends

Key messages

- Real gross domestic product (GDP) and global trade fell by 3.5 percent and 8.3 percent, respectively, in 2020. The contractions were of historic magnitude, comparable to those in the Great Recession of 2008–09. In 2020 the share of services and trade in GDP contracted disproportionately relative to that of goods. The contractions were concentrated in the second quarter of 2020, followed by a rapid recovery in many countries.

- The composition of merchandise trade underwent substantial shifts in response to changing consumer demand. In value terms, trade in medical supplies and food increased, whereas trade in minerals and fuels, motor vehicles, and footwear contracted.

- Contractions in trade largely took the form of reductions in volume (intensive margin) rather than the disappearance of country- and product-specific trade flows (extensive margin). However, the extensive margin was more fragile for low-income exporters. Aside from an increasing role of East Asian countries in light manufacturing, there is little evidence that global trade pivoted away from China in 2020; if anything, the opposite occurred.

- Multiple layers of uncertainty affected foreign direct investment (FDI) perhaps even more than trade. During 2020 and 2021, the value of global FDI declined by an estimated 40 percent to 50 percent, reaching levels not seen since 2005.

- Tourism and travel were affected the most negatively given the direct effects of border closures, travel restrictions, and the cancellation of many commercial flights. In February 2021, 32 percent of international borders remained closed, and almost all countries maintained some form of restrictions on travel. Commercial passenger flights, which had collapsed by 80 percent in April 2020, have partly recovered. However, much of the tourist ecosystem, which is based on small and medium enterprises, may simply have gone bankrupt, making consolidation among larger players likely.

- Participation in global value chains (GVCs) intensified the negative trade shocks arising from lost imports of intermediate goods and lost export markets but mitigated the negative effect of domestic lockdowns. The trade effects of the pandemic were smaller in industries where the possibility of working remotely was greater.

Introduction

This chapter builds on the review of historical experiences described in chapter 2. Using high-frequency monthly data, it assesses the immediate impact of the COVID-19 (coronavirus) shock on trade in both goods and services with a focus on low- and middle-income countries. It uses highly detailed data for the four main trading countries or regions—China, the European Union (EU), Japan, and the United States—to explore the main trends in the volume and value of trade, the relative importance of the intensive and extensive margins, and changes in the rate of trade flow deaths before and during the crisis. These detailed data are then explored using econometric analysis to identify the role of GVCs, the relative importance of the different channels through which domestic demand and supply as well third-country shocks affected trade flows, and the role that sector characteristics played in mitigating or augmenting the effect of such shocks.

Trends in trade and GDP

Aggregate trends for goods and services trade and GDP

During the COVID-19 crisis, global GDP plummeted at twice the rate seen during the Great Recession of 2008–09, and the global trade of goods and services dropped slightly less. In 2020 real GDP and the volume of global trade dropped by 3.5 percent and 8.3 percent, respectively, amid extensive COVID-19 lockdowns and border closures (figure 3.1, panel a). The drop in real GDP was the fastest since the Second World War and the Great Depression (World Bank 2021a). The 2020 drop in the global volume of goods and services trade was slightly smaller in magnitude than the drop in 2009 when trade declined by 11 percent. The ratio between trade and GDP growth rates was about 2:1 in the current crisis as opposed to 5:1 in 2009. The difference reflects, in part, the impact of the pandemic on services.

FIGURE 3.1 Volume and type of trade and GDP, 2005–20

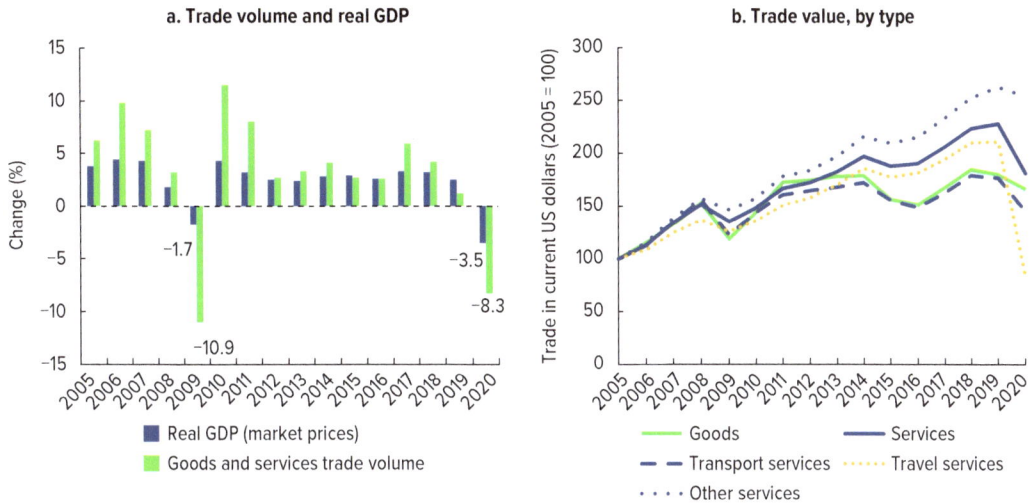

Sources: Estimates based on World Bank 2021a; CPB World Trade Monitor data; World Trade Organization data.

In a significant departure from the dynamic observed during the Great Recession, in 2020 services trade was affected more severely than goods trade. Relative to the Great Recession, the 2020 drop in goods trade was slightly milder, and the drop in services trade was more severe. The value of goods trade dropped by 8 percent in 2020 as opposed to 23 percent in 2009 (figure 3.1, panel b). In contrast, the value of services trade dropped by 21 percent in 2020, compared with a drop of 11 percent in 2009. Travel services were the most affected during the COVID-19 crisis. Transport services, which typically closely follow the trends in goods trade, declined faster than the latter because of the severe impact on passenger transport. "Other" services were relatively more resilient than transport and travel services as well as goods. This finding is consistent with the notion that some of these other services (information technology services, e-commerce) were able to function well and even flourish in an online environment.

An examination of monthly trade flows sheds light on differences in the dynamic of goods versus services (figure 3.2). Both merchandise trade and services trade plunged in April and May 2020 to a similar degree. Nevertheless, merchandise trade recouped much faster than services and faster than during the Great Recession: its rebound was under way as early as June 2020, and trade values caught up with the previous year's levels by the fourth quarter of 2020. By contrast, services trade remained depressed for the rest of 2020, trailing the 2019 level by 15 percent.

Impacts on tourism

Of all forms of international trade, tourism was affected the most negatively by COVID-19. Attempts to constrain the pandemic led to the closure of a majority of international borders by May 2020. Although some borders reopened in the

FIGURE 3.2 Monthly year-over-year change in the value of goods and services trade, 2019–21

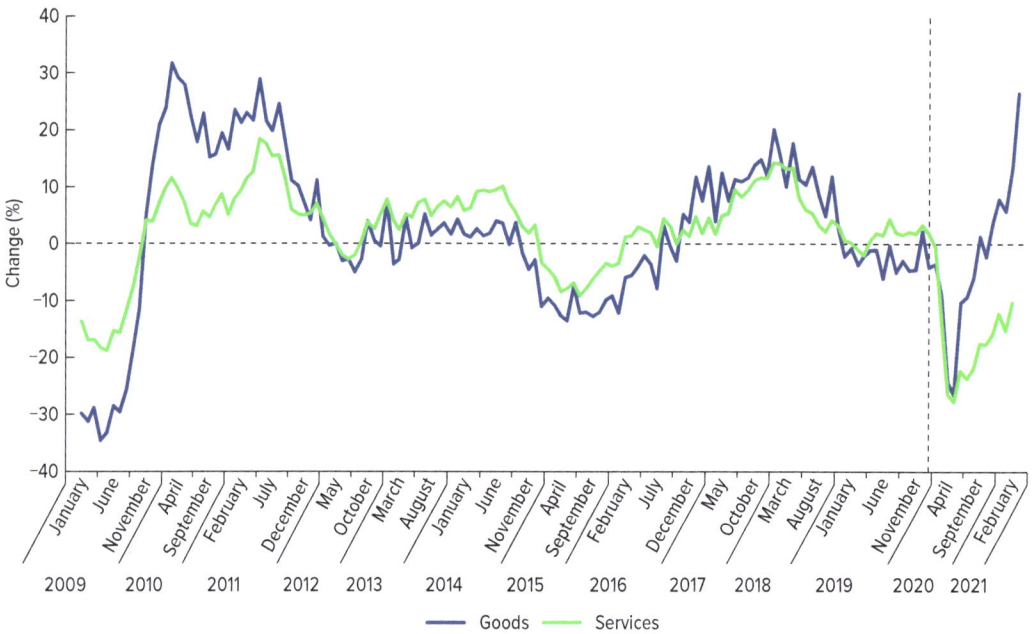

Source: World Bank 2021b.
Note: Vertical line indicates January 2020.

second half of the year, others closed again in early 2021, particularly in Europe. In February 2021, 32 percent of international borders remained closed (figure 3.3), and virtually all countries maintained some form of restrictions on travel, except for Tanzania (map 3.1). Commercial passenger flights, which had collapsed by 80 percent in April 2020, had partly recovered (figure 3.4). Thus, for tourism, the adjustment was primarily at the extensive margin. Because 80 percent of firms involved in the tourism industry are small and medium enterprises, it is likely that a significant part of the tourism ecosystem in many countries went bankrupt or otherwise shut down and will be difficult to restore, including hotels, lodging, tour operators, and local transport (World Bank 2020). The United Nations World Tourism Organization estimates that international arrivals declined by 74 percent in 2020, leading to a loss of US$1.3 trillion in export revenue (11 times the loss recorded during the financial crisis) and putting an estimated 100 million to 120 million jobs in tourism at risk (UNWTO 2021).

The pandemic is likely to have lasting effects on the tourism exports of low- and middle-income countries. A significant number of airlines have faced bankruptcy pressure, including Alitalia, American, Czech, and Interjet. The latter ceased operations in December 2020. State-owned airlines or airlines in countries with sector-specific bailout programs are likely to do better. Consolidations are also likely among large firms in air transport and hotels. As of March 2021, the global cruise line industry is experiencing a year-long shutdown, with plans for reopening still tentative and dependent on the implementation of systems for proof of vaccination (Grimaldi 2021).

FIGURE 3.3 Share of borders closed, by region, May 2020–February 2021

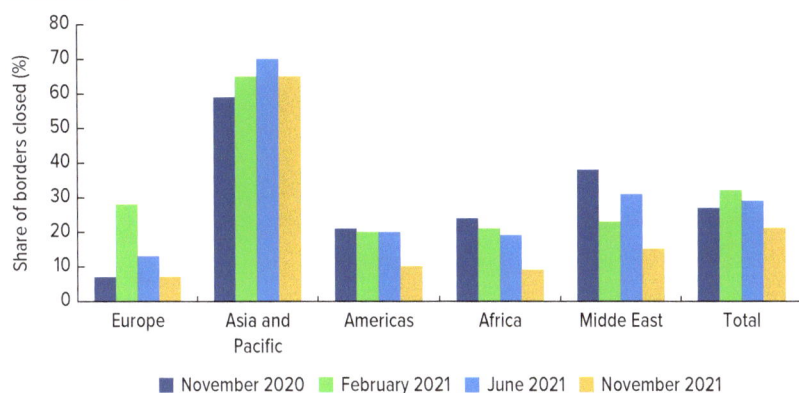

Source: UNWTO 2021.

MAP 3.1 COVID-19-related travel restrictions, February 2021

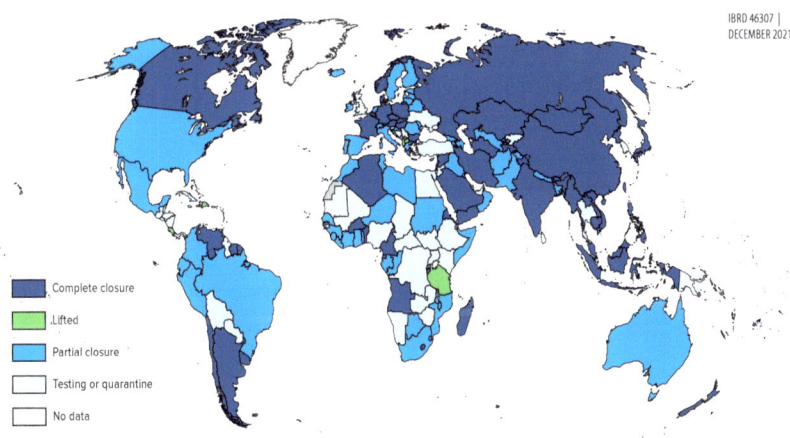

Source: United Nations World Tourism Organization data.

Trends in the unit value of traded goods

The drop and recovery in the value of merchandise trade reflect mostly the dynamic in traded volumes, but prices also changed. By the end of 2020, the overall price index exceeded the 2019 levels, albeit with significant variation by type of product (figure 3.5, panel a). Thus, whereas the price of fuels did not recover until the end of the first quarter of 2021, the price of nonfuel commodities rose by more than 20 percent in the fourth quarter of 2020 relative to 2019 and continues to surge (figure 3.5, panel b). The price of China's exports of medical products, including those related to COVID-19, rose about tenfold (figure 3.5, panel c). Going forward, semiconductor prices are expected to rise amid pent-up demand and limited supply due to capacity constraints.

FIGURE 3.4 Number of commercial flights, by month, 2019–21

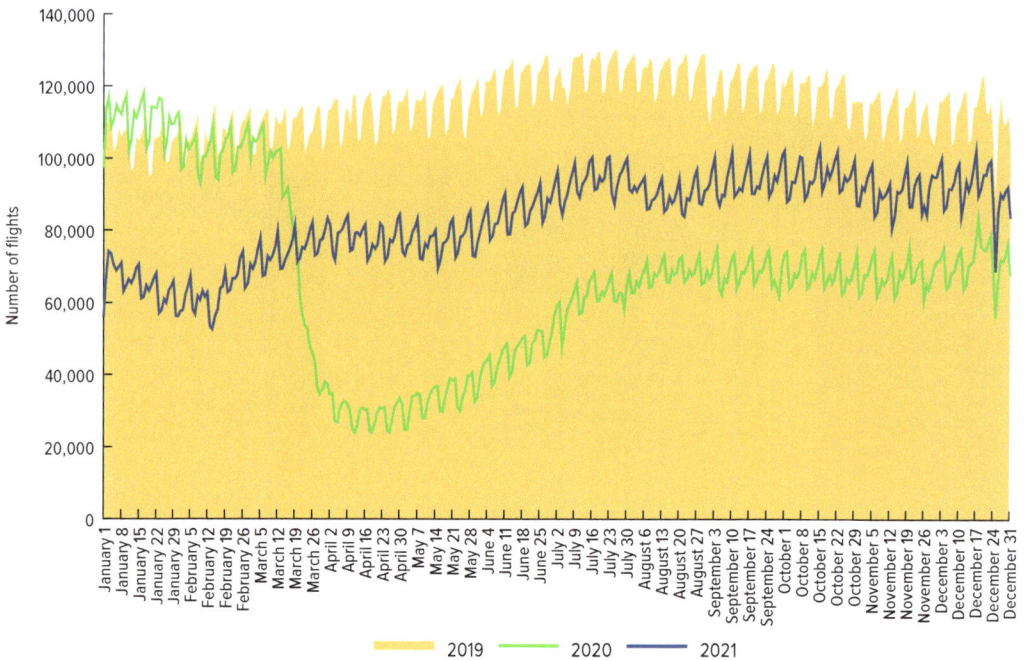

Source: Flightradar24 data.
Note: Commercial flights include commercial passenger flights, cargo flights, charter flights, and some business jet flights.

Merchandise trade by country

Merchandise trade shrank in 2020 for all regions and income groups, albeit at different rates. Declines in exports varied from 24 percent for the Middle East and North Africa, reflecting the impact of the fall in oil prices, to 0.7 percent for East Asia and Pacific, given robust exports in countries such as China and Vietnam (table 3.1).[1] Declines in imports ranged from 21.7 percent for South Asia to 4.7 percent for East Asia and Pacific and were generally deeper than the declines in exports because of the impact of low fuel prices on the value of the imports of oil-importing countries. The exports and imports of upper-middle-income countries were more resilient than those of high-income and lower-middle-income countries. High-income countries accounted for 90 percent and 70 percent of the global decline in export and import values, respectively.

Merchandise trade by product

For most broad product categories, trade in 2020 remained below the level in 2019. The largest contributors to the slack in trade values (from January to December 2020) relative to 2019 were fuels and transport equipment, which saw a double-digit drop in annual trade value. For example, exports of transport equipment shrank in 2020 to three-quarters of the 2019 level. By contrast, consumer goods and agriculture and food products contributed positively to the growth in both imports and exports in

FIGURE 3.5 Value, volume, and price of merchandise trade

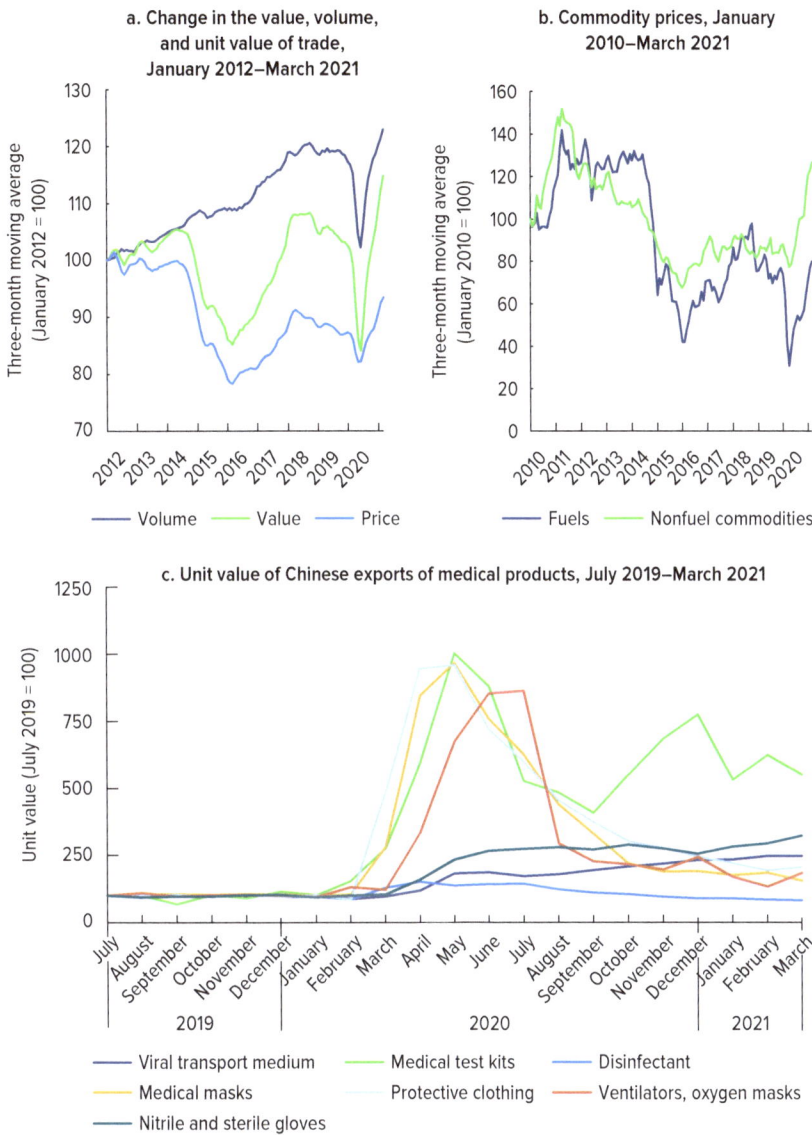

a. Change in the value, volume, and unit value of trade, January 2012–March 2021

b. Commodity prices, January 2010–March 2021

c. Unit value of Chinese exports of medical products, July 2019–March 2021

Sources: CPB World Trade Monitor data; World Bank 2021b.

TABLE 3.1 Growth of exports and imports, by region and income group, 2020 vs. 2019

Region	Exports		Imports	
	Change (%)	Contribution to total	Change (%)	Contribution to total
East Asia and Pacific	−0.7	−0.2	−4.7	−1.5
China	3.6	0.5	0.0	0.0

Table continues next page

TABLE 3.1 Growth of exports and imports, by region and income group, 2020 vs. 2019 (*continued*)

Region	Exports		Imports	
	Change (%)	Contribution to total	Change (%)	Contribution to total
Japan	−9.1	−0.4	−11.9	−0.5
Europe and Central Asia	−7.7	−3.3	−7.2	−2.9
EU-27	−6.2	−2.1	−7.3	−2.2
Latin America and the Caribbean	−8.2	−0.5	−15.5	−0.8
Middle East and North Africa	−24.0	−0.6	−14.1	−0.3
North America	−12.8	−1.5	−7.1	−1.2
United States	−12.9	−1.2	−6.4	−0.9
South Asia	−14.5	−0.3	−21.7	−0.7
Sub-Saharan Africa	−4.4	0.0	−20.5	−0.1
High income	−8.3	−5.8	−7.3	−5.2
Upper-middle income	−1.1	−0.3	−5.4	−1.2
Lower-middle income	−5.6	−0.3	−15.3	−1.2
Total	−6.4	−6.4	−7.5	−7.5

Source: World Bank 2021b.
Note: EU-27 = Austria, Belgium, Bulgaria, Croatia, Cyprus, Czechia, Denmark, Estonia, Finland, France, Germany, Greece, Hungary, Ireland, Italy, Latvia, Lithuania, Luxembourg, Malta, Netherlands, Poland, Portugal, Romania, Slovakia, Slovenia, Spain, and Sweden.

2020 (figure 3.6). China's exports of COVID-19 medical products almost doubled in 2020 compared to 2019.

Trade in medical supplies and equipment, consumer electronics, and office equipment benefited throughout the year from buoyant demand triggered by the medical crisis, the extensive lockdowns, and the switch to home-based work and education. These notable developments are most evident in the monthly trade data (figure 3.7). Demand for the products in question was met by East Asian suppliers to a large extent (more than 90 percent in the case of the EU, Japan, and the United States). The value chains of vaccines are particularly concentrated—88 percent of ingredients for producing vaccines are sourced from vaccine-producing nations.

The effects of COVID-19 on the intensive and extensive margins of merchandise trade

In 2020 the impact of the contraction in trade was more significant on the intensive margin than on the extensive margin. Changes on the intensive margin refer to changes in the value of existing product-partner trade flows, whereas changes on the extensive margin refer to the appearance or disappearance of product-partner trade flows. The flows associated with the net intensive margin drove the sharp year-over-year drop in the value of exports and imports in April and May 2020 and the recovery in the following months (figure 3.8). This finding, which is consistent with

FIGURE 3.6 Merchandise trade of major trading countries, 2020 vs. 2019

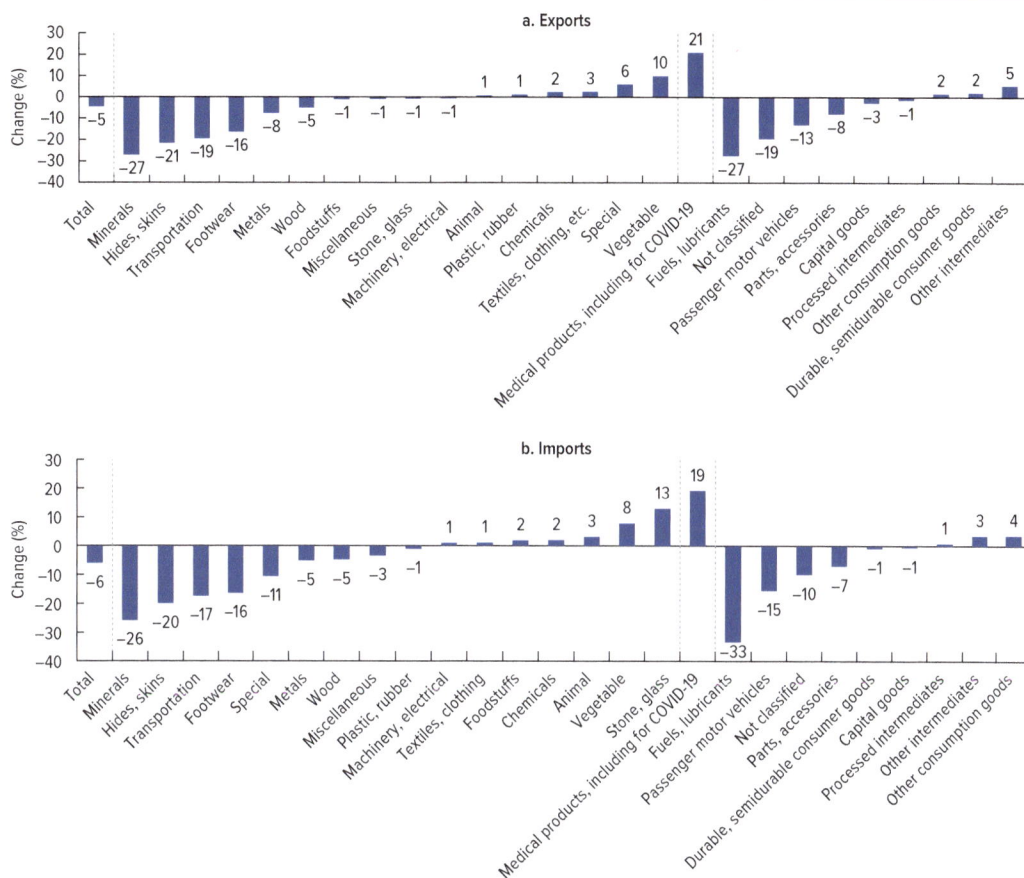

Source: World Bank 2021b.
Note: Trade is in current US dollars. Sum of national data from China, EU-27 (external trade), Japan, and the United States.
EU-27 = Austria, Belgium, Bulgaria, Croatia, Cyprus, Czechia, Denmark, Estonia, Finland, France, Germany, Greece, Hungary, Ireland, Italy, Latvia, Lithuania, Luxembourg, Malta, Netherlands, Poland, Portugal, Romania, Slovakia, Slovenia, Spain, and Sweden.

the literature focusing on other crises,[2] emerges from an examination of the monthly trade data reported by China, Japan, the United States, and each of the 27 EU countries over the past three years.[3] The intensive margin is captured by looking at the number and value of the trade of exporter-product-partner combinations that survive two adjacent years (that is, flows observed in any month m of years t and $t+1$). The extensive margin is captured by looking at exiting export-product-partner combinations (that is, combinations existing in month m of year t but not in month m of year $t+1$) as well as entering combinations (that is, combinations observed in month m of year $t+1$ but not in month m of year t). Figure 3.8 shows the full decomposition of monthly trade growth in 2020.

For low-income countries, the contribution of the extensive margin to the overall growth of goods trade is larger than that of the intensive margin (figure 3.9). By contrast, the trends in middle-income countries closely resemble global trends. This finding suggests that the COVID-19 crisis worsened the problem of low trade flow survivability in low-income countries. The negative contribution of the extensive

FIGURE 3.7 Imports of China, EU-27, Japan, and the United States, January 2019–February 2021

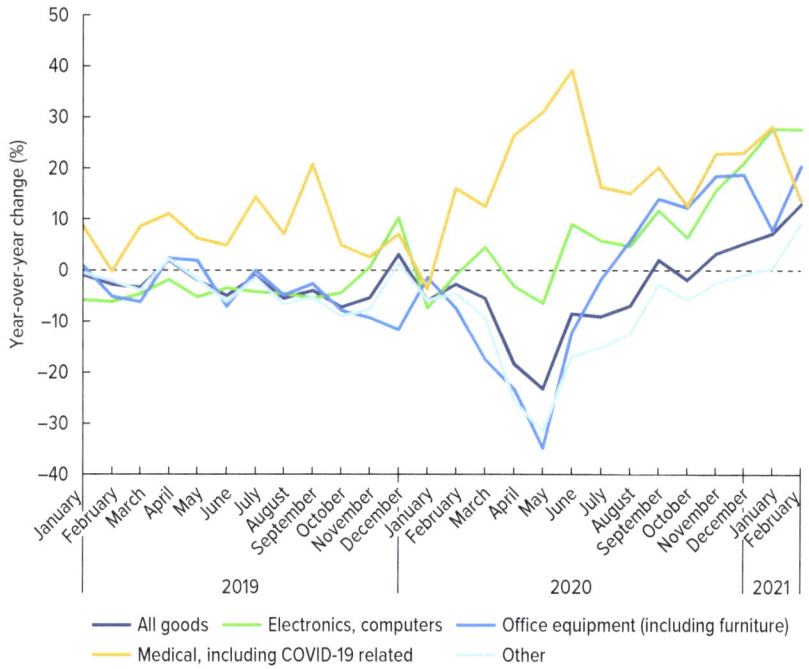

Source: World Bank 2021b.
Note: EU-27 = Austria, Belgium, Bulgaria, Croatia, Cyprus, Czechia, Denmark, Estonia, Finland, France, Germany, Greece, Hungary, Ireland, Italy, Latvia, Lithuania, Luxembourg, Malta, Netherlands, Poland, Portugal, Romania, Slovakia, Slovenia, Spain, and Sweden.

margin in the last quarter of 2020 deserves attention if confirmed by future data revisions.

The propensity for new and lost trade flows in the pandemic differed markedly from the historical trends, pointing to significant changes in the extensive margin, despite the latter's small contribution to the drop in trade values (figure 3.10). On the one hand, the propensity for trade death (the number of reporter-product-partner combinations available in month m of year t but not available in month m of year $t+1$, as a share of the reporter-product-partner combinations in month m of year t) increased by about 9 percentage points for exports and 6 percentage points for imports at the peak of the crisis (April, May 2020) and remained a few percentage points above the 2019 level in the following months. On the other hand, the propensity for new trade (the number of reporter-product-partner combinations not available in month m of year t but available in month m of year $t+1$ as a share of reporter-product-partner combinations in month m of year t) dropped by about 8 percentage points for exports and 6 percentage points for imports at the peak of the crisis. Thereafter, it remained slightly below the level in the corresponding months of 2019.

How soon have trade flows that exited at the peak of the COVID-19 crisis reappeared? Depending on the country group, up to 30 percent of the reporter-product-partner trade combinations that exited from March to May 2020 were still

FIGURE 3.8 Contribution of the intensive and extensive margins to the year-over-year change in global trade, 2019 and 2020

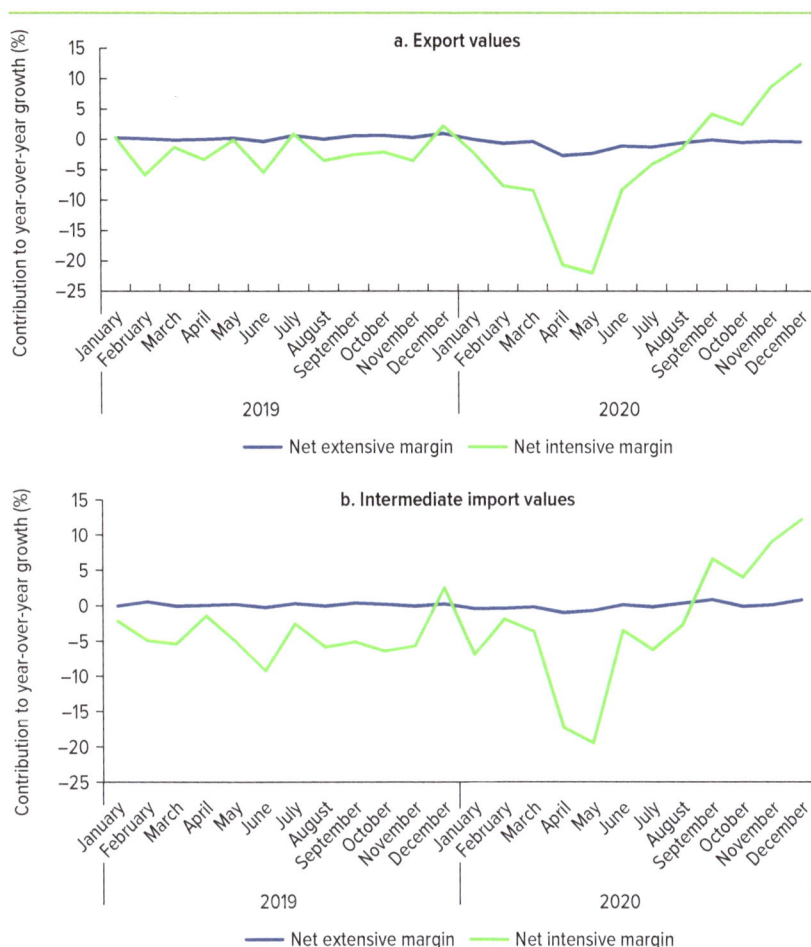

a. Export values

b. Intermediate import values

Source: World Bank staff calculations based on data from China Customs, Japan Customs, Eurostat's Comext, and US Census.

Note: Global trade is proxied by the trade of 30 large reporting countries: China, EU-27, Japan, and the United States. Trade flows below US$1,000 are excluded. EU-27 = Austria, Belgium, Bulgaria, Croatia, Cyprus, Czechia, Denmark, Estonia, Finland, France, Germany, Greece, Hungary, Ireland, Italy, Latvia, Lithuania, Luxembourg, Malta, Netherlands, Poland, Portugal, Romania, Slovakia, Slovenia, Spain, and Sweden.

lost by the end of the year (table 3.2). However, the revival rates do not differ significantly from the ones in the corresponding months of 2019, suggesting that the pandemic did not delay the revival of lost trade flows.

Low-income countries' propensity for lost intermediate imports is higher for imports from rich partner countries than for imports from China (figure 3.11). The survivability of intermediate imports from China is relatively higher than that of imports from other countries. This finding is true for all country groups, including low-income countries and irrespective of the presence of COVID-19. Nevertheless, for middle-income and low-income countries, the propensity for lost imports from

FIGURE 3.9 Contribution of the intensive and extensive margins to the year-over-year change in global trade of low-income countries, 2019 and 2020

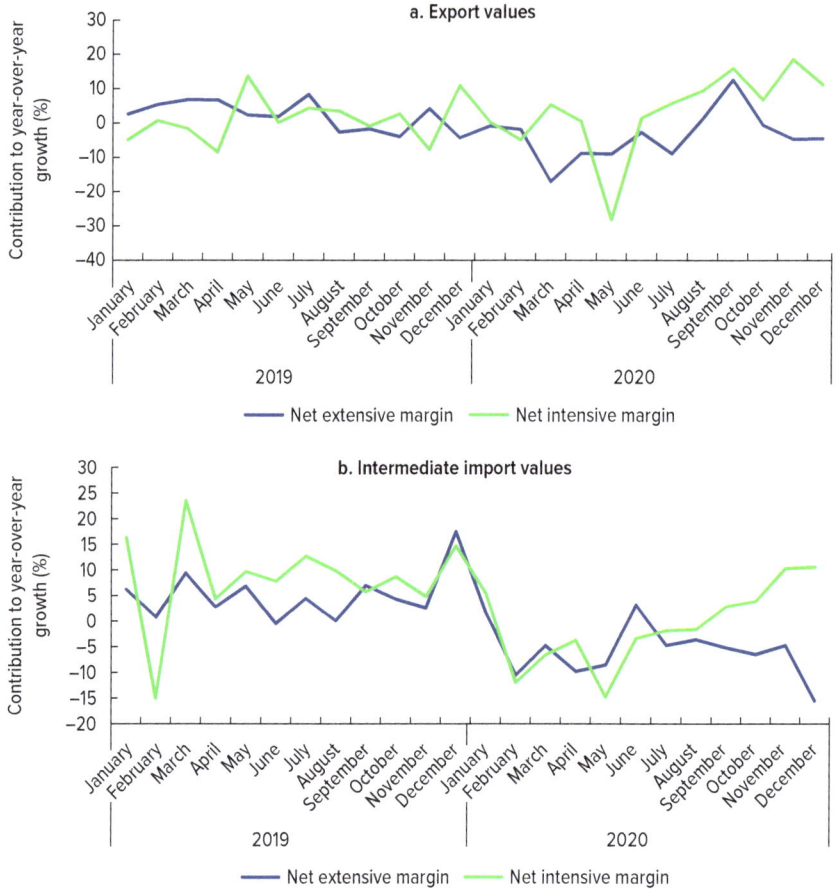

Source: World Bank staff calculations based on mirror trade data from China Customs, Japan Customs, Eurostat's Comext, and US Census.
Note: Trade flows below US$1,000 are excluded. Contribution of net extensive margins to import growth became positive in the first quarter of 2021.

China spiked in February 2020, when China was most affected by COVID-19, to levels above those seen for imports from rich partners. Moreover, for low-income countries, the propensity vis-à-vis China remained elevated throughout most of 2020 relative to the previous year.

Country experiences with the pandemic reinforce these trends. In Vietnam, sectors exposed to GVCs were the most affected during the pandemic. The acceleration of e-commerce provided resiliency (box 3.1). In Cambodia, firms linked to GVCs were the most negatively affected during the decline but the quickest to bounce back during the recovery (box 3.2).

FIGURE 3.10 Propensity for lost and new trade flows at the extensive margin, 2019 and 2020

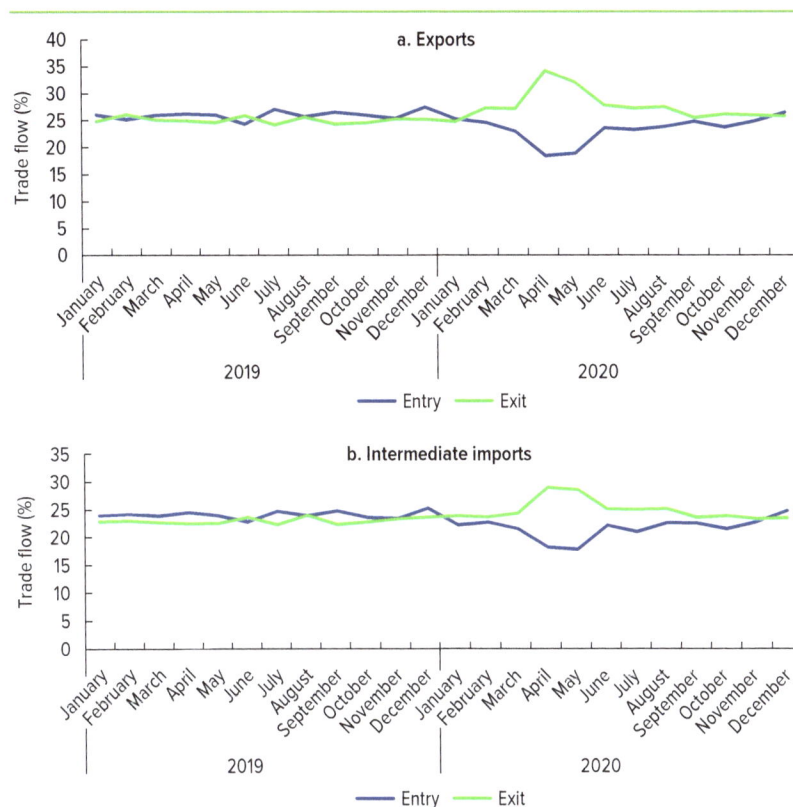

Source: World Bank staff calculations based on data from China Customs, Japan Customs, Eurostat's Comext, and US Census.
Note: Global trade is proxied by the trade of 30 large reporting countries: China, EU-27, Japan, and the United States. Trade flows below US$1,000 are excluded. EU-27 = Austria, Belgium, Bulgaria, Croatia, Cyprus, Czechia, Denmark, Estonia, Finland, France, Germany, Greece, Hungary, Ireland, Italy, Latvia, Lithuania, Luxembourg, Malta, Netherlands, Poland, Portugal, Romania, Slovakia, Slovenia, Spain, and Sweden.

TABLE 3.2 Share of exiting trade flows that did not reappear by the end of the year, 2019 and 2020

Percent

Indicator	2019			2020		
	March	**April**	**May**	**March**	**April**	**May**
Exports						
All reporting countries	27	26	26	27	21	22
Low-income countries	41	43	46	48	39	38
Middle-income countries (excluding China)	33	33	35	34	28	28
China	14	16	18	16	17	17

Table continues next page

TABLE 3.2 Share of exiting trade flows that did not reappear by the end of the year, 2019 and 2020 (*continued*)
Percent

Indicator	2019			2020		
	March	**April**	**May**	**March**	**April**	**May**
High-income countries	28	27	27	28	22	23
Imports						
All reporting countries	29	29	29	30	25	26
Low-income countries	36	33	35	36	34	34
Middle-income countries (excluding China)	27	27	27	29	23	23
China	27	27	29	28	27	26
High-income countries	29	29	29%	30	25	26

Source: World Bank staff calculations based on data from China Customs, Japan Customs, Eurostat's Comext, and US Census.
Note: Global trade is proxied by trade of the 30 large reporting countries: China, EU-27, Japan, and the United States. Trade flows below US$1,000 are excluded. EU-27 = Austria, Belgium, Bulgaria, Croatia, Cyprus, Czechia, Denmark, Estonia, Finland, France, Germany, Greece, Hungary, Ireland, Italy, Latvia, Lithuania, Luxembourg, Malta, Netherlands, Poland, Portugal, Romania, Slovakia, Slovenia, Spain, and Sweden.

Focus on the changing role of China

Early in the pandemic, there was much discussion of a global pivot away from China. The medium-run effect of relative increases in Chinese wages and the United States–China trade conflict, beginning in 2018, led some observers to speculate that global GVCs were moving away from China. This idea intensified when COVID-19 emerged in China early in 2020. Speculation focused on South Asia, Southeast Asia, and Sub-Saharan Africa as places that might gain market share from such a pivot.

In recent years, China has lost market share in key groups of exported products, but this trend was reversed in 2020. Since 2015, China's share of global merchandise exports has plateaued and then declined slightly, interrupting years of steady increase (figure 3.12). Yet, in 2020, preliminary high-frequency data for some countries suggest that China's share may have gained 1.5 percentage points, reflecting a surge in demand for pandemic-related products (medical and lockdown related) that China was well equipped to meet as well as China's quicker recovery from COVID-19 in general.

The erosion in China's aggregate share of global exports up to 2019 is associated primarily with light manufacturing products and electronics equipment. China's largest losses occurred in the share of footwear, apparel, and hides or skins as well as miscellaneous categories including toys and furniture (figure 3.13, panel a). Some of these losses or stagnation started around 2011 (figure 3.13, panel b). Since 2015, China's share of global exports of electronics and computer equipment has also experienced mild losses. By contrast, China's share of chemicals and plastics and rubber products has increased. The decline in China's global share of some manufacturing products intensified in 2019 following the US imposition of import duties on certain products.

FIGURE 3.11 Propensity for lost imports of inputs from China and other countries, by country income level, 2019 and 2020

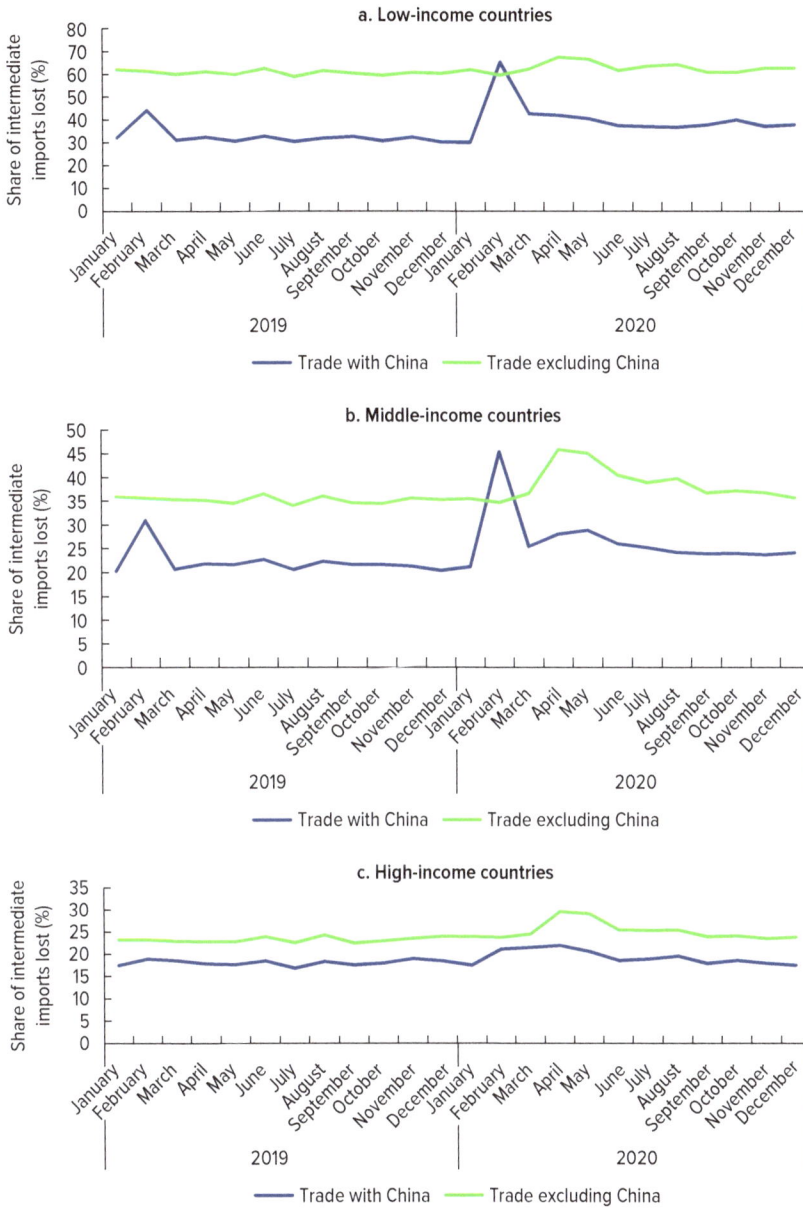

a. Low-income countries

Trade with China — Trade excluding China

b. Middle-income countries

Trade with China — Trade excluding China

c. High-income countries

Trade with China — Trade excluding China

Source: World Bank staff calculations based on reported and mirror trade data from China Customs, Japan Customs, Eurostat's Comext, and US Census.
Note: Trade flows below US$1,000 are excluded.

BOX 3.1 Vietnam's trade experience during the pandemic

The COVID-19 (coronavirus) pandemic affected firms' production and trade activities in Vietnam, leading to lower revenues from and lack of cash flow for their operations. Surveys in 2020 indicate that 85.7 percent of enterprises were adversely affected by COVID-19. Firms emphasized loss of domestic and foreign demand primarily and loss of foreign and domestic inputs secondarily: 50.2 percent and 47.2 percent of respondents considered a shrinking domestic market and inability to export, respectively, to be major constraints, whereas 39.9 percent and 16.8 percent of respondents identified lack of imported inputs and lack of domestic inputs, respectively.

Although Vietnam's total exports grew 7.3 percent in 2020, strong by international standards, certain key exports suffered negative growth in 2020. Exports of food products, garments, and footwear fell by 2.1 percent, 9.6 percent, and 8.3 percent, respectively, largely because of disruptions in the supply of inputs. Imports of semifinished materials for producing textiles and garments and leather and footwear products fell by 10.7 percent. The impacts of the pandemic were evident throughout 2020 and in the first quarter of 2021, but the second quarter of 2020 suffered the most, with exports falling 6.5 percent. Firms were less affected in the first quarter of 2021, when the inventory of materials was adequate to serve production, and from the second quarter of 2020 onward, because of the government's efforts to contain the pandemic and firms' efforts to adjust.

The structure of Vietnam's participation in global value chains (GVCs) contributed to the vulnerability of its exports of labor-intensive goods during the pandemic. First, Vietnam's backward participation, measured by the foreign value content in gross exports, grew from 36.1 percent in 2005 to 44.5 percent in 2015, indicating a high and growing reliance on imported intermediate inputs for export production and low domestic value added, a factor vulnerable to supply chain disruption. Second, Vietnam's specialization in finished products in some subsectors led to a lower level of diversification and made it incapable of adjusting quickly to producing domestic materials to substitute for disrupted imports. The share of the top-three subsectors in total exports increased from 60.2 percent in 2007 to 70.8 percent in 2017. In addition, in 2019 the share of finished processing products in total exports (compared to raw and semifinished processing exports) was high for key subsectors, including textiles and garments and leather and footwear, at 84 percent and 88 percent, respectively. This structure changed little over the past decade. Finally, Vietnam's semifinished inputs are mainly sourced regionally, especially from China, a country that was locked down for an extended period because of the pandemic. For example, China accounted for 58 percent of Vietnam's semifinished imports for textiles and garments in 2019.

Despite these constraints, Vietnam is a success story of resilience against the pandemic. Measures controlling the health crisis helped firms to sustain their operations during the pandemic. Exporters tried to tap local inputs to sustain export growth. Firms also accelerated the use of e-commerce and digital platforms to reach consumers, especially in the periods of reduced operations and mobility restrictions. In a World Bank survey in June, almost 50 percent of businesses reported increasing their use of digital platforms to adapt to the COVID-19 pandemic. As a result, Vietnam is one of the few countries whose gross domestic product grew in 2020 (2.9 percent). Gross domestic product is projected to grow 6.6 percent in 2021.

Vietnam may benefit from multinationals' attempts to build resilience in global supply chains. The "China plus one" trend emerged before the pandemic, under the assumption that labor costs in China would continue to rise. To seize the opportunity, Vietnam will need to upgrade its production infrastructure to produce more diversified products with enhanced domestic value added, more embedded technology, and more environmentally friendly processes. Strengthening the links between domestic firms and foreign domestic investment within Vietnam is key not only for minimizing the risks of external shocks in the future but also for enhancing the country's competitiveness.

BOX 3.2 Impact of the COVID-19 shock on the export performance of Cambodian firms

Since the early 2000s, Cambodia has used export-led growth to support poverty reduction and create jobs for low-skill workers, especially in the apparel industry. Before the COVID-19 (coronavirus) shock, exporter firms grew in number between 2016 and 2019 thanks to a combination of new firms entering, higher survival rates for entering firms, and fewer firms exiting. In addition to apparel, this trend was driven by emerging export sectors, such as leather and footwear and electronics.

Based on analysis using customs data from the Exporter Dynamics Database, Cambodia's participation in global value chains played a significant role in how the shock manifested itself (Engel et al. 2021). Overall, Cambodia's exports showed a V-shaped decline and recovery across many sectors, while the number of exporting firms declined. The average number of export destinations per exporter decreased by 24 percent between January and April 2020, while the number of exported products (measured at the eight-digit level of the Harmonized System [HS]) declined by 27 percent. The decline in destinations was more pronounced for firms exporting apparel, leather and footwear, and bicycles.

Participation in global value chains (GVCs) initially magnified the negative trade shock given firms' dependence on imported inputs and on destination markets for exports. Export values initially fell more strongly for GVC firms—that is, firms exporting and importing inputs and capital goods—than for non-GVC firms, as did the number of export destinations. The country's heavy specialization in traditional GVC-intensive sectors, such as apparel, combined with low sectoral diversification overall, likely contributed to its vulnerability. However, the value and diversification of exports tended to recover more quickly for firms participating in GVCs than for firms not in GVCs.

The COVID-19 shock induced downward pressure on export prices, especially in GVC-intensive sectors. Average export values per firm followed a V-shaped decline and recovery, both overall and in apparel, leather and footwear, and bicycles, with average export values per firm being significantly lower during the early months of the pandemic. Evidence suggests that apparel GVC firms were getting squeezed because of COVID-19, as unit values across the top apparel products declined, despite the overall recovery of export values.

Although many exporting firms in Cambodia exited during the early months of the pandemic, GVC firms were more resilient. Survival rates of exporters (relative to the same quarter in 2019) declined in all key sectors, particularly in food and beverages and electronics. But GVC firms had higher survival rates throughout the pandemic than firms that only export (figure B3.2.1, panel a), with larger GVC firms having consistently higher survival rates than smaller GVC firms (figure B3.2.1, panel b).

Overall, more integrated exporting firms were more resilient, likely reflecting their higher productivity and capital intensity. Specific policy measures could be used to support exporters' resilience to external shocks, such as measures targeting firms' survival and (re)entry into export markets. Policies should aim to support the resilience of small and medium enterprises in particular, given their lower survival rates.

Box continues next page

BOX 3.2 Impact of the COVID-19 shock on the export performance of Cambodian firms (*continued*)

FIGURE B3.2.1 Average firm survival rate in Cambodia, by type and size of firm, 2016 Q1 to 2020 Q3

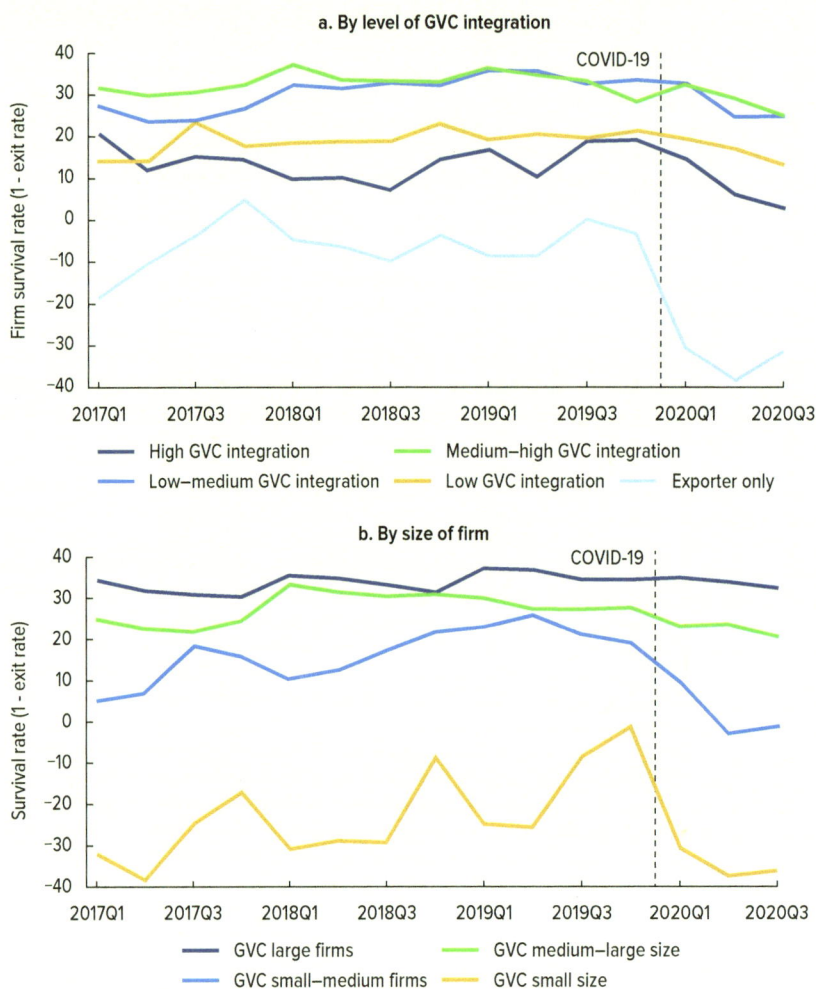

Source: Engel et al. 2021.
Note: GVC = global value chain.

FIGURE 3.12 China's share of global merchandise exports, 2002–20

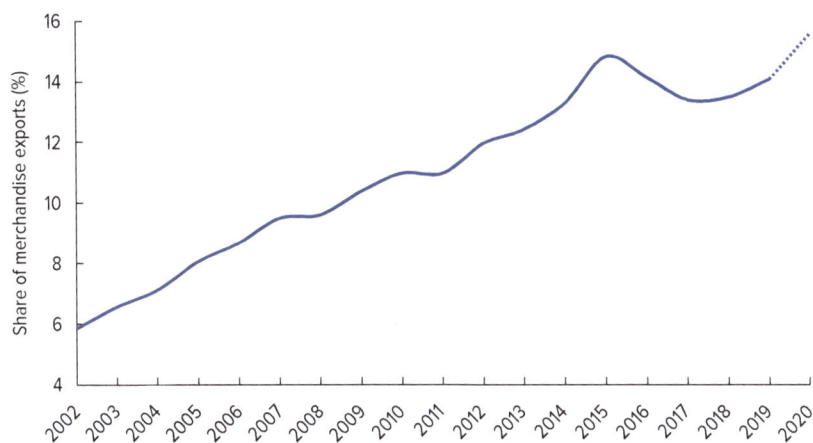

Sources: World Bank staff calculations based on World Integrated Trade Solution data for the period 2002–19 and on the World Bank's COVID-19 Trade Watch data for the 2020 estimate.
Note: The 2020 estimate is based on preliminary high-frequency export data available for select countries.

FIGURE 3.13 China's share of global exports, by product group, 2002–19

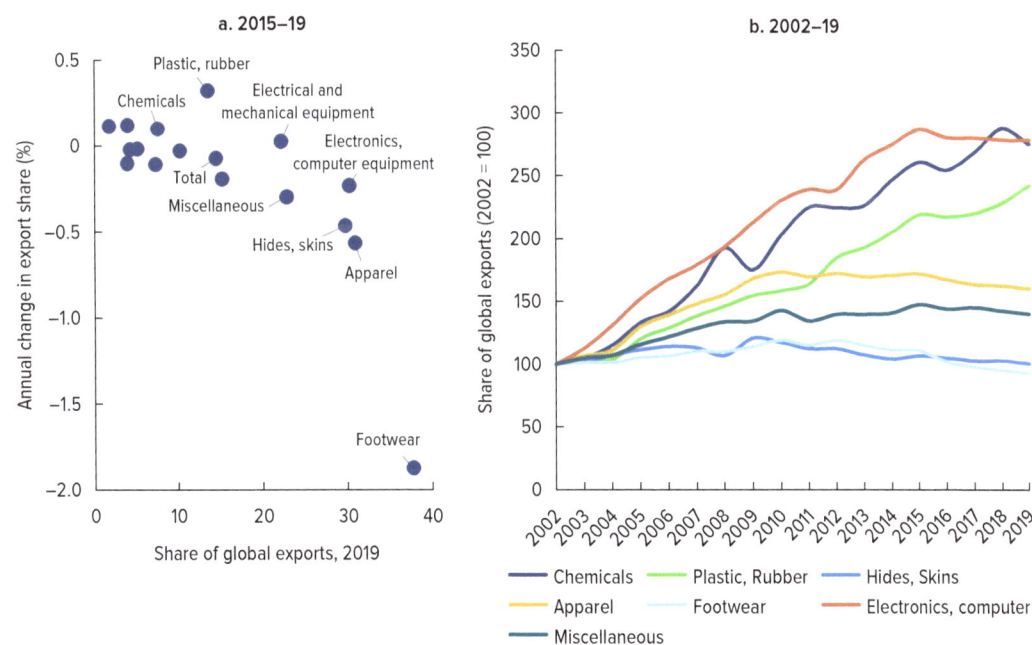

Sources: World Bank staff calculations based on Centre for Economic Policy Research BACI international trade database.

FIGURE 3.14 Change in the share of global exports, by country or region and sector, 2011–19

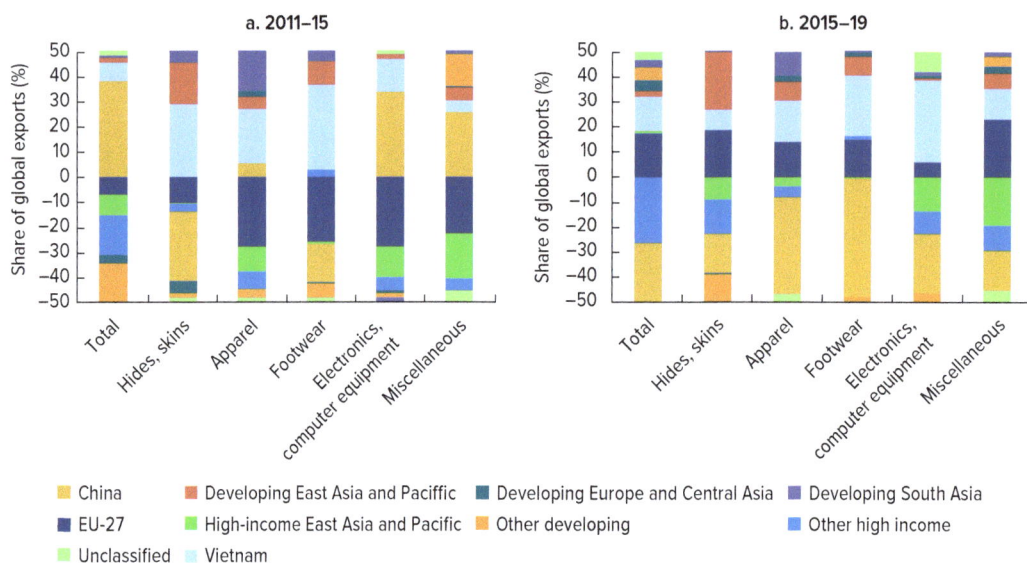

Sources: World Bank staff calculations based on Centre for Economic Policy Research BACI international trade database.
Note: Based on products in China's export basket. EU-27 = Austria, Belgium, Bulgaria, Croatia, Cyprus, Czechia, Denmark, Estonia, Finland, France, Germany, Greece, Hungary, Ireland, Italy, Latvia, Lithuania, Luxembourg, Malta, Netherlands, Poland, Portugal, Romania, Slovakia, Slovenia, Spain, and Sweden.

Vietnam and, to a lesser extent, other low- and middle-income East Asian countries have benefited the most from China's relative decline as an exporter of light manufacturing (figure 3.14). The decline in China's share of hides and skins and footwear since 2011 as well as apparel, electronics, and furniture and toys (included in miscellaneous) since 2015 correlates with increases in the market share of Vietnam and other low- and middle-income East Asian countries and, in some cases, South Asian countries. The concomitant rise in the share of the EU may be unrelated to China's shrinking share, reflecting instead exports of similar Harmonized System (HS) products of different sophistication levels, which do not compete directly with Chinese exports.

In 2020 the sudden changes in consumer preferences as a result of the COVID-19 crisis led to an increase in China's share of world exports. These trading patterns are apparent from the available trade data for the four major global economies (China, the EU, Japan, and the United States). The most striking increase in China's market share was in apparel, which relates primarily to products for medical use (figure 3.15, panel a). China's share in exports of electrical and machinery equipment also rose because of increased shipments of electrical devices needed for remote work and education. Plastics and rubber continued to show robust gains in share. In East Asia, the shares of both high-income and low- and middle-income countries increased, but less substantially than those of China (figure 3.15, panel b).

Impacts of COVID-19 on foreign direct investment

COVID-19 has had a profound effect on global FDI. Although comprehensive data are not yet available, the United Nations Conference on Trade and Development

FIGURE 3.15 Shares of mirror exports to four economies (China, EU-27, Japan, and the United States), by country and product group, 2019–20

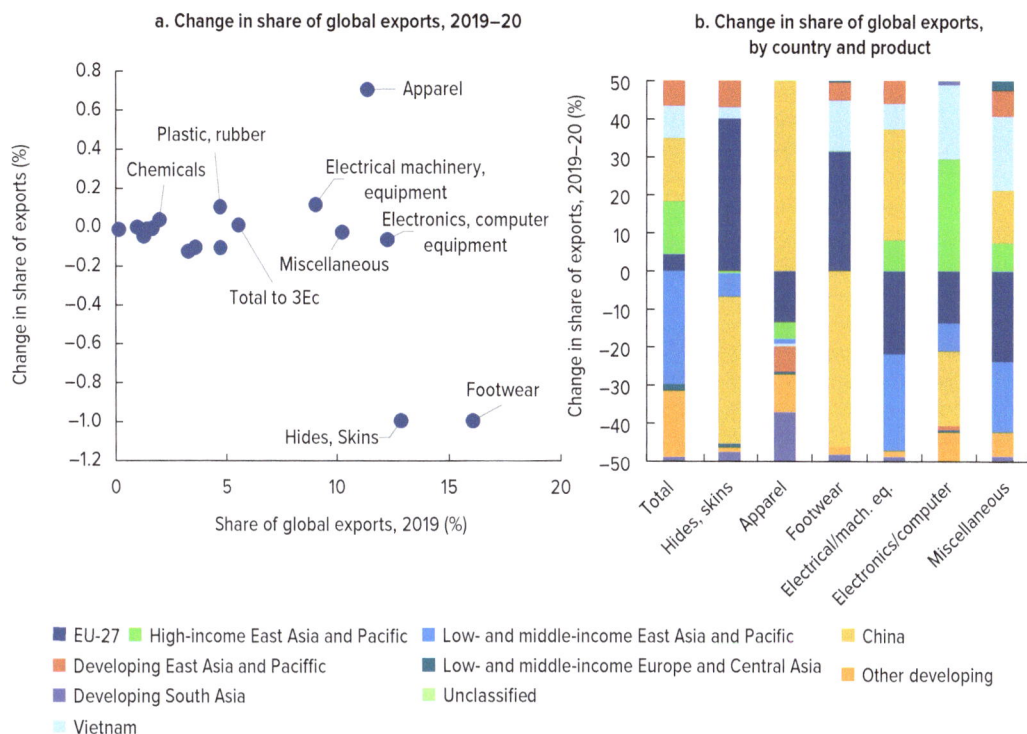

a. Change in share of global exports, 2019–20

b. Change in share of global exports, by country and product

Legend:
- EU-27
- High-income East Asia and Pacific
- Low- and middle-income East Asia and Pacific
- China
- Developing East Asia and Pacific
- Low- and middle-income Europe and Central Asia
- Other developing
- Developing South Asia
- Unclassified
- Vietnam

Sources: World Bank staff calculations based on World Bank 2021b.

Note: 3Ec is an aggregate that comprises EU-27, Japan, and the United States. Panel b is based on products in China's export basket.

estimated in June 2020 that global FDI flows could decline by up to 40 percent in 2020, falling below US$1 trillion for the first time since 2005, and by a further 5 percent to 10 percent in 2021, before recovering in 2022 (UNCTAD 2020). Uncertainty about the persistence of COVID-19, the speed of recovery, and the nature and extent of government stimulus interventions all contributed to a dampening of investment overall. The partial recovery of corporate profitability in the second half of 2020 suggests that global FDI did not fall as much as this initial estimate.

Governments responded to the impacts of the pandemic by promoting investment and imposing new restrictions. These efforts included facilitation of online investment, pandemic-related services of investment promotion agencies, and new incentives for investment in health care. The pandemic seems to have accelerated trends already visible in 2019, when some planned mergers and acquisitions were canceled for regulatory and political reasons and negotiations on international investment agreements slowed (UNCTAD 2020). As of August 18, 2020, out of a sample of 40 countries, 29 had tightened investment regulations, 7 had liberalized them, and 4 had taken both types of measures (Qiang, Liu, and Steenbergen 2021).

Short-term trade and GVC effects of the pandemic

The COVID-19 pandemic generated both a supply and a demand shock across many countries, affecting production, consumption, and trade patterns. Lockdowns and social distancing measures introduced to contain the pandemic across the globe exacerbated these direct effects. Factory closings led to a drop in the supply of exportable goods in affected countries. These supply shocks were compounded by demand shocks, as consumers and firms had to modify their spending decisions amid this new environment.

A closer look at the initial three months of the pandemic, when most of the countries examined here implemented lockdown policies, illustrates how restricted mobility—a proxy for the COVID-19 shock—is correlated with lower growth in industrial production (figure 3.16, panel a). The shift over time of the country sample toward the bottom left suggests that both work mobility and growth of the industrial production index (IPI) deteriorated as the pandemic advanced. Panel a of figures 3.17 and 3.18 suggest that mobility restrictions affected aggregate trade flows through supply and demand channels. Specifically, figure 3.17, panel a, shows the correlation between a lower IPI in exporting countries and falling export growth (supply shock), and figure 3.18, panel a, indicates a link between declining IPI and lower import growth in partner countries (demand shock). From the peak of the first wave of COVID-19 in April until June 2020, work mobility, industrial production, and trade improved gradually, as shown in panel b of figures 3.16, 3.17, and 3.18.

As the crisis unfolded, researchers asked whether the impact of the pandemic was different across sectors and whether GVC participation mitigated or magnified COVID-19 shocks (Baldwin and Tomiura 2020; Eppinger et al. 2020; Freund et al. 2021; Gerschel, Martinez, and Méjean 2020; Javorcik 2020; Miroudot 2020). This section is based on the analysis produced by Espitia et al. (2021), who investigate the short-term trade effects of COVID-19. Using bilateral monthly export data for 28 exporting countries (most EU members, Japan, and the United States) and multiple trading partners at a detailed sector level during the first wave of the pandemic (February and June 2020),[4] this study empirically assesses the trade impact of demand, supply, and third countries' shocks based on a sector-level gravity model (the empirical strategy to assess the impact of COVID-19 on trade is described in annex 3A). This methodology allows the authors to identify the role of sector characteristics in mitigating or magnifying COVID-19-related shocks in the exporting, destination, and source countries.

A simple conceptual framework helps to identify not only the various channels through which demand, supply, and third-country shocks affect trade flows but also the role that sectoral characteristics play in mitigating or augmenting the effect of such shocks. These shocks and channels work simultaneously, and their impact on trade depends on factors that vary at the country and sector levels.

A supply shock in the exporting country, induced by reduced worker mobility—the source of the supply shock—negatively affects export growth by lowering its production capacity. This impact depends on sector-specific characteristics such as the feasibility of remote work arrangements to maintain production processes once governments impose social distancing measures to limit the spread of the virus.

FIGURE 3.16 Change in IPI and work mobility in exporting countries, February to June 2020

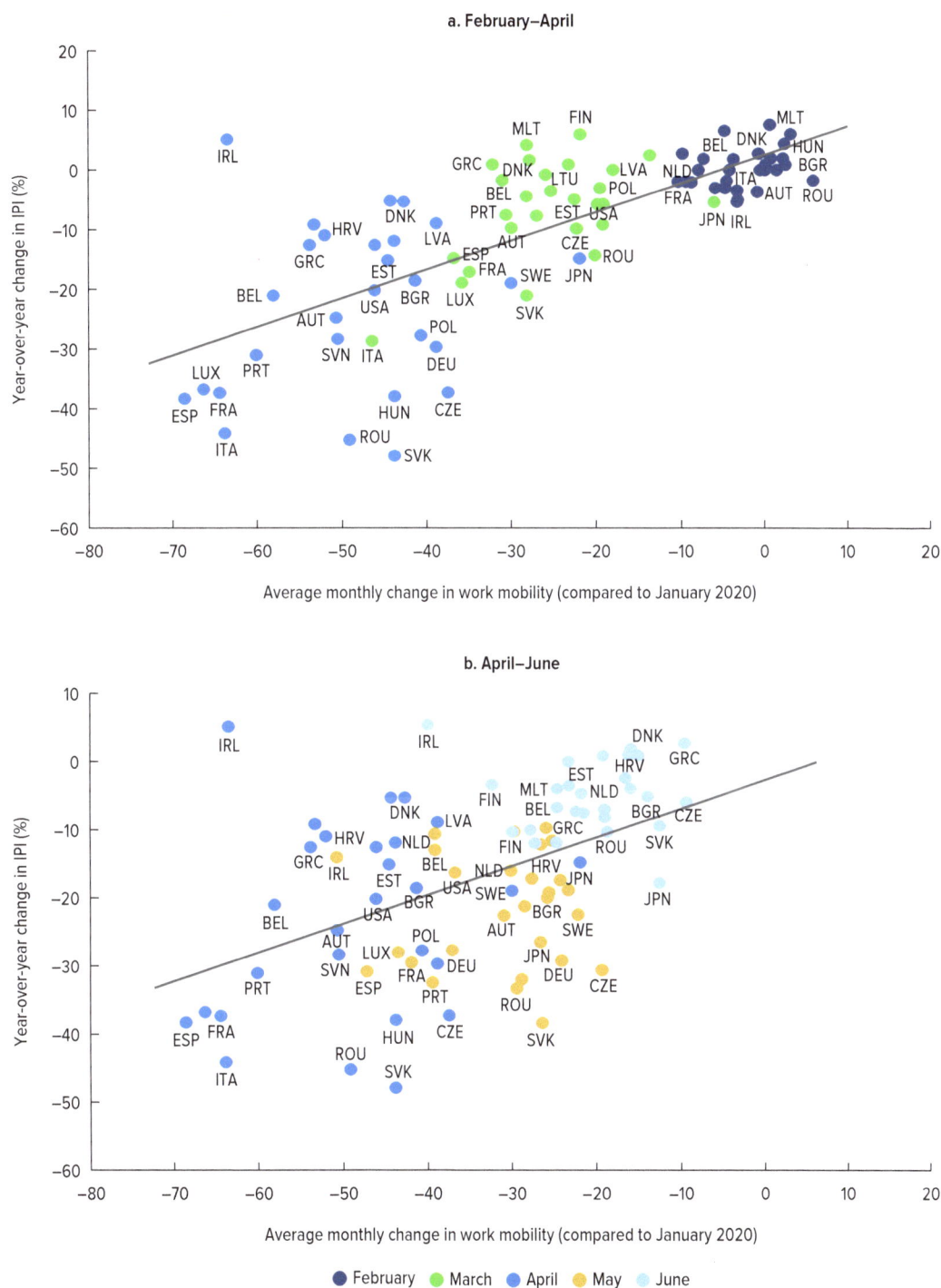

a. February–April

b. April–June

● February ● March ● April ● May ● June

Source: Espitia et al. 2021.

Note: IPI = industrial production index; UNIDO = United Nations Industrial Development Organization; yoy = year-over-year. P-value < 0.0001. For panel a, IPI yoy UNIDO supply = 0.483842*Avg Work + 0.025427. For panel b, IPI yoy UNIDO supply = 0.422401*Avg Work + −0.0264189.

FIGURE 3.17   Change in IPI and export growth in exporting countries, February to June 2020

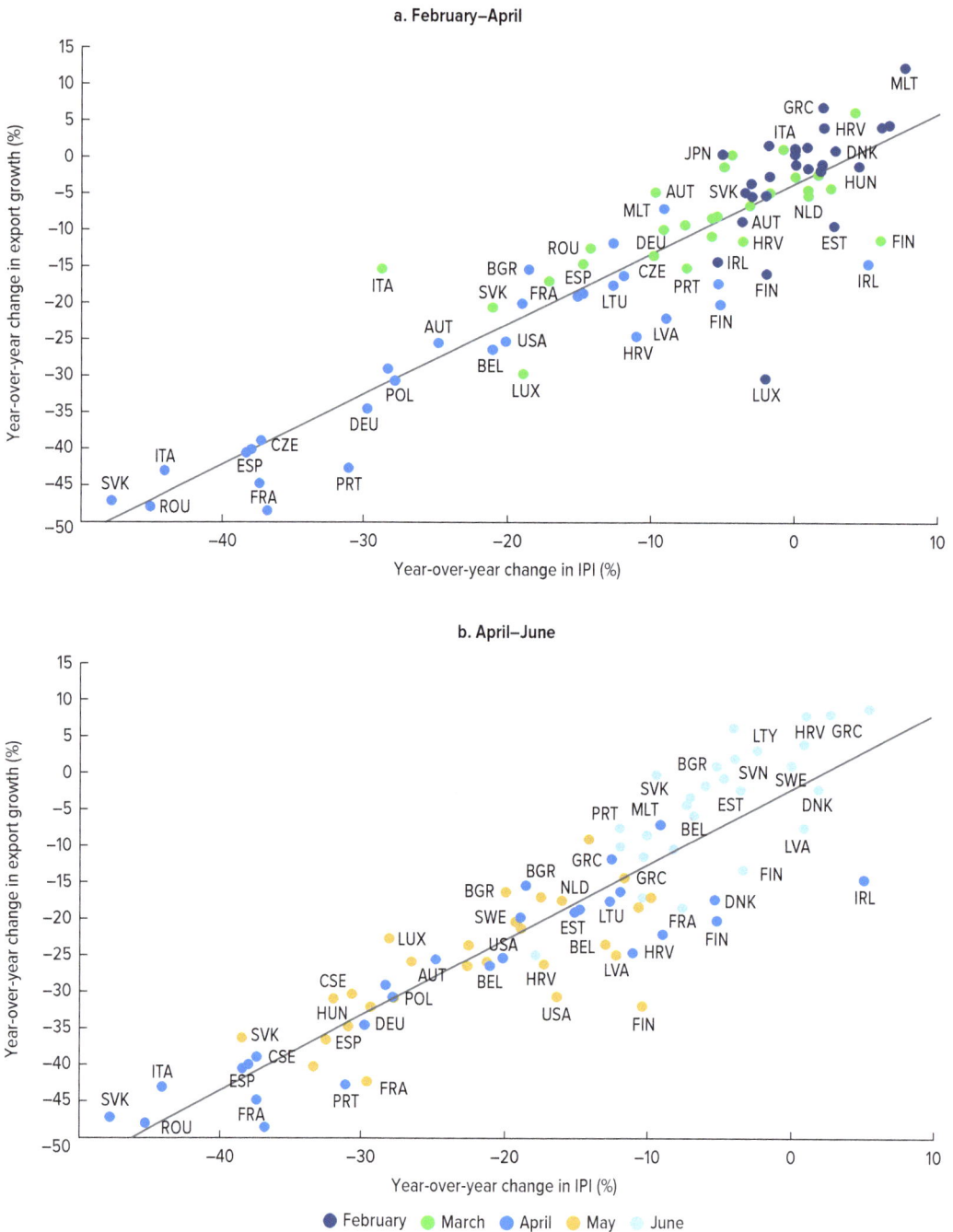

a. February–April

b. April–June

● February   ● March   ● April   ● May   ○ June

Source: Based on Espitia et al. 2021.
Note: Exports from 28 countries, including the EU-27 (excluding Cyprus), Japan, and the United States. EU-27 = Austria, Belgium, Bulgaria, Croatia, Cyprus, Czechia, Denmark, Estonia, Finland, France, Germany, Greece, Hungary, Ireland, Italy, Latvia, Lithuania, Luxembourg, Malta, Netherlands, Poland, Portugal, Romania, Slovakia, Slovenia, Spain, and Sweden; IPI = industrial production index; yoy = year-over-year. For panel a, Growth = 0.962113*IPI yoy + −0.0377225. For panel b, Growth = 1.03327*IPI yoy + −0.0222923.

FIGURE 3.18 Change in IPI and import growth in partner countries, February to June 2020

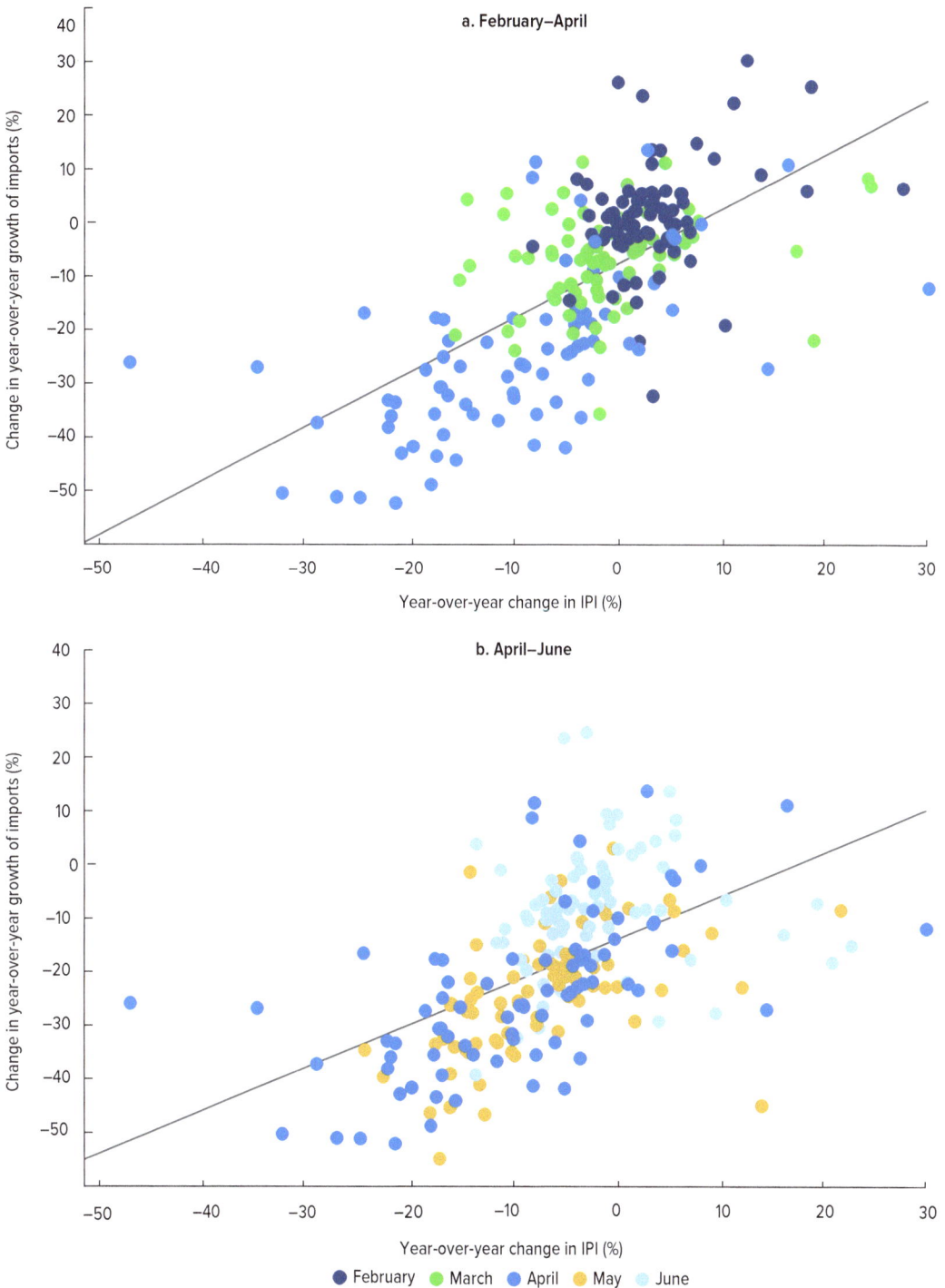

Source: Based on Espitia et al. 2021.

Note: Imports in more than 50 partner countries from 28 countries (EU-27 [excluding Cyprus], Japan, and the United States). EU-27 = Austria, Belgium, Bulgaria, Croatia, Cyprus, Czechia, Denmark, Estonia, Finland, France, Germany, Greece, Hungary, Ireland, Italy, Latvia, Lithuania, Luxembourg, Malta, Netherlands, Poland, Portugal, Romania, Slovakia, Slovenia, Spain, and Sweden; IPI = industrial production index. yoy = year-over-year. P-value < 0.0001. For panel a, Growth = 1.01546* IPI yoy + −0.0749845. For panel b, Growth = 0.802447* IPI yoy + −0.139168.

One can expect that the higher the share of occupations in a sector that can be performed remotely—that is, via the internet—the lower the negative impact of a supply shock in the exporting country.

Similarly, declines in retail mobility in the partner country, such as the closure of retail stores, reduce the demand for imported consumer goods (demand shock). Durable consumer goods tend to be affected by this shock more strongly during a crisis, because consumers may choose to postpone their purchase when uncertainty is high. Because retailers generally order durables in advance, this effect is likely to be transmitted to imports with a lag.

Supply shocks in third countries may also have an impact through the competition channel. If COVID-19 leads to the imposition of mobility restrictions in countries other than the exporting and partner countries, firms in the exporting country might take advantage of the production disruption of rivals and export more to their partner's markets. This effect is expected to be stronger in sectors in which third countries hit by a negative supply shock have a larger share of global exports and the exporter has the capacity to scale up production rapidly.

Participation in GVCs can mitigate or augment the negative trade effects of COVID-19-related shocks. The effect of a shock on bilateral export growth depends on the extent of a sector's reliance on imported inputs as well as on the geographic location of the shock (as indicated by the white boxes in figure 3.19). When the shock takes place in the exporting country, higher reliance of a sector's exports on imported inputs helps firms to withstand the disruption in domestic production, thus supporting export growth. When the shock takes place in the partner country, demand for the

FIGURE 3.19 A simplified framework of bilateral trade growth

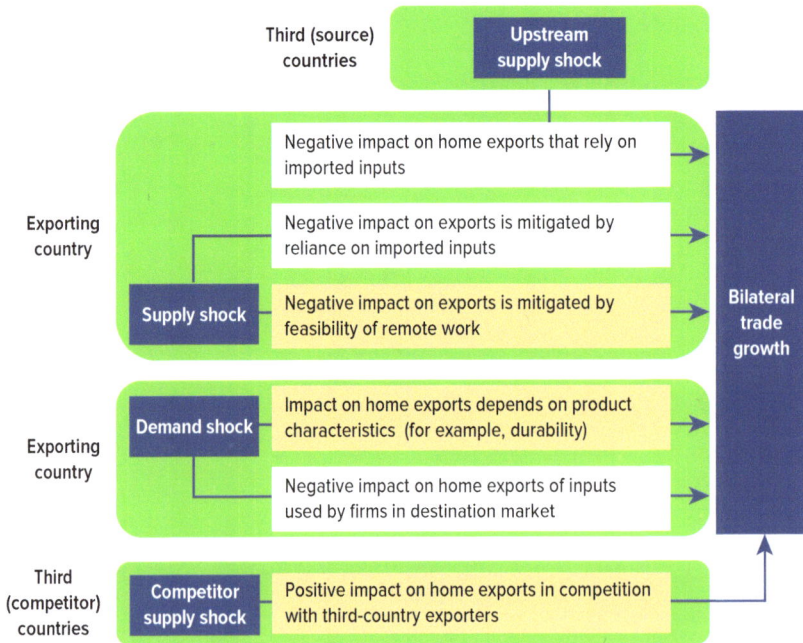

Source: Espitia et al. 2021.

exporter's intermediate inputs declines relative to demand for final goods as production is disrupted. When the shock takes place in a third source country that supplies inputs to the exporting country, the latter experiences a production disruption that hurts its exports.[5] From an exporter's perspective, the first channel captures the benefit of GVC participation in the presence of a domestic shock, whereas the second and third channels relate to foreign shocks either upstream or downstream that can disrupt supply chains.

The impact of demand, supply, and third-country shocks on trade

The analysis suggests that all types of shocks explain the impact of the pandemic on export growth (figure 3.20). Although bilateral export growth is positively correlated with both supply shocks in the exporting country (blue bar) and demand shocks in the partner country (green bar), the impact of supply shocks is stronger. A 1.00-percentage-point decline in worker mobility relative to January 2020 is associated with a 0.35-percentage-point decline in annualized export growth on average (blue bar), whereas a 1.00-percentage-point decline in retail mobility in partner countries is linked to a 0.31-percentage-point decline in export growth on average (green bar). By contrast, competition shocks are negatively associated with bilateral export growth (purple bar) because lower production in third competitor countries can boost export growth. Finally, the coefficient capturing the upstream shock is positive and significant (purple bar), suggesting that declines in industrial production in an exporter's source countries, weighted by a sector's reliance on imported inputs from them, translates into negative export growth.

FIGURE 3.20 Impact of demand, supply, and third-country COVID-19 shocks on bilateral export growth

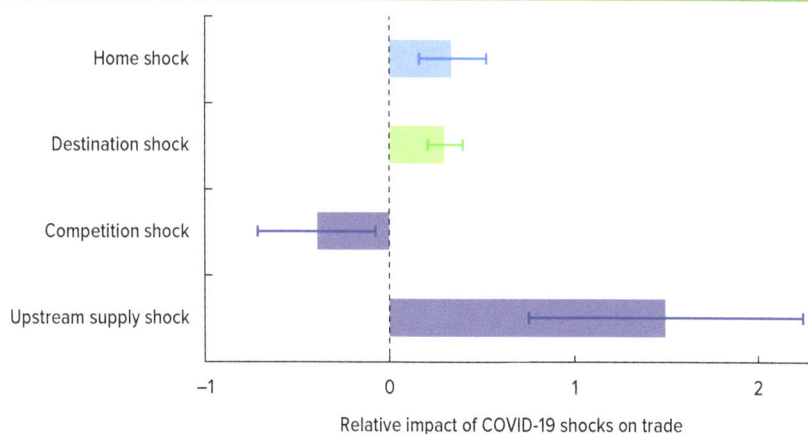

Relative impact of COVID-19 shocks on trade

Source: Based on Espitia et al. 2021.
Note: The figure plots the coefficients for home, destination, and third-country shocks (competition and upstream supply) obtained using a standard difference-in-differences method.

The heterogeneous impact of COVID-19 across sectors

The trade effects of the pandemic also vary across sectors. Figure 3.21 depicts the regression coefficients for sectors that are part of the first and third quartiles of the distribution of different sectoral characteristics. This finding shows the following:

- Sectors with a higher share of occupations that can be performed remotely were less severely affected during the pandemic, suggesting that the feasibility of remote work mitigated the negative effects of reduced worker mobility on export growth in the exporting country. For example, during the period February–June 2020, the negative effect of COVID-19 was 19 percentage points larger for the manufacture of pulp, paper, and paperboard in countries such as Hungary, where less than one-third of occupations can be performed remotely, than for the manufacture of electric motors, generators, and transformers in countries such as Japan, where more than two-thirds of production can be done remotely.

- A decrease in retail mobility in the partner country, such as the closure of retail stores, had a smaller negative impact on imports of durable goods in the same month but a larger impact in the following month, even though demand for certain durable goods may have increased because of lockdowns. Specifically, for

FIGURE 3.21 The impact of COVID-19 shocks on bilateral exports across sectors, 2020

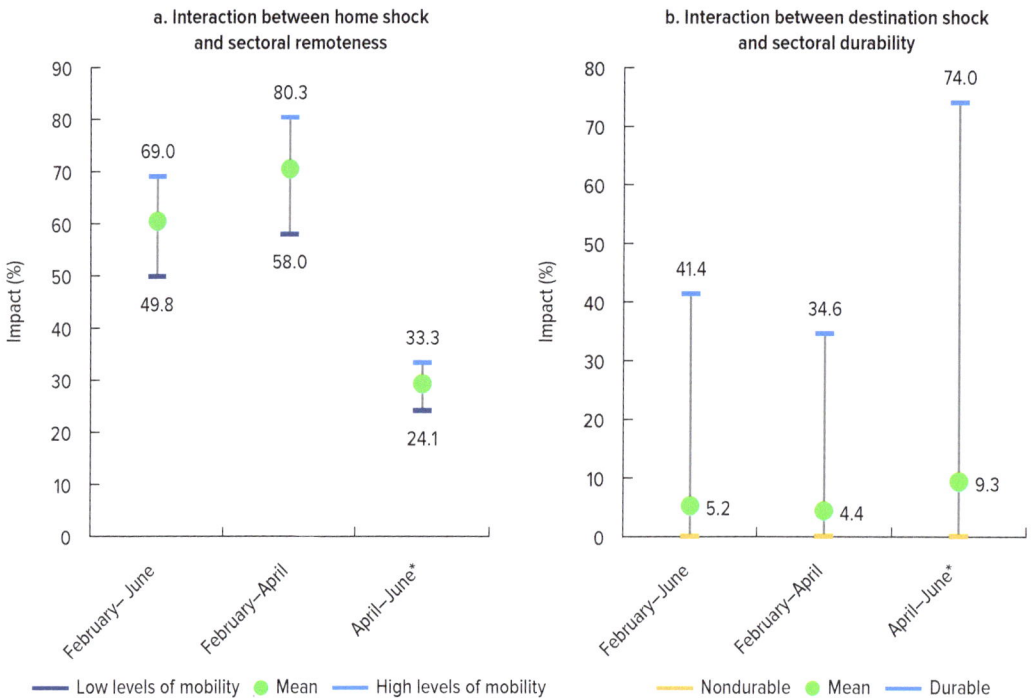

Source: Based on Espitia et al. 2021.
Note: Panel a plots the differential impact of the interaction between home shock and sectoral remoteness (the ability to perform tasks remotely) at two points of the distribution (third quartile and first quartile). Panel b plots the interaction between destination shock and sectors in which all underlying products are durable. Coefficients for the interactions are obtained using a standard difference-in-differences method.
* Not significant.

sectors in which all products are classified as durable or semidurable (for example, the manufacture of parts and accessories for motor vehicles), the negative impact is 41 percentage points smaller than for sectors in which no products are classified as durable or semidurable (for example, processing and preservation of fruit and vegetables).

• Although the demand and supply shocks generated by COVID-19 had a differentiated impact across sectors, the estimations do not support the view that shocks in third countries had a positive impact on exporters that were competing in the same destination markets. One explanation of this result is that shocks affected the set of 28 exporters in the sample simultaneously, restricting the potential for bilateral trade growth to adjust through the competition channel.

Transmission of foreign shocks and mitigation of domestic shocks through GVCs

The analysis suggests that GVC participation increased an exporter's vulnerability to foreign shocks generated by the pandemic but reduced its vulnerability to domestic shocks. In particular, importing inputs can alleviate some of the negative impacts of domestic supply shocks on trade. The estimated coefficient of the interaction term between the home supply shock and GVC participation suggests that the trade effect of a negative supply shock in exporting countries is lower in sectors that rely more strongly on imported inputs for their exports (figure 3.22). Specifically, the negative impact of a decrease in mobility for country-sectors in the first quartile of the distribution, where imported inputs account for less than one-quarter of total exports (for example, Spain's manufacture of agricultural and forestry machinery), is 20 percentage points higher than for country-sectors in the third quartile of the distribution, where shares of imported inputs in exports can reach 37 percent (for example, Austria's manufacture of other chemical products). The smaller role of an exporter's reliance on imported inputs in mitigating domestic shocks between February and April could reflect simultaneous production shocks in key source countries, such as China and Germany, which made importing inputs less viable.

By contrast, a demand shock in an exporter's destination countries more adversely affected its export growth in sectors where the share of intermediate inputs in exports was higher. More specifically, the impact of the demand shock for sector-countries with low shares (first quartile of the distribution) is almost 12 percentage points smaller than for those with high shares (third quartile of the distribution). There are several explanations for this result. Buyer firms in partner country-sectors hit by the COVID-19 shock could have imported fewer inputs from their suppliers and thus reduced their output. If firms in partner countries can no longer satisfy consumer demand, imports of final goods relative to intermediate inputs from the exporting countries may rise. The results also show that shocks in partner countries were more disruptive during the later phase of the first lockdown (April to June).

Finally, GVCs transmit foreign shocks in an exporter's source countries, resulting in negative export growth. Declines in industrial production in source countries affect the supply of intermediate inputs and thus lower export growth in the home country. Specifically, an average decline of 1.0 percentage point in the weighted annualized IPI growth in an exporter's source countries is linked to a 2.2-percentage-point decline in bilateral annualized export growth. The negative effect of upstream supply chain

FIGURE 3.22 The impact of COVID-19 shocks on bilateral exports through global value chain channels

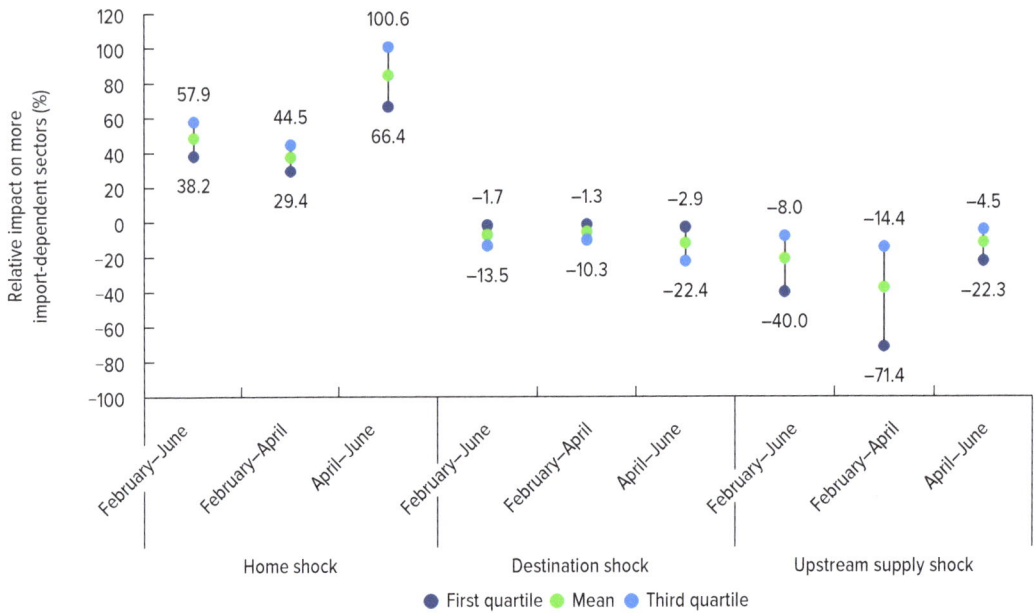

Source: Based on Espitia et al. 2021.
Note: The figure plots the coefficients for the interaction between the home, destination, and upstream supply shocks and global value chain variables obtained using a standard difference-in-differences method. The estimated positive coefficient on the upstream supply shock is translated into a negative shock to reflect that declines in industrial production in source countries go hand in hand with declines in the home country's exports.

disruptions was more severe during the earlier phase of the lockdown (February to April) but subsided in both size and statistical significance as China and other countries gradually increased industrial production (April to June).

The transmission of shocks is different in low- and middle-income countries and China. The analysis for 64 countries based on mirror trade data suggests that the possibility of remote work no longer offsets the negative trade effect of supply shocks, possibly because many occupations cannot be or are not performed remotely in low- and middle-income countries. Second, the impact of upstream shocks is smaller, possibly because goods exported by low- and middle-income countries tend to be located farther upstream in supply chains. That is, a negative shock in an exporter's source countries has a weaker negative impact on its export growth (see table 3A.1). The relative magnitude of effects also changes when China is included as an exporter in the baseline regressions. Third-country shocks induced by COVID-19 now affect bilateral export growth through the competition channel. This finding implies that China's exports expanded in destination markets when its competitor countries were hit by production shocks. Also, the upstream shock matters more strongly for bilateral trade growth, which is consistent with the centrality of China in modern GVCs.

Annex 3A Empirical strategy used to assess the short-term impact of COVID-19 on trade and GVCs

The empirical strategy used to identify the trade effects of COVID-19 is based on a sector-level gravity model (for example, Dai, Yotov, and Zylkin 2014). Following the approach in Rajan and Zingales (1998), the model estimates a difference-in-differences specification including interaction terms between a selected time-varying measure at the country level (reflecting the COVID-19 shock) and a time-invariant sector measure (reflecting the sector's vulnerability to the shock—for example, amenability to remote work or GVC participation).

The analysis includes 28 exporting countries and more than 50 trading partners at the International Standard Industrial Classification of All Economic Activities (ISIC) Rev. 3 four-digit level for February to June 2020:

$$Growth_{ijkt} = \underbrace{\alpha + \beta_1\ work\ mobility_{it} * remote_{ik} + \beta_2\ work\ mobility_{it} * gvc_{it}}_{Exporter\ supply\ shock}$$

$$\underbrace{+ \beta_3\ retail\ mobility_{jt} * durable_k + \beta_4\ retail\ mobility_{jt} * gvc\ parner_{jl}}_{Partner\ demand\ shock}$$

$$\underbrace{+ \beta_5\ competition\ shock_{ijkt} + \beta_6\ upstream\ shock_{ilt} + controls}_{Third\text{-}country\ supply\ shock}$$

where $growth_{ijkt}$ denotes bilateral annualized growth of exports from country i to partner country j in sector k at time t. The explanatory variables include the supply shock in the exporting country and demand shock in the partner country interacted with the relevant sector characteristics. The supply shock in the exporting country is captured by the variable work mobility, $work\ mobility_{it}$ while retail mobility, $retail\ mobility_{jt}$ measures the demand shock in the partner country. Both vary at the country-time level and are computed as monthly changes relative to January 2020.[6] As for sector intensities, the variable $remote_{ik}$ captures the feasibility of performing work remotely, and the variable $durable_k$ designates the average percentage of durable products (including semidurable and transport equipment) within a sector.

To capture the third-country competition channel, Espitia et al. (2021) compute a time-varying third-country shock at the exporter-partner-sector level. Three variables are considered to assess the impact of COVID-19 through the GVC channel. The first two are straightforward: gvc_{il} measures an exporter-sector's share of imported inputs in its exports, and $gvc\ partner_{jl}$ measures a partner-country-sector's reliance on imported inputs in its total imports. To account for shocks in an exporter's source (third) countries, the model includes an upstream shock variable.

The model also includes a set of controls—namely, exporter-partner-sector (γ_{ijk}), exporter-time (γ_{il}), partner-time (γ_{jl}), and sector-time (γ_{zt}) fixed effects—to account for potentially omitted variables; ε_{ijkt} is the error term. Standard errors are clustered at the exporter-partner level.[7] The sector-time fixed effects cannot be at a highly disaggregated level because of collinearity with some of the sector characteristics.[8] To account for differences in sectoral output growth and minimize the concern of possible omitted variable bias, Espitia et al. (2021) construct a global monthly IPI growth variable at the ISIC Rev. 3 two-digit level, $global\ output_{mt}$, as an additional control. See table 3A.1.

TABLE 3A.1 Short-term impact of COVID-19 on trade: Regression coefficients for different samples of countries

$growth_{ijkt}$

Framework	Variable	High-income countries	High-income countries plus China[a]	Low- and middle-income countries (excluding China)
Exporter supply shock* sector characteristic	*$supply\ shock_{it} \times remote_{ik}$*	1.587*** (0.375)	0.772* (0.469)	0.044 (0.353)
	$supply\ shock_{it} \times gvc_{il}$	1.564*** (0.522)	2.571*** (0.638)	1.647*** (0.517)
Partner demand shock* sector characteristic	*$demand\ shock_{jt} \times durable_{k}$*	0.414*** (0.097)	0.382** (0.167)	0.425*** (0.103)
	$demand\ shock_{jt} \times gvc\ partner_{jl}$	−0.234*** (0.074)	−0.239* (0.127)	−0.214*** (0.074)
Third-country supply shock	*$competition\ shock_{ijkt}$*	0.335* (0.181)	−0.244 (0.158)	0.203 (0.187)
	$upstream\ shock_{ilt}$	2.172** (0.891)	2.400*** (0.789)	1.673* (0.870)
	$global\ output_{mt}$	0.753*** (0.166)	0.611*** (0.153)	0.426** (0.179)
	Constant	1.243*** (0.103)	0.971*** (0.085)	0.906*** (0.094)
	Observations	496,295	487,264	323,998
	R-squared	0.424	0.433	0.446
	Exporter-time FE	Yes	Yes	Yes
	Importer-time FE	Yes	Yes	Yes
	Exporter-partner-sector FE	Yes	Yes	Yes
	Sector-time FE	Yes	Yes	Yes
	Cluster	Exporter-partner	Exporter-partner	Exporter-partner

Source: Based on Espitia et al. 2021.

Note: Sector-time fixed effects (FE) control for unobserved effects affecting aggregated sectors over time (see note 5). The variable *$global\ output_{mt}$* additionally controls for global sector-time trends. Robust standard errors are in parentheses.

a. Changes in worker mobility are replaced with annualized industrial production index (IPI) growth in exporting countries and retail mobility with annualized IPI growth in partner countries.

*** $p<0.01$ ** $p<0.05$ * $p<0.1$

Notes

1. Only 12 countries in the sample used in World Bank (2021b) had positive export growth in 2020.

2. See the literature review in chapter 2.

3. These data are used as a proxy for global trends; mirror trade data are used to identify trends in the trade of low- and middle-income countries.

4. The sample reflects primarily a period of sharp decline in merchandise trade, with the beginnings of recovery in June. As the first part of this chapter shows, the trade recovery in later months was sharp and robust. Had these data been available at the time of the analysis, the results presented here might have shown stronger evidence of the positive effects of GVCs on resilience of trade.

5. Production disruptions can also have trade effects if firms can switch input suppliers. However, switching input suppliers is difficult in the short term, particularly when inputs are customized in GVCs. Therefore, reshaping value chains in response to a shock is a longer-term process and especially difficult in the period considered in this chapter. For an empirical analysis of the longer-term effects of natural disasters on GVCs, see Freund et al. (2021).

6. Mobility data are not available for 2019, so annualized mobility changes are not computed.

7. This approach is the most commonly used in a sectoral bilateral gravity trade model because some of the explanatory determinants of bilateral trade (like distance) vary only by country-pair. See, for example, Dai, Yotov, and Zylkin (2014).

8. Sector-time fixed effects in this model control for unobserved effects affecting aggregated sectors over time. The fixed effects differentiate between GVC-intensive and nonintensive sectors, of which the first includes all subsectors in apparel, electronics, machinery, and transport.

References

Baldwin, Richard E., and Eiichi Tomiura. 2020. "Thinking Ahead about the Trade Impact of COVID-19." In *Economics in the Time of COVID-19,* edited by Richard Baldwin and Beatrice Weder di Mauro, 59–71. London: CEPR Press.

Dai, Mian, Yoto V. Yotov, and Thomas Zylkin. 2014. "On the Trade-Diversion Effects of Free Trade Agreements" *Economics Letters* 122 (2): 321–25.

Engel, Jakob, Deeksha Kokas, Gladys Lopez-Acevedo, and Maryla Maliszewska. 2021. *The Distributional Impacts of Trade: Empirical Innovations, Analytical Tools, and Policy Responses.* Washington, DC: World Bank.

Eppinger, Peter, Gabriel Felbermayr, Oliver Krebs, and Bohdan Kukharskyy. 2020. "COVID-19 Shocking Global Value Chains." CESifo Working Paper Series 8572, CESifo GmbH, Munich.

Espitia, Alvaro, Aaditya Mattoo, Nadia Rocha, Michele Ruta, and Deborah Winkler. 2021. "Pandemic Trade: COVID-19, Remote Work, and Global Value Chains," Policy Research Working Paper 9508, Macroeconomics, Trade, and Investment Global Practice, World Bank, Washington, DC.

Freund, Caroline, Aaditya Mattoo, Alen Mulabdic, and Michele Ruta. 2021. "Natural Disasters and the Reshaping of Global Value Chains." Policy Research Working Paper 9219, Macroeconomics, Trade, and Investment Global Practice, World Bank, Washington, DC.

Gerschel, Elie, Alejandra Martinez, and Isabelle Méjean. 2020. "Propagation of Shocks in Global Value Chains: The Coronavirus Case." IPP Policy Brief 53, Institut Polytechnique de Paris.

Grimaldi, Lisa A. 2021. "When Will Cruises Restart?" Northstar Meetings Group, Virginia Tech University, March 30, 2021. https://www.northstarmeetingsgroup.com/News/Industry /Cruise-Lines-Suspend-Sailings-Coronavirus.

Javorcik, Beata. 2020. "Global Supply Chains Will Not Be the Same in the Post-COVID-19 World." In *COVID-19 and Trade Policy, Why Turning Inward Won't Work,* edited by Richard Baldwin and Simon Evenett, ch. 8. Washington, DC: CEPR Press.

Miroudot, Sébastien. 2020. "Resilience Versus Robustness in Global Value Chains: Some Policy Implications." In *COVID-19 and Trade Policy, Why Turning Inward Won't Work,* edited by Richard Baldwin and Simon Evenett, ch. 9. Washington, DC: CEPR Press.

Qiang, Christine, Yan Liu, and Victor Steenbergen. 2021. *Global Value Chains: An Investment Perspective.* Washington, DC: World Bank.

Rajan, Raghuram G., and Luigi Zingales. 1998. "Financial Dependence and Growth." *American Economic Review* 88 (3): 559–86.

UNCTAD (United Nations Convention on Trade and Development). 2020. *World Investment Report 2020: International Production beyond the Pandemic.* Geneva: UNCTAD.

UNWTO (United Nations World Tourism Organization). 2021. "2020: Worst Year in Tourism History, with 1 Billion Fewer International Arrivals." UNWTO, Madrid, January 28, 2021. https://www.unwto.org/news/2020-worst-year-in-tourism-history-with-1-billion-fewer -international-arrivals#:~:text=Global%20tourism%20suffered%20its%20worst,World%20

Tourism%20Organization%20(UNWTO).&text=The%20crisis%20has%20put%20 between,small%20and%20medium%2Dsized%20enterprises.

World Bank. 2020. *Rebuilding Tourism Competitiveness: Tourism Response, Recovery, and Resilience to the COVID-19 Crisis.* Washington, DC: World Bank.

World Bank. 2021a. "Global Economic Prospects June 2021." World Bank Group, Washington, DC.

World Bank. 2021b. "Trade Watch Series: Underlying Data." World Bank, Washington, DC. https://www.worldbank.org/en/topic/trade/brief/trade-watch.

4

Responses of Firms and Governments to Supply Chain Shocks Surrounding COVID-19

Key messages

- Although firms have made significant investments in new data-driven methods of supply chain management (Supply Chain 4.0), many companies were caught off guard at the beginning of 2020 by the COVID-19 (coronavirus) crisis.

- The pandemic spawned multiple shocks in supply chains, including reductions in supplies of imported inputs, reductions in foreign demand, and direct impacts on domestic production due to lockdowns. Restrictions on the movement of people also negatively affected logistics at road border crossings and at seaports. Some producers experienced sudden cutoffs in payments for goods already produced.

- The pandemic also accelerated some preexisting mega trends, including automation, e-commerce, and working from home. Firms adapted by reducing the variety of products, increasing the flexibility in factory procedures and labor scheduling, and seeking alternate suppliers. Support of parent firms for affiliates—and affiliates for suppliers—was widespread but not universal.

- Although widely discussed, responses to COVID-19 such as near-shoring, reshoring, or international decoupling were limited. Most foreign investors that had been considering relocating from China before 2020 because of labor costs or trade tensions have already done so.

- Government trade policy responses to COVID-19 proliferated, particularly for medical goods and food. These policies included both restrictive and liberalizing measures.

- In Sub-Saharan Africa, shocks to international trade associated with the response to COVID-19 were particularly severe, with import and export bans resulting in cross-border disruption.

- The rapid but uneven recovery from COVID-19 saw new types of problems for supply chains, including shortages of containers and semiconductors and overlapping shocks such as the Texas freeze and the Suez Canal blockage.

- Greater transparency and collaboration through digital solutions, effective regulation of the logistics sector, and reforms in port governance and management, together with trade facilitation measures, will improve supply chain flexibility and help traders and policy makers to act more quickly if such problems arise in the future.

Introduction

This chapter seeks to understand the impact of the changes in trade due to the COVID-19 shock on firms in global value chains (GVCs), how the responses of firms and governments have been implemented, and whether these measures have enhanced the resilience of firms and GVC networks. The analysis is based on firm-level surveys and interviews with prominent lead GVC firms. The potential importance of firm and policy responses, such as measures to reshore production, for reshaping GVCs is explored, together with other factors that affect, or are expected to affect, global trade, including the rise of China.

Traditional supply chain management and its limitations

The events of 2020 gave rise to shocks to GVCs of unprecedented magnitude. Firms and governments responded to these shocks in both improvised and novel ways. Although some of the techniques for responding to supply chain shocks were well developed, they were not universally used in 2020. Even the best-managed firms were placed under unusual stress.

At the end of the twentieth century, the emergent managerial model for supply chains was the Supply-Chain Operations Reference (SCOR) model, originally developed in 1996 by the management consulting firm PRTM (now part of PricewaterhouseCoopers) and AMR Research (now part of Gartner) (Lambert 2008). The principles of SCOR were still widely employed in 2020[1] and are now part of a de facto strategic, management, and process improvement methodology for supply chain management. The ideas behind SCOR and their implementation have been important for the development of GVCs and for the coordination of supplies among networks of firms.

The SCOR model links each stage of the supply chain in a linear manner. Suppliers of raw materials and parts communicate with producers of goods, producers communicate with distributors, and distributors communicate with customers and consumers. Each stage of the supply chain is interlinked by a process of planning for future activity, ordering, and confirmation, leading to a limited view of the supply chain.

Information can be delayed as it is transmitted from one part of the organization (or network if multiple firms are involved). Different parts of the supply chain may operate in an unsynchronized way as information moves along the supply chain, leading to a distorted view of consumer demand.

One chronic problem in supply chains is the so-called bullwhip effect (McCullen and Towill 2002). Also called demand amplification, bullwhip refers to the magnification of small changes in customer demand at previous stages of the supply chain. This problem has long been documented (Forrester 1961), both for the general case and for many types of manufactured goods. Consequences of bullwhip include inventory costs, costs of stopping and starting up production, and sporadic availability of products leading to lost sales. Although appropriate management practices can reduce bullwhip and increase profitability, they are by no means universally applied, because many managers are not convinced that the issue is important or that the techniques are effective. The bullwhip effect has been implicated in the Great Trade Collapse of 2008–09, with Zavacka (2012) finding that, after the Lehman Brothers shock, the volatility of US imports was greater in upstream industries.

Problems in supply chain coordination can occur even when the supply chain is not exposed to an unusual external shock. In February 2018, supply chain problems caused two-thirds of the 900 Kentucky Fried Chicken restaurants in the United Kingdom to close because they had run out of chicken (Bomey 2018). Thus, better methods of managing supply chains were being sought even before the events of 2020 highlighted the need to respond to external shocks.

Supply Chain 4.0

More recently, Supply Chain 4.0, a model of supply chain management, offers the prospect of substantial improvement in the supply chain performance and profitability of firms (Ferrantino and Koten 2019). Supply Chain 4.0 is sometimes thought of as merely the application of Industry 4.0 technologies to supply chains, such as big data, the Internet of Things, artificial intelligence, and autonomous robots. The key principle, however, is end-to-end visibility of the supply chain. For example, the purchase of a single Barbie doll in a Walmart at the checkout counter should generate information not only for the regional warehouse to send more Barbie dolls but also for China to produce more Barbie dolls, for the input suppliers of Barbie dolls for the various providers of logistics, and so on. By the same token, the analysis of an entire supply chain with big data analytics should enable firms to ask deeper questions: What just happened? Why did this happen? What should I do next? This information, in turn, should lead to superior optimization of everything from inventories, to production, to which product varieties to offer at a particular retail location, to whether marketing ought to be done by store displays, advertisements, or e-commerce platforms.

Another type of chronic problem with supply chains is the bottleneck problem (Carvalho, Elliott, and Spray 2020). Certain firms may account for a high share of supply at certain stages of the supply chain—either final manufacturers or tier 1 or tier 2 suppliers that provide inputs to many firms. Bottleneck firms usually have high market shares at their stages of the supply chain and may operate in activities that have high barriers to entry. If a bottleneck firm is unable to produce at normal capacity for some reason, negative shocks are likely to be transmitted up and down the supply chain. Identifying bottleneck firms in advance and engaging in contingency planning in the event such firms should be shut down or constrained in activity are an important part of supply chain management.

The types of shocks that affect supply chains

Supply chain disruptions are having a substantial impact on firms. McKinsey Global Institute (2020) estimates that both small and large supply chain disruptions can cause a typical company to lose more than 40 percent of one year's profits in a particular decade. Supply chain disruptions have a skewed distribution in both their frequency and their magnitude—a disruption of 1 to 20 weeks may occur every 2 years on average, and a disruption of 2 or more months may occur once every 4.9 years.

Supply chain disruptions also vary according to the ability to forecast or anticipate the disruption. Theft, counterfeiting, and common cyberattacks are relatively small, frequent, and apparently random disruptions. Climate change gives rise to both moderate, predictable supply chain shocks (heat waves) and larger, less predictable shocks (hurricanes, tsunamis). Pandemics, financial crises, and trade disputes are predictable insofar as they can be expected to occur from time to time and to require at least some lead time to respond. At the far extreme are events whose impact is both massive and likely to strike suddenly without warning (extinction-level meteor strikes, solar storms, massive terrorist events, globally systemic cyberattacks).

Trends before COVID-19

Before the onset of COVID-19 in Wuhan in November 2019, various headwinds were facing potential foreign investors in the Chinese economy and economic links between China and the world in general. The sharp decline in Chinese economic activity in January and February 2020, associated with the lockdowns imposed by Chinese authorities to limit the spread of the virus, deepened these existing weaknesses. Although it does not reflect the full global impact of COVID-19, the European Union Chambers of Commerce and Business (EUCCB) survey, conducted in February 2020, provides a reasonable idea of the trends that were perceived as affecting business in China at the beginning of 2020 (EUCCB 2020). Table 4.1 presents the top concerns of European chamber members in 2019 and 2020.

TABLE 4.1 Top concerns of Chamber of Commerce members in Europe, 2019 and 2020

Percent of firms listing the item as a top-three concern

Issue	2020	Change from 2019
China's economic slowdown	40	−5
United States–China trade war	27	+4
Global economic slowdown	26	−1
Rising labor costs	22	−1
Ambiguous rules and regulations	17	+2

Source: EUCCB 2020.
Note: N = 626.

A US-China Business Council survey released in August 2020 reported the following as the top-five challenges for US firms operating in China (US-China Business Council 2020):

1. United States–China relations

2. COVID-19 impacts

3. Competition with Chinese companies

4. Tariffs

5. Cost increases

These findings are broadly consistent with those of the European survey.

Automation

In the 2010s a variety of mega trends emerged in manufacturing, often known collectively as Industry 4.0. These trends include, but are not limited to, smart automation and the Internet of Things, advanced robotics, and 3-D printing (Hallward-Driemeier and Nayyar 2017). Uptake of these technologies was well under way before 2020. Between 2010 and 2018, the operational stock of industrial robots doubled in North America, tripled in the Republic of Korea, and increased sixteenfold in China (Hallward-Driemeier and Nayyar 2017, 97). During COVID-19, the use of robots became increasingly profitable as social distancing reduced the number of human workers in factories. Similarly, the use of the Internet of Things to monitor and adjust factory conditions from a remote location became increasingly relevant.

Trade conflicts

During 2018–19, the trade policies of the major powers became completely unpredictable. The United States imposed tariffs on most Chinese imports in an escalating manner, to which China responded with tit-for-tat tariffs on most US imports. Additional US trade actions on steel and aluminum led to retaliation by many US trading partners. Other trade disputes involved washing machines and solar panels (Peterson Institute of International Economics 2021).

Some large firms describe the trade conflicts of 2018–19 as a sort of fire drill preparation for COVID-19. Because the imposition of the tariffs was haphazard and unpredictable, firms developed rapid response teams to decide whether or not to continue supplying from China. Merchandise finance, logistics, and government relations units of large firms had to cooperate on navigating the trade wars. The tariff response team could then become a COVID-19 response team, using the newly acquired skill sets.

Increased costs in China

According to the National Bureau of Statistics of China, nominal wages more than doubled from 2011 to 2019.[2] These wage increases were especially notable on China's east coast, where decades of rapid development led by foreign investment increased the demand for labor at a greater rate than the amount of permitted intracountry migration. These wage increases led firms to respond in one of two ways: by seeking cheaper labor inland (the "Go West" movement) or by seeking locations outside of China (for example, Vietnam). The increase in wages was a longer-run trend, as contrasted with the short, sharp contraction in Chinese manufacturing in the early stages of COVID-19 (January and February 2020).

According to interviews conducted for this study, most multinationals with concerns about higher wages in China had already relocated their production by 2018. To the extent that there is scope for further relocation away from China, it lies primarily in export-oriented production. A large share of China's inbound foreign direct investment (FDI) serves the domestic Chinese market and has no incentive to move. Moreover, the perceived instability of China as a source of supplies receded from March 2020 onward, because Chinese production recovered quickly thereafter.

Issues revealed by COVID-19

Lockdown-related shocks to supply and demand

The administration of lockdowns was, in many cases, the chief cause of the contraction in production. The imposition of lockdowns affected economic activity in several ways—direct orders to shut down production, orders to keep labor from moving to and from the production facility, and changes in the way production was carried out within the facility. The administration of lockdowns was often sudden, with unpredictable effects, and frequently revised. In Kenya, the original curfews prohibited movement across county lines. If a factory was on one side of the line and 95 percent of its workforce was on the other side of the line, the factory needed to shut down, even if no quarantine order had been issued for the factory itself.

One factor affecting the variability of lockdown severity across countries was the way in which "essential activities" were defined in the emergency. If a major manufacturer was defined as "essential," but its suppliers of goods and services were not, then the manufacturer would have to shut down anyway. A misunderstanding of how supply chains work led to lockdowns that were more severe than necessary in some countries. The experience of 2020 shows that, in an emergency, a negative list is preferable to a positive list. In a negative list, the government identifies what must be shut down, ideally consulting with private sector lead firms that will share information on their suppliers. With a positive list, the government identifies what can remain open. This model, which was followed in at least one Southeast Asian country, often led to unintended consequences. As an extreme example, a prohibition on physical movement by a supplier of business process services that were needed to maintain payroll systems nearly shut down the government's ability to meet its own payroll. The resulting high-level emergency, in which officials learned that government workers would go unpaid if an exemption was not immediately granted to the firm in question, could have been avoided by taking a negative-list approach.

Social distancing within factories imposes a severe constraint on production. US producers of dishwashers customarily had as many as 15 workers handling each machine. When the pandemic hit, the assembly line was reconfigured to require only five workers. This change caused output to drop by about two-thirds, leading to shortages of machines available at retail stores as well as of spare parts for repair. Many factories, cafeterias, tea break areas, and shuttle buses to workers' homes also had to be reorganized to respect social distancing, imposing further constraints on production. In industries with economies of scale, such as textiles and motor vehicles, operating the same factory with fewer workers led to an increase in the ratio of fixed to variable costs and thus an increase in unit costs. Running the factory at a fraction of capacity because of falling demand had the same effect. Some firms with pricing power passed these costs on to buyers, whereas others simply lost money.

Disruption of foreign supply of intermediate goods

Such disruptions could happen because the supplying countries were under lockdown or because logistics were difficult at the importing port of entry. During January and February, many producers of apparel in Africa, Bangladesh, and elsewhere were hit hard by the lack of Chinese supplies of yarn and cloth. By the time the shutdowns hit Europe later in February and March, shortages of import supplies were endemic. As a report by the EUCCB (2020) put it,

> Companies are still finding upstream supplies running dry, while demand downstream plummets. The fragility of highly efficient global supply chains has been exposed as economy after economy is hit by rolling outbreaks. For example, even if an automotive manufacturer somehow manages to get 95 percent of its global supply chain moving, it cannot sell a car without brakes, a steering wheel, or a radiator. Such single constraints then disrupt not only the demand for upstream inputs from manufacturers and their suppliers, but also the energy and financing that fuels the entire chain.

In Europe's auto industry, producing a vehicle required that quarantines be lifted in every country that produced a major subassembly or component. Makes and models of cars that depended on parts sourced from countries with longer quarantines, such as the United Kingdom, faced additional disruption.

Disruption of foreign demand

Sudden declines of European and US demand, precipitated by COVID-19-related lockdowns, led to widespread nonpayment of orders for imports from low- and middle-income countries, including orders for goods already handed over (Nilsson and Terazono 2020). In Bangladesh's apparel industry, many firms did not survive the crisis. After street conflicts in April, the government extended loans to support 65 percent of wages. At the same time, firms whose revenues declined passed the shock farther up the supply chain, both to suppliers of inputs, such as the cotton farmers in India's Maharashtra Province who have traditionally supplied the basic inputs for yarn and cloth in the region, and to banks, which found that payments on working capital loans had stopped. In Turkey, where more than 90 percent of automobiles produced are sold in Europe, most factories shut down from mid-March until early May. Domestic sales of autos continued out of inventory.

Unpredictable shifts in demand

The consumption patterns of people working from home and those quarantined at home were sharply different from those of people going to work. Major shifts in demand cascaded backward through global supply chains, for example, during March and April 2020 in the United States.[3] Demand shifted sharply away from clothing and autos and toward food and home equipment products as well as toward information and communication technology and furniture products used in home offices. Shifts also occurred within categories—from business clothes to yoga pants, for example. Demand for home workout equipment and sewing machines spiked. These shifts in demand were not forecasted and placed additional pressure on the planning of production and logistics. The V-shaped recovery of US demand in May and June required a sudden shift in the opposite direction. The timing of these shifts in demand varied from country to country.

Disruption of transport and logistics

Disruptions to the physical movement of persons in the pandemic led to backlogs both at road borders and at the intersection of seaports and port networks in many places. These disruptions often happened because truckers were prevented from moving, due to very general lockdowns or positive test results. In the port of Djibouti, customs brokers and freight forwarders were accustomed to deliver paperwork by hand to the port, because there was no electronic means of submission. When quarantines made hand delivery impossible, trucks began to back up in the port for lack of documents. The pandemic led simultaneously to an increase in smaller parcels due to the expansion of e-commerce and the reduction in larger, heavier packages.

Lack of transparency in supply chains

Firms often know their primary suppliers and their shipment schedules to primary customers but have little knowledge of suppliers farther up the chain (Frikkee 2020). Information about tier 2 and higher suppliers may be revealed only when they become bottlenecks in a crisis. Another issue with transparency relates to the ability of buyers and shippers to identify counterfeit products. This issue arose in a variety of forms with respect to counterfeit personal protective equipment (PPE) and COVID-19 testing kits originating from China. Frequently changing rules placed additional burdens on shippers. In early April 2020, China identified a "white list" of factories from which supplies were guaranteed not to be counterfeit. Difficulties in getting certifications for supplies originating from these factories created bottlenecks, coinciding with arbitrary warehouse closures. These issues reportedly eased in subsequent months.

Firm-level adaptations in 2020

Increased demand for supply chain mapping

More and more firms turned to outside suppliers of supply chain mapping services, including third-party logistics firms, specialized supply chain mapping firms, and supply chain finance firms. For the first time, many firms needed PPE on the factory floor. Because many firms acquired PPE in small, rather than large, quantities, this situation itself led to major shifts in supply systems. Other drivers of increased demand for supply chain mapping were corporate social responsibility and human rights issues.

Reduction in product varieties offered

Firms experiencing sharp declines in output lose economies of scale and face rising unit costs. Firms have several logical responses to this situation, short of shutting down completely. If the firm has significant market power, it may try to raise prices, as some automakers did. For firms that produce differentiated products, there is a trade-off between the number of product varieties offered and the economies of scale obtainable from producing each variety. Thus, reducing the number of varieties can help to retain economies of scale on each individual variety, holding down costs and making profitability more likely. In 2020 some firms reduced the availability of their product offerings. Both Coca-Cola and Procter and Gamble strategically reduced the number of individual SKUs (stock-keeping units) offered (Cosgrove 2020).[4]

Support of affiliate and network partners

Lead firms, especially buyers, vary widely in how they treat suppliers during a demand shock. Buyers with falling demand may assert force majeure and simply not pay. The mechanics of international trade facilitate this approach—in many cases, the ownership of goods is not transferred from the buyer or the seller until the ship reaches the port of importation, so orders can be canceled. But some buyers agreed to absorb the risks of falling demand, because they were better able to bear the risks than small suppliers in low- and middle-income countries. Such an agreement can include accepting orders of finished products even when not required, selling goods out of season, and making arrangements whereby suppliers can obtain liquidity by taking purchase orders to a global bank associated with the lead firm.

Within the domestic economy, lead firms are responsible for maintaining networks of both suppliers and dealers. In industries such as motor vehicles, there is a greater incentive to support suppliers rather than dealers because suppliers produce specialized parts and components and dealers are more easily replaced if they go under.

Support of parent firms for their affiliates and affiliates for their suppliers was widespread but not universal during the COVID-19 supply chain stresses of 2020. The World Bank's Global Pulse Survey for the third quarter of 2020 revealed that globally 61 percent of affiliates of multinational enterprises (MNEs) received some type of support from their parent company in response to COVID-19 and 55 percent extended some type of support to their suppliers. The most common types of support provided were new technology or managerial guidance to allow operations to continue, followed by financial support, new technology, or managerial guidance to help with product differentiation and new technology for supply chain mapping and management. The Global Pulse Survey also found that large firms were more likely to survive the shocks of 2020 than medium or small firms.

The Global Pulse Survey for the third quarter of 2020 reports that the vast majority of MNE affiliates (97 percent) received some type of government support to counter the effects of the pandemic. Of these, the most common type of support was information about COVID-19 (69 percent), followed by support with operational issues and grievances (59 percent), trade finance (57 percent), relaxation of regulations (55 percent), tax relief (55 percent), financial support (54 percent), and restructuring or postponing of debt (52 percent). Going forward, MNE affiliates reported that the most important form of government support to deal with COVID-19 would be tax relief, with 53 percent identifying tax relief as "critically important" and 39 percent as "somewhat important."

Internal flexibility

In the face of uncertainty about the epidemiological course of COVID-19 and associated lockdowns, some firms needed to upscale and downscale production several times. This change in production indicates that firms with an advantage in flexible rescaling are likely to do better than firms without it (PwC Global 2020). On the staffing level, human resources models of the 60:40 type—planning around a 60 percent core workforce and a 40 percent flexible workforce—are likely to gain ground. Various aspects of strict separation, hygiene, and control may need to be stepped up and down flexibly; choosing these aspects strategically is key. Flexibility also includes shifting to different customers, depending on circumstances. In Kenya, small logistics firms, frustrated by cross-border transport bottlenecks, pivoted to the domestic delivery of essential goods.

E-commerce and digitization

In every region of the world, the use of e-commerce by consumers exploded in 2020 as a result of COVID-19 lockdowns. Globally, the share of e-commerce in retailing increased from 14 percent in 2019 to 17 percent in 2020 (e-Trade for All 2021). In individual markets, the increase was even more marked. In Latin America, the platform Mercado Libre sold twice as many articles per day in the second quarter of 2020 as in 2019. The African e-commerce platform Jumia saw a 60 percent increase in the volume of transactions in the first six months of 2020 compared to 2019. From August 2019 to August 2020, the share of online retailing in Kazakhstan rose from 5.0 percent to 9.4 percent. In Thailand, downloads of shopping apps rose 60 percent in a single month, from February to March 2020 (e-Trade for All 2021). Moreover, the shift toward e-commerce is likely to be sustained even after recovery—a majority of consumers expect to continue shopping more online than they did before, and the share of internet retailing compared to store-based retailing has very likely increased permanently. Locally, there are numerous reports of online food delivery businesses appearing and flourishing, for example, in Sub-Saharan Africa. In Rwanda, e-payments increased by 400 percent after the government required all firms to have an identifying code to receive such payments.

Remote working

COVID-19 accelerated many preexisting trends in technology. Firms that had already invested in remote work technologies and behaviors did better in 2020 than those that had not (PwC Global 2020). The share of workers able to work from home is much smaller in low- and middle-income countries than in rich countries (Sanchez et al. 2021), because of both a different mix of occupations and less internet connectivity. In interviews, firms in East Africa indicated that initiating remote working was initially problematic, both because of lack of preparedness of workers and because of perceived difficulties in monitoring firms' output. In Bangladesh, apparel firms that invested in automation before 2020 were likely to be relatively more resilient when lockdowns limited the ability of workers to come into factories (Obe 2018).

Working from home provided a challenge for many firms in low- and middle-income countries that had not tried it before. Home-based work provides a classic instance of the principal-agent problem: How can the employer tell how hard the employee is working? Some African employers reported lower productivity early in the transition to home-based work, until employers and employees learned to function under the new conditions.

Making medical products

Some firms were able to pivot to making PPE or other medical equipment. In the United States, spontaneous innovation enabled auto companies to begin making ventilators, further incentivized by the Defense Production Act. At Tropic Knits, a company of CIEL Textile, based in Mauritius but also operating in India and Madagascar, innovations in materials and methods enabled some production facilities to pivot to PPE from apparel at a time when demand for PPE was exploding and demand for apparel was collapsing.[5] This switch, in turn, supported employment for migrant workers who otherwise would have had to return to their home countries. In Ethiopia, some of the textile manufacturers located across special economic zones diverted their lines of production to PPE. In South Africa and Uganda, companies previously engaged in the production and manufacturing of alcoholic beverages diverted their production to hand sanitizers.

Seeking alternate suppliers: Near-shoring, reshoring, and decoupling

In February 2020, at the onset of the global COVID-19 crisis, only 11 percent of European companies were considering shifting current and planned investments in China to other markets (EUCCB 2020). This figure was down from 15 percent in 2019 and 22 percent in 2012. The most frequently mentioned alternate locations were Europe (27 percent), Association of Southeast Asian Nations (ASEAN) (23 percent), other Asia-Pacific (12 percent), Middle East (12 percent), North America (11 percent), South Asia (10 percent), South America (4 percent), and Africa (2 percent).

The US-China Business Council reported that, in 2020, 87 percent of US-based companies said that neither had they moved operations out of China recently nor did they plan to do so; 11 percent said they planned to move to a location other than the United States, with Mexico and Thailand being the leading alternative destinations (US-China Business Council 2020). Only 4 percent planned to move operations back to the United States. However, 24 percent said that they reduced or stopped planned investment in China in 2020, up from 8–17 percent during 2012–18. The main reasons for this decision were higher costs or uncertainties from United States–China tensions (52 percent) and uncertainty stemming from COVID-19 (42 percent).

At the onset of the crisis, some firms in Rwanda received government support for finding alternative suppliers in countries other than China—for example, in the Arab Republic of Egypt and Turkey. The need for this support appears to have been short-lived.

Automation

COVID-19 accelerated the move toward automation. Automation can help simultaneously to raise productivity and to reduce the risk of virus transmission (Frikkee 2020). Automation of industrial processes is one way to deal with the need for social distancing in industrial establishments. The changes are not limited to the use of robots. The increase in remote connectivity and visibility of industrially generated data has allowed cooperation among teams of workers thousands of miles away. ExxonMobil had recently established a machinery monitoring group in Malaysia when it became necessary for its facility in Beaumont, Texas, to engage in an orderly shutdown because of the onset of Hurricane Laura in August 2020. Remote monitoring capabilities allowed engineers in Malaysia to guide the staff in Beaumont through the shutdown (Greenfield 2021). Use of robotic inspections and operator assistants driven by artificial intelligence also increased during the pandemic.

Private sector views of the transition

World Bank Group staff members conducted a series of 30 in-depth interviews with representatives of global companies, consultancies, trade associations, and the private sector in Africa, Asia, Europe, and North America. The interviews took place from April 2020 through February 2021. Some participants were interviewed twice, covering views early and later in the COVID-19 crisis. Participants were selected on the basis of GVC participation and insight, rather than systematic geographic or sectoral coverage. Interviewees were all senior executives positioned at levels with strategic corporate insight. The interviews focused on how COVID-19 affected GVCs. Whereas the early interviews focused on the immediate COVID-19 situation, later interviews shifted toward lessons learned and the post-COVID-19 outlook for the future of GVCs and sourcing. All interviews took place under Chatham House rules, so views cannot be traced back to any entity or person.

During COVID-19, the global economy and GVCs changed dramatically in a very short period. Global companies experienced serious disruption of supply chains, demand, and other shocks, such as lack of availability of affordable transportation. Part of this disruption was due to fragile trade facilitation, with bottlenecks at borders and ports as well as in inland supply networks.

As a result, many MNEs are reassessing their global production and sourcing. It appears likely that this reassessment will lead to changes in GVCs and global sourcing, but how and to what degree are unclear. Although one or two MNEs had already decided to diversify and seek suppliers in Asia beyond China, interviewees explained that most companies will not make strategic decisions until the global economy has turned a corner and they can reassess GVC vulnerabilities under clearer conditions. One respondent explained that changing supply chains in Western markets would entail traveling to new suppliers to verify labor and environmental conditions. This verification cannot take place until travel resumes after COVID-19.

MNEs see COVID-19 as the latest development in a series of shocks to GVCs and global production and sourcing. Because of its GVC importance and market size, China is central to companies' outlook. Global companies were hit first by rising costs in China, then by international trade tensions and US tariffs on China and other countries, and now by COVID-19. These developments raised the priority given to managing and mitigating risk in corporate agendas. Interviewees spoke about strategic reflections on GVCs and sourcing in terms of on-shoring or near-shoring, GVC resilience, diversification and moving away from single-sourcing, and GVC simplification. One interviewee said that corporate thinking had gone from being "efficiency themed" to being "resiliency themed" and that the company planned to diversify suppliers further. Several said that post-COVID-19 concerns would likely lead to reductions in just-in-time GVCs. They expected more redundancy to reduce supply chain concentration, especially for low-value manufacturing and especially for export markets. Many companies had risk management strategies in place before COVID-19, but they said that they intended to revisit them postcrisis. Firms that did not have such strategies were less agile in responding to the changes in orders, inventories, and other external circumstances.

Looking ahead, MNE reflections evolve around the following considerations:

- *Global decoupling is widely expected to continue to challenge GVCs and sourcing.* Tariffs have not been effective and sometimes have even been counterproductive, as Western producers in some cases have moved production to China. In the middle to longer term, interviewees said that they expect increasing pressure to decouple GVCs, driven by geopolitics and by differences in national regulatory setups and disruptions of financial flows, but also pushed by the market power that big economies can force onto such divisions.

- *Irrespective of the pressures to look beyond China, GVCs have not left China in any significant numbers to date.* Although China was hit first by COVID-19, the Chinese economy was back up and running before any other economy because of its determined handling of the pandemic. China appears to be important for MNEs, as well as for the broad spectrum of supply-side efficiencies. China is a cluster in itself. For example, one interviewee said that he could find only 1 copper supplier in Malaysia, but found 10 within an hour in Guangdong. He also said that Chinese approvals are typically instant, whereas his company had encountered a difficult bureaucratic environment when moving to India. Another reason for continued attachment to China is that MNE production in China increasingly serves markets beyond the European Union and the United States, including China's own strong domestic market as well as other regional markets. One respondent said that the company expects 60 percent of global growth to be in China over the next decade. China is considered to be an innovation leader, and this innovation leadership will help companies to achieve continued economic success, despite tariffs and other measures. This view is particularly true for high-tech, chemicals, coating, and inputs to artificial intelligence. Whereas some companies may diversify more into non-Chinese suppliers in the longer term, multinational companies in China said that they are increasingly unlikely to leave. However, as companies look beyond COVID-19, human rights are a rising concern in their China operations, particularly in certain regions.

- *Long-term relationships with suppliers had a stabilizing effect during COVID-19.* These relationships will continue beyond the crisis. One interviewee said that suppliers are harder to replace than dealers. In the short run, MNEs will go to relatively great lengths to help an established supplier to navigate the crisis, including suppliers with short-term financial difficulties.

- *COVID-19 triggered a significant shift to e-commerce.* One major global distributor explained that, whereas business was 50 percent e-commerce in 2019, it is now 70 percent e-commerce. A significant part of this change is expected to remain beyond the crisis. The shift highlights the importance of global information and communication technology networks. As one interviewee commented, when WhatsApp goes down, the company's communications go down. In Africa, business associations stressed the difference between e-commerce in urban areas with good connectivity and e-commerce in rural communities with poor connectivity.

- *Global trade rules largely held up.* Apart from relatively limited export restrictions on medical supplies and food, interviewees expressed satisfaction with the robustness and relevance of trade rules through the crisis. One interviewee said that he hoped that by the next crisis more countries will have implemented the World Trade Organization Trade Facilitation Agreement.

- *Climate change is expected to become a more important GVC parameter.* One interviewee explained that climate change had been higher on the company's global agenda before the pandemic, but that the recent trade tensions and tariffs had pushed climate change completely aside. The company expected climate change considerations to return. Although positive incentives are better tools for influencing company decisions, MNEs expected carbon border taxes to be a bigger concern than US tariffs on China.

- *The regionalization of global trade architecture is expected to provide an impetus for the regionalization of GVCs.* One interviewee said that, although regionalization appeared likely, in particular regarding aligned rules of origin, this aspect of GVC regionalizing was "far from baked yet." In general, free trade agreements remain an element in company decisions regarding supply chains.

Government responses to supply chain issues during COVID-19

The unpredictable nature of COVID-19, particularly in its initial stages, resulted in unprecedented policy measures to mitigate the transmission of the virus. Strict lockdowns, curfews, suspension of flights, border closures, and import-export bans were common, affecting the flow of goods across GVCs. This section analyzes the effects of these shocks from two perspectives: first, domestic shocks associated with measures of public health and, second, shocks to external trade related to supply-demand and international logistics constraints.

Domestic shocks associated with measures of public health

Lockdowns, curfews, and similar measures partially or fully disrupted business operations. Severe lockdown measures, including restricting gatherings, canceling public transportation, and implementing stay-at-home requirements, limited the operations of all but essential businesses from the early days of the pandemic. As of February 1, 2021, some of these policies were still being implemented in some economies in East Asia and Pacific,[6] the Middle East and North Africa,[7] Europe and Central Asia,[8] South Asia,[9] and Latin and North America[10] (University of Oxford 2021).

Shocks to external trade

The pandemic drove an overall increase in import and export policies associated with supply-demand characteristics. Supply conditions and concentrated markets for crucial COVID-19 essential goods led to shortages of medical supplies and foodstuffs, fomenting a global spike in tariff liberalizations and export restrictions for these items (Espitia, Rocha, and Ruta 2020a, 2020b). Trade interventions involving other products included temporary import bans on alcoholic beverages and tobacco products in Sub-Saharan Africa and South and Central Asia,[11] import bans on wild animals in East Asia,[12] and a rise in import tariffs on fuel in East and Central Asia.[13] Despite initial fears that some governments would impose protectionist measures to gain comparative advantage in infant or protected industries, such policies were rare, except in Iraq, which imposed additional duties on imports of agricultural products and gypsum.[14]

Supply chain bottlenecks due to international logistics constraints were a key issue. Trade facilitation was one of the biggest challenges triggered by COVID-19 safety measures. Challenges to crossing borders in Central and North Asia, Europe, Latin America, and the Middle East and North Africa included obligatory quarantine before the trip or on arrival, mandatory escorting of cargo freight in transit, cumbersome transshipment regulations, a shortage of border officials due to capacity restrictions, lack of coordination by neighboring countries, and limited cooperation between national administrators.[15] For instance,

- Huge bottlenecks delayed road freight in the weeks following the closure of Europe's internal borders around March 17, 2020. Although the border closures did not target freight transportation directly, the collateral effects created traffic jams for as long as 50 kilometers (31 miles) on the Germany-Poland border (Knowler 2020a). Widespread disruptions to cargo flows were also registered at the France-Germany and Hungary-Austria border crossings (Knowler 2020b). In North and Central Asia, strict border health checks, quarantine, and driver replacement measures exacerbated an existing connectivity problem, prompting greater disruptions of transport operations (UNESCAP 2021).

- Similar constraints were faced in Latin America. The most notable example was in early May, when hundreds of freight trucks were stuck on the border between Costa Rica and Nicaragua because of uncoordinated efforts in testing protocols (Guzman 2020; Logistics Cluster 2020).

- The situation in the Middle East and North Africa region was no different, with Kuwait's and Saudi Arabia's land border experiencing some of the most severe difficulties. At the start of the pandemic, customs in Kuwait reportedly restricted the entry of trucks to a maximum of 25–30 per day, resulting in long queues at the border with Saudi Arabia and up to three days waiting time (Logistics Cluster 2020; UNECE 2020).

- Cargo and maritime freight was generally permitted across all regions, although in certain locations priority was reserved for cargo designated as "essential." As for the operation of maritime ports, shore leave and crew changes were ordinarily prohibited, and delays resulted from restrictions on operational capacity (Gondwe 2020; Logistics Cluster 2020).

Policy responses from governments in Sub-Saharan Africa

A series of unprecedented containment measures was implemented to curb the spread of the virus, with governments imposing partial or full lockdowns, limiting the movement and activities of people.[16] This analysis relies on available data from data centers[17] as well as anecdotal evidence from GVC participants and value chain experts located in Angola, Ethiopia, Kenya, Namibia, Nigeria, and South Africa. Government measures were the main catalysts of trade disruptions in the Sub-Saharan Africa region, first, by limiting the operations of local businesses and thus restraining their participation in global and regional trade and, second, by causing disruptions to cross-border trade in both goods and services.

Initial responses to contain the pandemic affected the operations of domestic value chain participants. Challenged by experts to prevent a worst-case scenario, most African governments started implementing strict COVID-19 preventive measures by early March 2020. The nature of such measures paused economic activity partially or completely for a prolonged period, resulting in negative shocks to local businesses involved in global and regional trade. The following are a few examples:

- *Kenya.* Nonessential workers were unable to enter or exit counties under lockdown, thus limiting the capacity and productivity of firms. In addition, a ban on alcohol sales was imposed on restaurants and eateries (Ikade 2020). Sorghum farmers across East Africa's alcohol value chain were reported to be strongly affected.

- *South Africa.* Government ordered the closure of all nonessential businesses, including factories. A total ban on alcohol and tobacco sales halted production for export for five weeks. Informal traders were not considered essential and were ordered to cease activities temporarily, creating a hiatus in the downstream end of supply chains, particularly in the agriculture sector.

- *Ethiopia.* Government containment responses resulted in the closure of industrial parks in special economic zones.

In Sub-Saharan Africa, the initial responses to the pandemic were marked by uncoordinated efforts between neighboring states. Consequently, their implementation and complexities varied across the region, as did their impact on trade and supply chains in general. Experiences from Eastern and Southern Africa land borders included the following:

- *Rwanda.* Delays of two to three days were reported at land border entries, due to slow testing protocols. In response to such delays, Rwanda established the Kiyanzi Logistics Platform, a dry port facility designed to facilitate a driver swap system and conduct COVID-19 tests for all truck drivers and assistants entering the country (Gahigi 2020).

- *Tanzania.* Slow testing protocols at the border led to long queues of trucks. Responding to protests from Tanzanian drivers following the implementation of Rwanda's relay system, Tanzanian authorities began to reject COVID-19 certificates from Rwanda. The waiting time for COVID-19 test results lasted between four and seven days.

- *Kenya and Uganda.* Both countries required new COVID-19 certificates at border entries, with costs varying depending on the port of entry. In addition, slow testing protocols caused excruciating traffic jams. As a result, the cargo transit time between Mombasa and Busia (Kenya-Uganda) rose from 4 days in January to 12 days in March (Mold and Mveyange 2020). As of November 2020, the line of trucks at the Busia border was 60 kilometers long (Ratner 2020), while queues at the Malaba border post exceeded 30 kilometers (Wasike 2020). Corruption by border officials also reportedly increased.

- *Southern Africa.* In Southern Africa, long queues of trucks, due to bottlenecks from customs clearing, were registered in the following ports of entry: Kasumbalesa border post (Zambia–Democratic Republic of Congo), Kazungula (Botswana-Zambia), Kopfontein/Skilpadshek (South Africa–Botswana), Beitbridge (South Africa–Zimbabwe), Lebombo (South Africa–Mozambique), Chirundu (Zimbabwe-Zambia), Forbes (Mozambique-Zimbabwe), and Nkonde (Zambia-Tanzania) (Goddard 2020; Logistics Cluster 2020).

Globally and in Sub-Saharan Africa, there was a surge in new export and import policies. Export policies were mainly restrictive, whereas import policies were almost always liberalizing. Worldwide, as of January 25, 2021, 140 of 142 export measures announced to the International Trade Centre were restrictive, whereas 163 of the 264 import measures announced were liberalizing. The vast majority of these measures covered medical supplies and food. Likewise, import restrictions increased because of sanitary and phytosanitary concerns and technical barriers to trade. Although often related to the agriculture sector, a few exceptions included the ban on used garments reported in Kenya, Zimbabwe, and briefly in Uganda, as well as on tobacco in Botswana, Namibia, and South Africa. Namibia and South Africa also imposed an import ban on alcoholic beverages for purposes of public order. The ban on imports of alcoholic beverages and tobacco products in South Africa stopped the production of products for export for approximately five weeks.

Border closures halted in-person services trade almost completely. In Africa 32 countries restricted flights. Some suspended all commercial passenger flights, others blocked international flights, and a few limited the restrictions to countries with high infection rates. Anecdotally, some countries permitted entry to international experts providing essential services, whereas others permitted entry to international experts on a case-by-case basis.

Attempting to overturn the general downward trend in the services sector, some governments in the region included e-commerce businesses on the list of essential services and adjusted fiscal policies to facilitate the inclusion of e-payments. For example, in Rwanda mobile payment became one of the obligatory methods of payment for all businesses, and cash was highly discouraged. As a result, e-payments increased by 400 percent during the pandemic.

Issues with the recovery: Containers, semiconductors, and overlapping shocks

As trade and production began to recover in the second half of 2020 and into 2021, different activities returned at different speeds. Although this happens in any recovery, the abruptness of the current episode was particularly striking. Demand for motor vehicles and electronics recovered sharply, whereas demand for services continued to lag (see chapter 3). The variable-speed recovery caused bottlenecks in both transportation and production, as economic activity was constrained by the activities whose recovery lagged in relative terms or by the inability of firms to forecast the pace of recovery accurately. Unprecedented shortages of shipping containers and semiconductors in late 2020 and early 2021 were emblematic of this problem. Moreover, the presence of a major shock to supply chains, such as a pandemic, does not stop additional shocks from taking place, requiring firms to manage multiple bottlenecks simultaneously.

Global prices for shipping containers began to rise sharply in November 2020, with prices tripling on some routes. A primary source of the disequilibrium was that retail demand in Europe and the United States outpaced the increase in production capacity in China (Liu and Hale 2021; Steer, Eley, and Romei 2021; Steer and Romei 2020). As a result, containers could not be repositioned rapidly enough, with queuing in some ports and relative vacancy in others. In addition, some ports in the western United States faced labor-induced capacity constraints due to the pandemic. The mislocation of containers also affected trade in the Southern Hemisphere, where one of the first places hit was India. Demand for India's exports of rubber, plastics, and vegetables surged in late 2020, whereas demand for imports was suppressed because of relatively severe lockdowns (Findlay 2020). As a result, containers were frequently empty on the return trip to India. Prices of container services rose sharply, and typical wait times to book containers increased from two weeks to more than three weeks.

In early 2021, a number of auto manufacturers began to experience shortages of the types of semiconductors increasingly used in today's data-intensive vehicles (Beresford 2021). After the collapse in demand for autos in the second quarter of 2020, automakers ordered too few semiconductors, and semiconductor manufacturers pivoted to serve demand for gaming consoles and other electronic products that use more specialized kinds of chips. The chip shortage may be a short-run planning problem that the auto industry will resolve relatively quickly (Lincicome 2021). Nonetheless, US President Biden identified semiconductors as part of his executive order on supply chain management, and proposals for tax credits, matching grants, and research and development subsidies for semiconductors have received growing support in Congress (Mingas 2021).

In February 2021, record cold temperatures and snowstorms knocked out the electricity supply in Texas, causing shutdowns to the state's petrochemical supply chain. As much as 80 percent of chemicals production came to an abrupt halt, disrupting most US production of the world's three most widely used plastic polymers: polyethylene, polypropylene, and polyvinyl chloride (Jacobs and Dempsey 2021). Because of the disorderly nature of the factory shutdowns, recovery of supply was expected to be time-consuming and costly, taking perhaps months. Interviews conducted for this study indicate that by March the impacts were being felt as far away as the medical devices industry in Southeast Asia, suggesting that specialty plastic resins were also affected. The Texas freeze in the middle of COVID-19 was not related to the pandemic and shows that shocks to supply chains can overlap in unpredictable ways.

Another example of a shock unrelated to COVID-19 is the blockage of the Suez Canal in late March 2021. This blockage happened when the giant container ship *Ever Given*, weighing 224,000 tons and longer than the Eiffel Tower, ran aground in the southern part of the canal. About 12 percent of global trade, 8 percent of liquefied natural gas, and 1 million barrels of oil pass through the Suez Canal daily. Although blockages of the canal happen periodically, they can usually be cleared in a few hours. This blockage, which occurred on March 24, was not cleared until March 29 (Koh, El Wardany, and Clark 2021).

Thus, although merchandise trade recovered strongly and stabilized above pre-COVID-19 levels through 2021, global supply chains were subject to substantial stress during the latter part of the year. Bottlenecks in ports and logistics facilities at key nodes led to substantial disruption that was transmitted along GVCs, bringing consequences across the world—notably delivery delays and rising shipping costs. These challenges in global supply chains highlighted the need to advance port reforms and trade facilitation measures, promote supply chain digitization, and improve oversight and regulation of shipping lines and logistics operators. If measures to improve global shipping and logistics are introduced, there is little to suggest that the COVID-19-induced supply chain disruptions will have long-term impacts on the structure of global value chains. Box 4.1 summarizes the main factors behind the supply chain disruptions of 2021, the impact they had, and the measures that can be taken to prevent them from recurring.

BOX 4.1 Global supply chain disruption in 2021: Causes, consequences, and solutions

Three factors are responsible for the disruptions in global supply chains experienced in the later part of 2021. First, there was an unprecedented *surge in demand for goods*. The release of pent-up demand in early 2021 combined with a substantial shift in consumer expenditures toward durable goods triggered a rapid increase in containerized exports starting in May 2020, especially from East Asia to Europe and the United States. In the first quarter of 2021, expenditures for furniture and household equipment in the United States increased by 28 percent and motor vehicles and parts increased by 31 percent.

Second, a *series of chokepoints at ports and hinterlands* interfered with the global circulation of ships, with the impact cascading around the world. Shipping capacity stalled at a few ports located in Asia and the United States. For example, Yantian, the third-busiest port in the world, was operating at 30 percent capacity during parts of the year because of measures to prevent the spread of the Alpha variant, causing the dwell time of ships at the port to double to 16 days. On the US west coast, ports were unable to cope with the additional stress due to a combination of pandemic measures, lack of 24/7 port operation, lack of investment in modern handling equipment and information technology solutions, and a shortage of skilled logistics operators and truckers.

Third, *limited availability of ships and containers* constrained the supply-side response. After scaling down operations during the initial stage of the pandemic, the capability of shipping lines to move goods peaked in October 2020, reaching full capacity. Together with the declining circulation of ships, this situation limited the ability of shipping lines to respond to the surging demand. Shipping lines ordered new ships, but they take two to three years to be delivered. Further, the repositioning of empty containers to export locations where they were needed when the surge occurred was disrupted during the early months of 2020 because of the pandemic. In addition, production of new containers declined by 40 percent in 2020, as large manufacturers in China shut operations for several months.

This combination of strong demand and capacity constraints caused *an increase in shipping rates,* which rose considerably above prepandemic levels. By the end of 2020, freight rates had increased by 60 percent for trade between Asia and North America, 51 percent for trade between Asia and Europe, and 84 percent for intra-Asia trade compared to rates at the start of the year. Increases were highest for goods originating from China, with an eightfold increase to Europe and a fourfold increase to the US west coast. Freight rates to low- and middle-income regions, including Sub-Saharan Africa and South America, skyrocketed as well. By early 2021, freight rates from China to South America had jumped 443 percent.

In addition to higher shipping rates, trade was affected by *slower and less reliable supply chains,* with reliability and timeliness falling to levels not seen in modern logistics. The Trans-Pacific lead time, for example, rose threefold, while the proportion of container ships arriving on schedule dropped from 75 percent to 35 percent.

Finally, *profits in the container shipping industry rose to unprecedented heights*, potentially as much as 10 times higher in 2021 than in 2020. Shipping companies used these large profits to expand vertical integration into landside logistics and air cargo, leading to greater concentration of activity in the sector. As a result, regulators placed the industry under growing scrutiny, which may have moderated the increase in shipping rates because the major lines announced voluntary caps and rates dropped by 4 percent in October 2021. Some governments, including the United Kingdom and United States, are now looking more closely at some of the practices of shipping companies.

Box continues next page

BOX 4.1 Global supply chain disruption in 2021: Causes, consequences, and solutions (*continued*)

This crisis highlights how constraints at key logistics can affect the costs, reliability, and timeliness of global trade. In the short run, measures were introduced—for example, moving to 24/7 operations at US west coast ports. But additional measures are required to prevent such crises in the future and build global supply chain resilience:

- *Improving transparency and collaboration through digital solutions* can improve supply chain flexibility and help traders and policy makers to act more quickly when a crisis hits logistics. Private digital platform initiatives can improve coordination and forecasting of logistics activities in port, such as programing rail capacity well before ships arrive.

- *Improving the regulation of the logistics sector* would help to ensure effective competition and limit any negative impacts of the increasing vertical integration of the industry.

- *Advancing reforms in port governance and management, together with trade facilitation measures* would help to streamline port and customs clearance procedures.

- *Improving regulations* not only would reduce trade costs and improve timeliness but also would enable the design of effective continuity plans for maintaining ports and customs operations during a crisis, such as operating with a limited workforce under social distancing.

Source: The box draws heavily on Arvis et al. 2021.

Notes

1. See, for example, the description of SCOR by the Association for Supply Chain Management, https://www.apics.org/apics-for-business/frameworks/scor.
2. As cited in https://tradingeconomics.com/china/wages.
3. For US retail sales data, see https://www.census.gov/retail/index.html.
4. A SKU is a product defined at the finest level of detail by having a unique bar code.
5. See https://apparelcoalition.org/some-good-news-ciel-textile/.
6. Australia; Guam; Hong Kong SAR, China; Japan; Korea; Timor-Leste; and China, with six areas in Beijing subject to localized lockdown.
7. Iraq, Israel, Lebanon, Libya, and Morocco.
8. Azerbaijan, 30 percent capacity; Cyprus, Denmark, Norway, and United Kingdom, all non-essential business required to close.
9. Bhutan and Sri Lanka, all nonessential business closed.
10. Bolivia, industry-specific requirements; Brazil, Belo Horizonte e Piracicaba, all nonessential business; Guyana, 40 percent capacity; Honduras, national curfew plan; Panama, all nonessential business; and Puerto Rico, 30 percent capacity.
11. Bhutan, Botswana, India, Namibia, and South Africa. Namibia was the exception regarding the ban on sales of tobacco.
12. China, Korea, and Vietnam.

13. Fiji, Kazakhstan, and the Philippines.

14. International Trade Centre, Market Access Map, htpps://www.macmap.org.

15. This information was obtained in literature available at the International Trade Centre, United Nations Conference on Trade and Development, United Nations Economic Commission for Africa, United Nations Economic and Social Commission for Asia and the Pacific, United Nations Economic Commission for Europe, and World Bank and on logistics information platforms, including Journal of Commerce, Logistics Cluster, and Reuters.

16. A special thanks to the governments of Angola, Rwanda, and South Africa for sharing their experiences on this topic and to experts and business representatives in Ethiopia, Kenya, Namibia, and Rwanda for their valuable insights.

17. International Trade Centre, Market Access Map, https://www.macmap.org.

References

Arvis, Jean Francois, Michael Ferrantino, Martin Humphreys, Cordula Rastogi, and Daria Ulybina. 2021. "Global Supply Chain Disruptions: Putting Trade Recovery at Risk." Special Focus: Trade Watch, November 16, 2021, Global Trade and Regional Integration Unit, World Bank, Washington, DC.

Beresford, Colin. 2021. "Semiconductor Shortage Halting Car Production across North America." *Car and Driver*, February 20, 2021.

Bomey, Nathan. 2018. "KFC Is Suffering from a Chicken Shortage in the U.K. Yes, You Read That Right." *USA Today*, February 19, 2018. https://www.usatoday.com/story /money/2018/02/19/kfc-chicken-shortage-u-k-restaurants-close-amid-delivery-mishaps /350698002/.

Carvalho, Vasco M., Matthew Elliott, and John Spray. 2020. "Supply Chain Bottlenecks in a Pandemic." Note, University of Cambridge. https://covid.econ.cam.ac.uk/files/carvalho -files/BottlenecksPandemicNote.pdf.

Cosgrove, Emma. 2020. "Coca-Cola, Mondelez Trim SKUs as CPGs Tackle Pandemic Stresses." *Supply Chain Dive*, June 2, 2020. https://www.supplychaindive.com/news /coronavirus-supply-chains-SKUs-pandemic-Mondelez-Procter-Gamble-Coca -Cola/579017/.

Espitia, Alvaro, Nadia Rocha, and Michele Ruta. 2020a. "COVID-19 and Food Protectionism: The impact of the Pandemic and Export Restrictions on World Food Markets," Policy Research Working Paper 9253, Macroeconomics, Trade, and Investment Global Practice, World Bank, Washington, DC.

Espitia, Alvaro, Nadia Rocha, and Michele Ruta. 2020b. "Trade in Critical COVID-19 Products." Trade and COVID-19 Guidance Note, World Bank, Washington, DC. http:// documents1.worldbank.org/curated/en/764011585606299529/pdf/Trade-and-COVID-19-Guidance-Note-Trade-in-Critical-COVID-19-Products.pdf.

e-Trade for All. 2021. *COVID-19 and E-Commerce: A Global Review.* New York: United Nations Publications for UNCTAD.

EUCCB (European Union Chamber of Commerce and Business). 2020. *Business Confidence Survey 2020.* Munich: Roland Berger, August.

Ferrantino, Michael Joseph, and Emine Elcin Koten. 2019. "Understanding Supply Chain 4.0 and Its Potential Impact on Global Value Chains." In *Global Value Chain Development Report 2019: Technological Innovation, Supply Chain Trade, and Workers in a Globalized World*, 103–19. Geneva: World Trade Organization.

Findlay, Stephanie. 2020. "Container Shortage Exposes India's Struggle to Recover from Virus." *Financial Times*, October 31, 2020.

Forrester, J. W. 1961. *Industrial Dynamics.* Cambridge, MA: MIT Press.

Frikkee, Tineke. 2020. "COVID-19 Crisis Has Laid Bare Weaknesses in Supply Chains." *Financial Times,* May 11, 2020.

Gahigi, Moses. 2020. "High Costs, Delays as Rwanda Truckers Stopped over COVID-19." *The East African*, September 23, 2020. https://www.theeastafrican.co.ke/tea/business/high-costs-delays-as-rwanda-truckers-stopped-over-covid-19-2370286.

Goddard, Eugene. 2020. "South and East Africa Border Crossings Congested by COVID-19." *Southern Africa's Freight News,* May 29, 2020. https://www.freightnews.co.za/article/south-and-east-africa-border-crossings-congested-covid-19.

Gondwe, Grace. 2020. "Assessing the Impact of COVID-19 on Africa's Economic Development." United Nations Conference on Trade and Development (UNCTAD), New York. https://unctad.org/system/files/official-document/aldcmisc2020d3_en.pdf.

Greenfield, David. 2021. "How COVID-19 Pushed ExxonMobil's Automation Technology Limits." *Automation World*, May 4, 2021.

Guzman, Hector. 2020. "Nicaragua–Costa Rica Coronavirus Dispute Stalls Hundreds of Trucks at Border." *Reuters*, May 22, 2020. https://www.reuters.com/article/us-health-coronavirus-costa-rica-nicarag-idUSKBN22Y2HR.

Hallward-Driemeier, Mary, and Gaurav Nayyar. 2017. *Trouble in the Making? The Future of Manufacturing-Led Development.* Washington, DC: World Bank.

Ikade, Faith. 2020. "Kenya Alcohol Ban to Cost Billions, Thousands of Jobs in Three Months." *Ventures Africa*, September 7, 2020. https://venturesafrica.com/kenya-alcohol-ban-cost-billions-thousands-jobs-three-months/.

Jacobs, Justin, and Harry Dempsey. 2021. "Global Supply Chains Face Months of Disruption from Texas Storm." *Financial Times*, March 24, 2021.

Knowler, Greg. 2020a. "Border Bottlenecks Freed up after EC Intervenes." *Journal of Commerce,* March 27, 2020. https://www.joc.com/trucking-logistics/border-bottlenecks-freed-after-ec-intervenes_20200327.html.

Knowler, Greg. 2020b. "Bottlenecks Delaying Road Freight at EU's Internal Borders." *Journal of Commerce,* March 19, 2020. https://www.joc.com/bottlenecks-delaying-road-freight-eu%E2%80%99s-internal-borders_20200319.html.

Koh, Ann, Salma El Wardany, and Aaron Clark. 2021. "Suez Canal Snarled by Giant Ship Choking Key Trade Route." *Bloomberg,* March 24, 2021.

Lambert, Douglas M. 2008. *Supply Chain Management: Processes, Partnerships, Performance.* Tempe, AZ: Supply Chain Management Institute.

Lincicome, Scott. 2021. "A Reality Check on the Pandemic, Supply Chains, and Our 'April 2020' Mindset." *The Dispatch*, March 3, 2021.

Liu, Nicolle, and Thomas Hale. 2021. "China's Exporters Hit by Global Shortage of Shipping Containers." *Financial Times*, February 28, 2021.

Logistics Cluster. 2020. "COVID-19 Global Response Overview." Logistics Cluster, June 15, 2020. https://logcluster.org/document/global-logistics-cluster-covid-19-cargo-entry-points-updates-15-june-2020.

McCullen, Peter, and Denis Towill. 2002. "Diagnosis and Reduction of Bullwhip in Supply Chains." *Supply Chain Management* 7 (3): 164–79.

McKinsey Global Institute. 2020. "Risk, Resilience, and Rebalancing in Global Value Chains." McKinsey Global Institute, August 6, 2020.

Mingas, Melanie. 2021. "Why US Chip Manufacturing Is in Line for a $37 Billion Windfall." *Capacity* (blog), February 25, 2021.

Mold, Andrew, and Anthony Mveyange. 2020. *The Impact of the COVID-19 Crisis on Trade: Recent Evidence from East Africa.* Washington, DC: Brookings Institution. https://www.brookings.edu/research/the-impact-of-the-covid-19-crisis-on-trade-recent-evidence-from-east-africa/.

Nilsson, Patricia, and Emiko Terazono. 2020. "Can Fast Fashion's $2.5 Tn Supply Chain Be Stitched Back Together?" *Financial Times*, May 17, 2021.

Obe, Mitsuru. 2018. "Bangladesh Fights for the Future of Its Garment Industry." *Business Trends*, November 4, 2018.

Peterson Institute of International Economics. 2021. "Trump's Trade War Timeline: An Up-To-Date Guide." *Trade and Investment Policy Watch* (blog), October 31, 2021. https://www.piie.com/blogs/trade-investment-policy-watch/trump-trade-war-china-date-guide.

PwC (PricewaterhouseCoopers) Global. 2020. "Energy Industry and COVID-19: Strategizing for the New Normal." https://www.pwc.com/gx/en/issues/crisis-solutions/covid-19/energy-utilities-resources-coronavirus.html.

Ratner, Baz. 2020. "Sixty KM Queues as COVID Turns Kenyan Border Crossing into Lorry Park." *Reuters*, November 26, 2020. https://www.reuters.com/article/health-coronavirus-africa-trade-idUSL8N2IB3BB.

Sanchez, Daniel, Nicolas Parra, Caglar Ozden, Bob Rijkers, Mariana Viollaz, and Hernan Winkler. 2021. "Who on Earth Can Work from Home?" *The World Bank Research Observer* 36 (1): 67–100. https://academic.oup.com/wbro/article/36/1/67/6158069.

Steer, George, Jonathan Eley, and Valentina Romei. 2021. "European Retailers Face Goods Shortages as Shipping Costs Soar." *Financial Times*, January 31, 2021.

Steer, George, and Valentina Romei. 2020. "Shipping Costs Quadruple to Record Highs on China-Europe 'Bottleneck.'" *Financial Times*, January 19, 2020.

UNECE (United Nations Economic Commission for Europe). 2020. "Observatory on Border Crossing Status due to COVID-19." UNECE, updated July 9, 2020. https://wiki.unece.org/display/CTRBSBC/Saudi+Arabia.

UNESCAP (United Nations Economic and Social Commission for Asia and the Pacific). 2021. "COVID-19 in North and Central Asia: Impacts, Responses, and Strategies to Build Better." Policy Brief, UNESCAP, Bangkok. https://www.unescap.org/sites/default/d8files/knowledge-products/NCA%20Covid19%20Policy%20Brief_final.pdf.

University of Oxford. 2021. "COVID-19 Government Response Tracker." Blavatnik School of Government, University of Oxford. https://www.bsg.ox.ac.uk/research/research-projects/covid-19-government-response-tracker.

US-China Business Council. 2020. *Member Survey 2020*. US-China Business Council, Washington, DC, August 2020.

Wasike, Andrew. 2020. "East Africa Urges to Recognize Neighbor Virus." Anadolu Agency, Ankara, October 30, 2020. https://www.aa.com.tr/en/africa/eafrica-urges-to-recognize-neighbor-virus-certificates/2005070.

Zavacka, Veronika. 2012. "The Bullwhip Effect and the Great Trade Collapse." Working Paper 148, European Bank for Reconstruction and Development, London.

5

The Key to COVID-19 Recovery and Poverty Alleviation: Globalization, Not Localization

Key messages

- Globalization will strengthen the recovery from the COVID-19 (coronavirus) pandemic, whereas localization will weaken it. Both high-income and low- and middle-income countries are better off in a globalized world.

- Policies that are supportive of, not hostile to, trade could prove critical to strengthening recovery from the pandemic, supporting greater diversification, and reducing extreme poverty.

- Low- and middle-income countries stand to gain the most from strengthening trade and global value chains (GVCs). In a globalized world, the overall increase in real income in low- and middle-income countries between 2019 and 2030 could be 10 percentage points higher.

- In a globalized world, global trade could grow by 25 percent between 2019 and 2030, whereas in a world where countries reshore their production, global trade could instead decline by 22 percent by 2030.

- A more hostile environment for trade, with a shift toward global reshoring, could drive an additional 52 million people into extreme poverty. The hardest hit would be the poor in Sub-Saharan Africa, with 80 percent of the new poor caused by reshoring.

- Measures to enhance trade could boost incomes, spur integration into GVCs, and lift almost 22 million additional people out of poverty by 2030. Such measures would also improve the incomes of the bottom 40 percent of the income distribution. A more supportive environment for trade would boost resilience to future supply shocks, widening access to raw materials, goods, and services.

- Low- and middle-income countries can take steps to strengthen their resilience to future shocks by unilaterally reducing tariffs on inputs, implementing trade facilitation measures, and diversifying sources of inputs.

- After COVID-19, most countries will need to boost their climate mitigation efforts to reach the Nationally Determined Contributions (NDCs) targets under the Paris Agreement. Each region and sector will be affected differently, as countries strive to reach their NDC targets, with countries heavily dependent on coal being the hardest hit.

- Depending on how policies are implemented, climate mitigation measures in high-income economies could reshape GVCs away from carbon-intensive activities. Climate policies would affect low- and middle-income countries differently, depending on the extent of carbon-intensive sectors in their economies, with countries in Europe and Central Asia potentially the most vulnerable.

- The European Union (EU) Green Deal, which would raise the implicit price of carbon by more than the Paris commitments, is also bound to have an impact on trade. EU countries would likely reduce imports of fossil fuels and other carbon-intensive products because of lower EU-wide demand. The impact of EU climate policies on other countries will depend on the degree of carbon intensity of their exports and links with the EU.

- Stylized modeling suggests that a carbon border adjustment mechanism (CBAM), as part of the EU Green Deal, would have relatively little impact on archetypal GVCs such as electronics, motor vehicles, and apparel. However, computers and electronics, motor vehicles and parts, and other light manufacturing could become even more deeply integrated into GVCs under CBAM.

- Low- and middle-income countries can mitigate the potential negative impacts of climate policies on certain sectors through their own policy responses.

Introduction

This chapter builds on the insights from data and firm responses presented in chapters 3 and 4, which will be updated as the COVID-19 pandemic continues to affect economic activity around the world. It explores simulations from a global model to enhance understanding of the potential longer-term impacts of COVID-19 on low- and middle-income countries and the possible policy responses. The model is used to assess the likely impacts of measures designed to reshore production and reduce reliance on imports as well other key factors shaping the global economy, including stylized scenarios to capture the essential elements of policies to reduce carbon emissions that will have an impact on trade.

Trade-enhancing policies will aid global recovery and poverty reduction. Chapter 4 shows that low-income countries may be the most vulnerable to GVC fragility.

The resilience of GVCs has been put to the test by the COVID-19 pandemic, extreme weather events, and trade tensions spurred by growing economic nationalism and protectionism. The sudden drop in global trade in the first half of 2020 was massive by historical standards. Econometric evidence shows that GVCs can transmit shocks in production and trade from one country to another, although participation in GVCs may help to lessen the blow of a domestic shock such as a lockdown. But GVCs can also drive recovery, spreading the benefits as, for example, countries come out of lockdowns at different times. In light of this experience, is it possible to design policies that enhance resilience to trade shocks in low- and middle-income countries without endangering growth?

The past three decades of globalization have lifted international trade to new heights, while helping to drive extreme poverty to new lows. GVCs have become longer and stronger to provide countries and consumers worldwide with vital goods and services, from vaccines to vacuum cleaners. The scenarios in this chapter provide emphatic evidence of the economic and social benefits of GVCs: globalization will strengthen a recovery, whereas localization will weaken it. Moreover, localization could drive more people into extreme poverty, whereas globalization could lift millions above the poverty line by 2030. In short, both high-income and low- and middle-income countries are better off in a globalized world.

Policies that are "friendly" rather than "hostile" to GVCs could prove critical to strengthening the economic recovery from the pandemic. Low- and middle-income countries stand to gain the most. Three scenarios examining the potential impact of "GVC-friendly" and "GVC-hostile" policies in 2020–30 show that shortening supply chains through reshoring or localization would short-change both low- and middle-income countries and high-income countries. The first scenario, *reshoring leading economies*, examines a case in which high-income economies and China raise barriers to imports and increase subsidies to agriculture and manufacturing in an attempt to achieve reshoring. The second scenario, *reshoring all*, looks at the impact of even wider localization and diminished globalization when low- and middle-income countries join the reshoring efforts. The third scenario, *GVC-friendly liberalization + trade facilitation*, examines a case in which low- and middle-income countries seek to lower trade costs and make it easier to use imports in domestic production. These scenarios are evaluated for 2030 against a baseline in which the economic recovery from COVID-19 is L-shaped—that is, growth rates before the pandemic are achieved, but the loss of potential output suffered in 2020 is permanent. The main messages would, however, remain the same under different recovery scenarios.

In a world where major countries try to reshore their production through subsidies and tariffs, global income would decline by 2.2 percent and global exports would decline by 17 percent by 2030 relative to the baseline. If low- and middle-income countries also decide to reshore, global income would drop by 2.2 percent and global exports would drop by 21.4 percent relative to the baseline. By contrast, if these countries move to lower trade costs, global income would increase by 0.4 percent relative to the baseline. A "hostile" environment with a shift toward global reshoring could drive an additional 51.8 million people into extreme poverty, whereas a more "friendly" one could lift 21.5 million additional people out of poverty by 2030 relative to the baseline.

The post-COVID-19 recovery in low- and middle-income countries will be much stronger in a globalized world. The simulations indicate that, in a globalized world, the overall increase in real income in low- and middle-income countries between 2019 and 2030 could be 10 percentage points higher.

This chapter examines three main trends with implications for GVCs and their potential impact on economic growth and poverty reduction:

- First, the COVID-19 crisis has had a significant impact on GVCs and government policies to support domestic industry and reshoring efforts, which will have a lasting impact on jobs, income, and poverty. Given the complexity of the policy and economic environment in which firms and governments are responding to COVID-19, a global computable general equilibrium (CGE) model is used to assess the impacts of COVID-19 and various policy changes on economic growth, sectoral trade flows, output, and employment.

- Second, trade tensions have created new challenges and uncertainties, including United States–China trade barriers and challenges to the legitimacy of the World Trade Organization (WTO). These tensions have led to swift changes in bilateral trade flows.

- Third, new carbon regulations to combat climate change are creating new complexities and competitive challenges for some industries, changing the comparative advantages of countries. As part of attempts to mitigate climate change and meet obligations under the Paris Agreement, several countries are developing domestic carbon regulations that could dramatically alter the comparative advantages of countries as well as the taxation of imported goods, which could have significant effects on their trading partners. For example, the European Commission has announced that a CBAM will be part of the ambitious EU Green Deal (European Commission 2019, 2021). This scheme will be the first to use a major border tax adjustment in climate policy.

The CGE tool can inform an understanding of the medium- to long-term implications of recalibrating GVCs. The analysis designs forward-looking scenarios to anticipate the medium-run impacts of COVID-19 and potential policy changes on trade in goods and services; employment and wages by sector, skill, and gender; and poverty and income inequality. The analysis builds on a global dynamic CGE model—the multiregional input-output (MRIO) version of the ENVISAGE model and the global microsimulation framework Global Income Distribution Dynamics (GIDD). This application extends the standard modeling framework by incorporating MRIO tables that distinguish between imports of intermediate, final, and investment goods to capture the nature of trade typical for GVCs. The CGE model relies on the Global Trade Analysis Project (GTAP) 10 Data Base, which has 2014 as the reference year and runs until 2030. The analysis covers 27 sectors and 21 countries and regions (see annex 5A).

The CGE tool provides inputs to a microsimulation tool, which translates the CGE results into implications for poverty and income distribution. These implications include the impacts on employment and wages of female and male workers. The GIDD simulations are based on a Global Micro Database, which covers 90 percent of the global population and gross domestic product (GDP) and includes harmonized household surveys for 124 countries. This chapter presents scenarios of globalized or segmented worlds and analyzes the implications of various shocks, such as future changes in trade policies, disruptions in production, and changes in climate mitigation policies. Their impacts on patterns of international trade, including GVCs, along with their implications for poverty and distribution, are the key questions addressed.

Methodological framework and scenarios: Using data and tools to find answers

The global recursive dynamic CGE model ENVISAGE is used here to provide a quantitative assessment of the policy scenarios considered in this chapter (van der Mensbrugghe 2019). The model is solved as a sequence of comparative static equilibria, in which the factors of production accumulate over time. Nested constant-elasticity-of-substitution (CES) functions are used to represent production technologies.

Key data are from the GTAP 10 MRIO Data Base, with 2014 as the reference year (Aguiar et al. 2019; Carrico, Corong, and van der Mensbrugghe 2020). Relying on the MRIO data, which distinguish agent-based demand for imports by region of origin, selected manufacturing sectors in the ENVISAGE model are represented using the MRIO specification; all other sectors are represented using the Armington assumption, treating imports as imperfect substitutes with domestically produced commodities. The current assessment aggregates 141 regions and 65 sectors of the GTAP 10 Data Base to obtain 21 countries or regions and 27 sectors. Annex 5A reports sectoral and regional mappings and identifies the sectors of the model that are represented using MRIO specification. Chepeliev et al. (forthcoming) provide technical details of the modeling framework.

Scenarios: COVID-19, climate change, and protectionist shocks to GVCs

Measuring the impact of the pandemic

The COVID-19 L-shape recovery baseline scenario is implemented using World Bank Macro and Poverty Outlook (MPO) projections from Fall 2020 (World Bank 2020). The pre-COVID-19 baseline scenario uses MPO projections from 2019 (World Bank 2019). GDP forecasts are extended after the period reported in each version of the MPO using per capita GDP growth rates from the Shared Socioeconomic Pathways (SSP) database relying on the SSP2 scenario (IIASA 2016). Several COVID-19-specific shocks are introduced into the COVID-19 L-shape recovery baseline scenario (the no-COVID-19 baseline does not have these shocks), relying partially on Maliszewska, Mattoo, and van der Mensbrugghe (2020), who simulate the impacts of COVID-19 in a comparative static CGE framework. Several COVID-specific shocks are implemented in the model for 2020 as the simulated year, including (a) higher cost of trade, (b) sharp drop in international tourism, (c) pandemic-induced changes in patterns of demand, (d) postharvest loss in production, (e) sharp decline in the use of public transportation, and (f) historical developments in oil prices (for details, see Chepeliev et al., forthcoming).

The COVID-19 L-shape recovery baseline also reflects the trade frictions between the United States and its trading partners (mainly China), which are implemented in the model via higher import tariffs based on the detailed tariff line data from the CARD database (Li 2018). These trade policy shocks are assumed to remain throughout the simulated time frame—that is, until 2030. Also included are all existing and ongoing trade agreements with a predefined set of tariff changes based on the published tariff schedules reported by the International Trade Centre (ITC 2020). This scenario is referred to as the COVID-19 L-shape recovery, because it represents the continuation of past trends.

Policy scenarios: Two that are "hostile" to GVCs and one that is "friendly"

The policy scenarios examine the impact of changes in trade and climate policies, including reshoring and carbon taxes, on the pace of economic recovery from the COVID-19 pandemic. This scenario explores how such policies affect high-income and low- and middle-income countries and what actions the latter can take to cushion the impact of policy shocks. It also discusses the construction of the corresponding policy shocks. Figure 5.1 summarizes all of the scenarios.

The reshoring leading economies scenario examines the impact of reshoring policies by high-income countries and China. This scenario assumes a subsidy to local production of agricultural and manufacturing products amounting to 1 percent of GDP in the corresponding region (through capital and labor subsidies), putting up barriers to imports—a 25-percentage-point surcharge—and making it harder to substitute imports for domestic production by, for example, tightening product standards (reducing trade elasticities by 50 percent). These shocks are phased in over five years, from 2022 to 2026.

FIGURE 5.1 Computable general equilibrium modeling scenarios

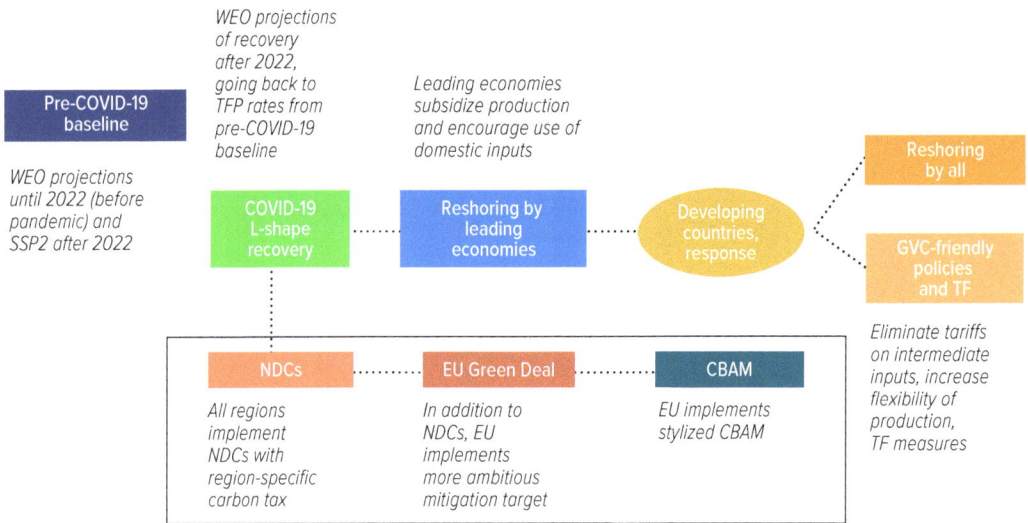

Source: Chepeliev et al., forthcoming.
Note: CBAM = carbon border adjustment mechanism; CGE = computable general equilibrium; EU = European Union; NDCs = Nationally Determined Contributions; SSP = Shared Socioeconomic Pathways; TF = trade facilitation; TFP = total factor productivity; WEO = World Economic Outlook.

The reshoring all scenario examines the impact if low- and middle-income countries respond in kind by implementing their own reshoring efforts. This scenario is similar to the localized world scenario in OECD (2020).

The GVC-friendly liberalization scenario is "friendly" rather than "hostile" to globalization. This scenario assumes that low- and middle-income countries implement three sets of policies to become more GVC-friendly. First, they eliminate tariffs on all intermediate inputs (MRIO sectors as identified in annex 5A). Second, they take steps to increase the flexibility of production by making it easier to substitute imported inputs for domestic production by streamlining nontariff, behind-the-border measures to reduce the costs of trade—for example, through mutual recognition of testing and conformity assessment relating to product standards. These policies are mimicked by increasing the trade substitution elasticity by 50 percent. Finally, low- and middle-income countries reduce the costs to trade by implementing trade facilitation measures in line with implementation of the WTO Trade Facilitation Agreement, which, according to estimates by Moïsé and Sorescu (2013) and WTO (2015), reduce trade costs by between 14 percent and 16 percent.[1] As in the case of reshoring, these policies are phased in between 2022 and 2026.

Another set of policy options deals with climate change mitigation, which has significant implications for the comparative advantages of countries. These policies may be viewed as slow-acting shocks to GVCs. There is much uncertainty over the exact shape that these policies will take and how they will be implemented. In order to explore their potential consequences for GVCs, the discussion includes a stylized interpretation of the Paris Accord and the EU Green Deal, with implementation of CBAM. First, NDCs, which refer to emissions reduction targets agreed under the Paris Accord, are implemented, following Böhringer et al. (2020) and Chepeliev, Osorio-Rodarte, and van der Mensbrugghe (2021). These targets are specified in the form of carbon dioxide (CO_2) emissions reductions in 2030 relative to the pre-COVID-19 baseline scenario. Countries are assumed to implement carbon pricing policies to reach their NDC commitments. The model estimates the carbon price level (for each region) consistent with these emissions reduction targets.

In addition to NDC targets, more ambitious climate mitigation efforts by the EU are considered in a stylized EU Green Deal scenario. This effort is consistent with the recently announced EU Green Deal plans to cut emissions by 55 percent in 2030 relative to 1990 levels (European Commission 2019). This more ambitious emissions reduction policy in the EU is achieved by further increases in carbon prices in the model. First, the impact of the EU Green Deal with and without implementation of a CBAM[2] is explored. In the assessment, CBAM is implemented as an ad valorem equivalent tax imposed on the region- and commodity-specific carbon content of imports to the EU. The carbon price level that is used to determine the CBAM rate is estimated as the difference between the carbon price in the EU and the carbon price in the country or region of origin of the imported commodity. Only imported commodities that correspond to the EU's emissions trading scheme (ETS) sectors are assumed to be covered by the CBAM.

The CBAM scenario covers a stylized modeling of the carbon taxes imposed by the EU. The CBAM is imposed on all energy-intensive, trade-exposed sectors (not only selected commodities within these sectors) and covers all emission scopes (that is, direct and indirect emissions). The assessment only considers CO_2 emissions from fossil fuel combustion. A "0" share of free ETS allowances is assumed, resulting in EU trading partners facing a full carbon price through implementation of the CBAM.[3]

In this assessment, the EU-wide carbon price reaches over US$210 per ton of CO_2 equivalent to be consistent with the "Fit for 55" mitigation targets. Thus, the results are likely to provide an upper bound of the potential impacts of CBAM on EU trading partners.

To provide an account of the CO_2 emissions embodied in bilateral trade, the discussion follows an approach outlined in Peters (2008).[4] Country-specific CO_2 emissions per unit of output by sector are used to estimate emissions associated with bilateral trade flows. Essentially, the role of the CBAM is to bring the level of emissions per unit of imported output to the average sectoral level in the domestic economy, in this case the EU.

The risks of GVC reshoring

The COVID-19 shock and recovery in a postpandemic world

GVC-friendly policies would provide a shot in the arm for the recovery. Low- and middle-income countries would be the most affected in the COVID-19 L-shape recovery scenario, in which pre-COVID-19 growth rates are achieved, but the loss of potential output suffered in 2020 would be permanent. South Asia would recover the slowest, with a difference of 34 percentage points between real income growth between 2019 and 2030 in the pre-COVID-19 baseline and growth in the L-shape recovery from COVID-19. The real income levels of high-income countries also would be lower in an L-shape recovery scenario, with China and the United States losing, respectively, 8 and 5 percentage points, but still doing better than Western Europe (with a drop of 9 percentage points by 2030) (figure 5.2).

FIGURE 5.2 Change in real income in 2030 relative to 2019, by region and scenario

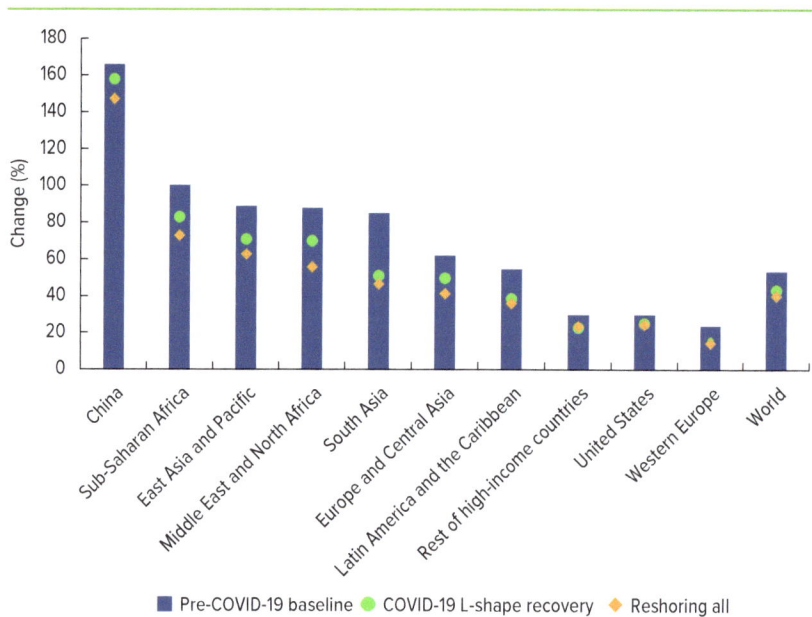

Source: Original calculations for this publication.

Welfare in China, Europe and Central Asia, the Middle East and North Africa, and the rest of East Asia and Pacific would be hit the hardest by the reshoring of production.[5] In the Middle East and North Africa, the real income growth between 2019 and 2030 would amount to 70 percent in an L-shape recovery compared with a 56 percent increase in a reshoring all world. Low- and middle-income countries also would recover more slowly: China's real income growth would be 11 percentage points lower (from the L-shape recovery scenario) in a world where all countries attempt to reshore. In the rest of East Asia and Pacific, real income growth could fall from 71 percent under an L-shape recovery to 62 percent under the reshoring all scenario. Lower growth would be driven by the high levels of openness and integration in GVCs in the East Asia and Pacific region.

In a reshoring all scenario, South Asia would suffer the biggest drop in exports and China would record the biggest drop in imports (figure 5.3). When all countries reshore their production, South Asia would see the biggest reduction in exports (a 45-percentage-point drop from a global world with COVID-19 to a reshoring all world), followed by China (a 37-percentage-point reduction) and the rest of East Asia and Pacific (a 34-percentage-point difference). All of these regions are deeply integrated in GVC networks. The highest reduction in imports between a globalized and a reshoring world would occur in China (a drop of 42 percentage points), the rest of East Asia and Pacific (a drop of 35 percentage points), and Sub-Saharan Africa (a drop of 33 percentage points). In a world where all countries attempt to reshore their

FIGURE 5.3 Real exports and real imports in 2030 relative to 2019, by region and scenario

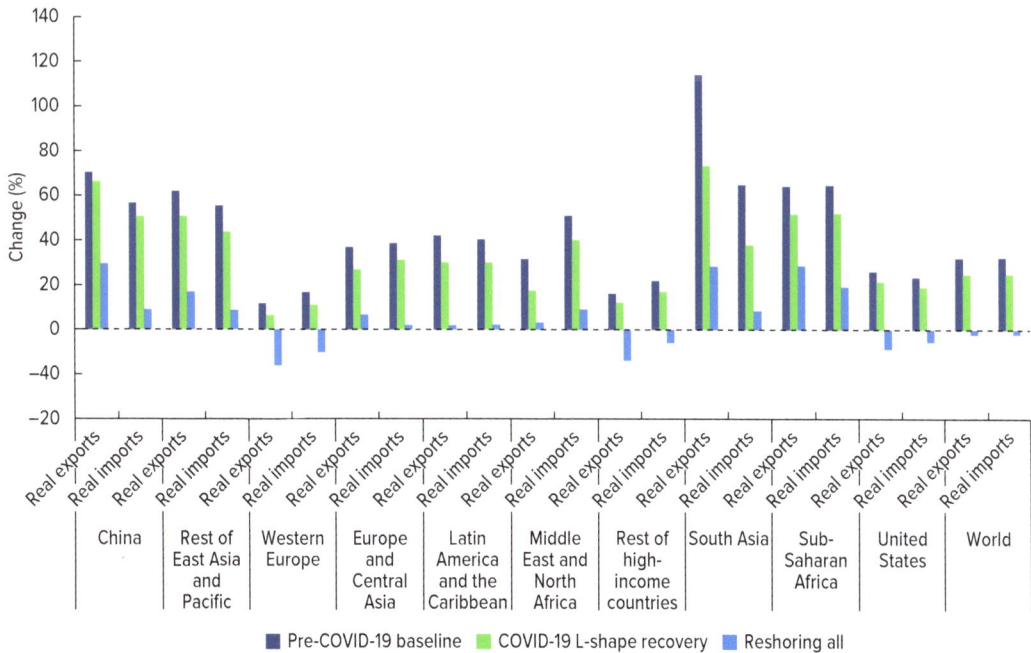

Source: Original calculations for this publication.

production, global trade would fall by 27 percent, changing from 25 percent growth in the COVID-19 scenario without reshoring to a 2 percent decrease in the scenario with reshoring.

Rethinking GVC restructuring

Low- and middle-income countries stand to gain significantly from stronger GVCs. The economic impact of COVID-19 has fueled an already heated debate about the benefits and costs of global supply chains, yet reshoring would have a negative impact in most regions. The pandemic has highlighted the role of GVCs in accelerating the spread of shocks, resulting in higher risks and vulnerabilities to external disruptions. With this role in mind, countries might be tempted to restructure their GVCs. A possible scenario is for the leading economies and China to reshore production, which would have a negative impact in most regions, particularly in developing regions, leaving them more vulnerable. Global real income would decrease by 1.5 percent by 2030, compared with the COVID-19 L-shape recovery. In this scenario, China's real income would fall by 2.6 percent. More negatively affected would be the Middle East and North Africa, with a drop in real income of 5.1 percent, followed by East Asia and Pacific, with a drop of 3.8 percent, and Europe and Central Asia, with a drop of 3.5 percent.

The best policy response to reshoring by leading countries would be for low- and middle-income economies to become more GVC-friendly and not respond in kind. To counter the sharp negative impact on regions that are highly dependent and integrated in GVCs, countries may be tempted to pursue their own reshoring policies. As the analysis indicates, having all economies reshore would compound the damage done by reshoring the production of leading economies. In fact, global real income would drop by 2.2 percent versus 1.5 percent if only leading economies reshore. The real income of China would fall 4.2 percent, a further loss of 1.6 percentage points compared to the previous scenario. The most negatively affected regions once more would be the developing regions, with the real income of the Middle East and North Africa declining up to 8.3 percent in a global reshoring war. The rest of the high-income countries would see a slight increase in real income, due mainly to the terms of trade effect.

Closer integration in the global economy through a GVC-friendly approach would pay dividends for low- and middle-income countries. Eliminating input tariffs and implementing trade facilitation measures would strengthen the integration of these countries in regional and global value chains. The gains would be evident in all developing regions. In this scenario, global real income would increase by 0.4 percent compared to the COVID-19 L-shape recovery. East Asia and Pacific (excluding China) and South Asia would benefit the most, with real income rising 4.7 percent and 4.3 percent, respectively. Countries that are already deeply integrated into GVCs would see the biggest gains, with Thailand (10.7 percent), Malaysia (7.2 percent), Turkey (7 percent), and Vietnam (6.8 percent) registering the highest gains in income. In other words, GVC-friendly policies could reverse the real income losses inflicted by the reshoring efforts of the leading economies (figure 5.4).

Reshoring by the leading economies would drastically reduce exports and imports for most regions (table 5.1). Global trade would decline 17 percent in this scenario in 2030, compared to the L-shape recovery scenario. The deepest declines in trade would be for countries engaging in reshoring policies, with declines in exports for China, the United States, and Western Europe, ranging from 20 percent to

FIGURE 5.4 Real income compared with COVID-19 L-shape recovery, by region and scenario, 2030

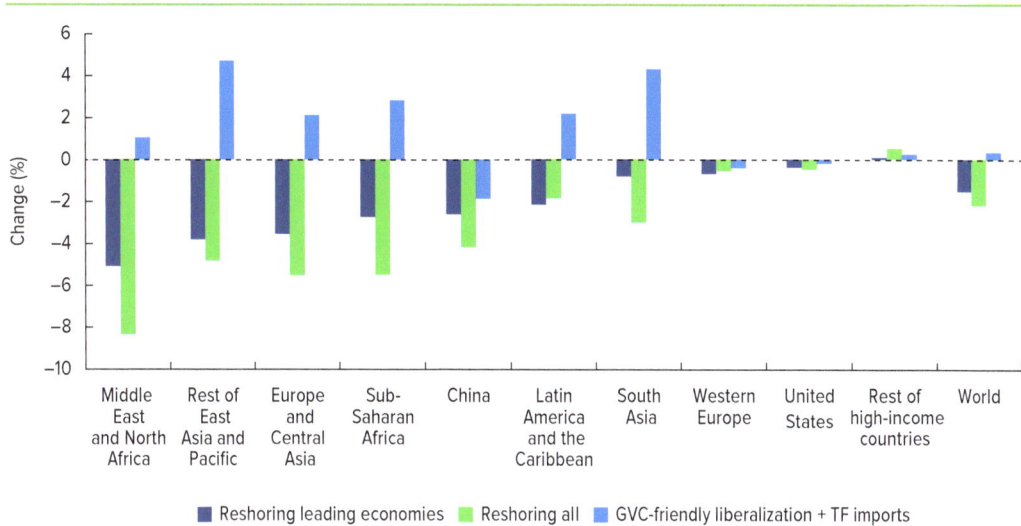

Source: Original calculations for this publication.
Note: GVC = global value chain; TF = trade facilitation.

25 percent. Developing regions would suffer collateral damage, with exports declining in the range of 1 percent to 5 percent. But, in the scenario in which low- and middle-income countries also attempt to reshore, losses in trade for these countries would be much larger. Compared to a scenario in which only leading economies reshore, in a scenario in which low- and middle-income countries also reshore, losses in exports would increase from 4.3 percent to 26.0 percent in South Asia, from 2.9 percent to 21.7 percent in Latin America, and from 1.3 percent to 12.1 percent in the Middle East and North Africa.

However, if developing regions choose to follow the GVC-friendly path, the reduction in global exports and global imports would be less pronounced. Compared with doing nothing or reshoring, both of which would lead to declining trade for low- and middle-income countries, a policy of GVC-friendly liberalization would increase trade in developing regions, ranging from an increase of about 12 percent for imports and exports in the Middle East and North Africa to an increase of 18 percent for exports and more than 25 percent for imports in South Asia. Similarly, developing regions would enjoy higher real income in the GVC-friendly liberalization + trade facilitation scenario. Despite choices made by the high-income economies and China, low- and middle-income countries can be in control of their own trade outcomes rather than passive victims of the decisions of others.

Reshoring by leading economies would hit low- and middle-income countries hard, but some sectors could see their exports expand as trade is diverted from leading economies to the rest of the world (table 5.2). When leading economies reshore their production, exports in some sectors would expand, even in regions that were badly hit, such as the Middle East and North Africa, whose computer and electronics sector would expand by US$13 billion compared to the COVID-19 L-shape recovery

TABLE 5.1 Real income, real exports, and real imports compared with a COVID-19 L-shape recovery, by region and scenario, 2030
Change (%)

Region	Real income			Exports			Imports		
	Reshoring leading economies	Reshoring all	GVC-friendly liberalization + TF imports	Reshoring leading economies	Reshoring all	GVC-friendly liberalization + TF imports	Reshoring leading economies	Reshoring all	GVC-friendly liberalization + TF imports
Middle East and North Africa	-5.1	-8.3	1.1	-1.3	-12.1	11.6	-9.9	-22.2	12.3
Rest of East Asia and Pacific	-3.8	-4.8	4.7	-4.7	-22.6	14.2	-9.4	-24.4	20.4
Europe and Central Asia	-3.5	-5.5	2.1	-0.8	-16.1	12.0	-8.4	-22.2	14.2
Sub-Saharan Africa	-2.7	-5.5	2.8	-3.0	-15.2	11.3	-9.0	-21.6	15.8
China	-2.6	-4.2	-1.9	-20.8	-22.1	-20.4	-22.8	-27.7	-20.5
Latin America and the Caribbean	-2.1	-1.8	2.2	-2.9	-21.7	12.6	-8.2	-21.4	17.1
South Asia	-0.8	-3.0	4.3	-4.3	-26.0	18.3	-6.7	-21.3	25.5
Western Europe	-0.7	-0.6	-0.4	-22.2	-21.1	-22.8	-19.7	-19.0	-19.7
United States	-0.4	-0.5	-0.2	-24.9	-24.7	-25.2	-20.1	-20.5	-19.4
Rest of high-income countries	0.1	0.5	0.3	-24.2	-23.0	-25.0	-20.9	-19.5	-21.0
World	-1.5	-2.2	0.4	-17.0	-21.4	-12.6	-16.9	-21.5	-9.2

Source: Original calculations for this publication.
Note: GVC = global value chain; TF = trade facilitation.

TABLE 5.2 Top-three increases in export sectors for the reshoring leading economies scenario: Change in the value of exports compared with the COVID-19 L-shape scenario, by region
Change in value (2014 US$, billions)

Region	Sector	Reshoring leading economies	Reshoring all	GVC-friendly liberalization + TF imports
China	Livestock	2	4	2
	Meat products (including fisheries) and other food	1	9	−2
	Accommodation, food, and service activities	0	1	0
East Asia and Pacific	Computer, electronic, and optical products	26	−104	157
	Motor vehicles, parts, and transport equipment	14	−15	49
	Refined oil	5	−6	10
Western Europe	Electricity	−1	−2	−3
	Coal extraction	−1	−2	−2
	Natural resource products	−2	−1	−4
Europe and Central Asia	Metals	12	−10	10
	Other manufacturing	11	−11	29
	Motor vehicles, parts, and transport equipment	8	−7	18
Latin America and the Caribbean	Computer, electronic, and optical products	16	−9	31
	Motor vehicles, parts, and transport equipment	13	−15	29
	Chemical products (including rubber and plastics)	9	−10	20
Middle East and North Africa	Computer, electronic, and optical products	13	−2	37
	Refined oil	12	−24	7
	Metals	9	−10	13
Rest of high-income countries	Natural resource products	11	8	7
	Electricity	0	0	0
	Air transport	0	1	−2
South Asia	Motor vehicles, parts, and transport equipment	17	−17	45
	Refined oil	8	−5	20
	Meat products (including fisheries) and other food	4	3	10
Sub-Saharan Africa	Metals	8	−7	14
	Motor vehicles, parts, and transport equipment	3	−2	14
	Other manufacturing	3	−3	9
United States	Natural resource products	1	0	0
	Electricity	0	0	0
	Water transport	0	0	0
World	Electricity	−2	−5	−4
	Natural resource products	−11	−31	−23
	Nonmetallic minerals	−12	−28	−16

Source: Original calculations for this publication.
Note: GVC = global value chain; TF = trade facilitation.

(the highest increase within the region). Some of the biggest increases would be in computers, electronics, and optical products in East Asia and Pacific (US$26 billion), in motor vehicles, parts, and transport equipment in South Asia (US$17 billion), and in computers and electronics in Latin America and the Caribbean (US$16 billion).

Sectoral exports would be hit hard if low- and middle-income countries decide to reshore. Responding in kind to reshoring by leading economies would aggravate the impact on exports. Low- and middle-income countries, which were expanding in certain sectors before the reshoring, would now contract. In East Asia and Pacific, exports of computer, electronic, and optical products, which were increasing by US$26 billion, would now contract by US$104 billion. In Europe and Central Asia, metals, which were expanding by US$12 billion, would now decrease by US$10 billion.

Eliminating intermediate input tariffs and implementing trade facilitation measures under the GVC-friendly scenario would lead to faster integration of low- and middle-income countries into regional and global value chains. Exports of several sectors deeply integrated into GVCs would expand, such as motor vehicles and transport equipment in Sub-Saharan Africa (by US$14 billion) or in South Asia (by US$45 billion). The sector that would experience the highest gains is computer, electronic, and optical products in the East Asia and Pacific region, with an increase of US$157 billion. Table 5.3 displays the changes in value of the top-three increases in imports in the GVC-friendly scenario as compared to the COVID-19 L-shape recovery scenario. Computer, electronic, and optical products in East Asia and Pacific would experience the biggest gains in imports for the reshoring leading economies scenario, with an increase of US$8 billion. However, if low- and middle-income countries respond in kind, this sector could decline by US$74 billion. In the GVC-friendly liberalization scenario, in contrast, gains in imports could rise to US$23 billion. In the reshoring all scenario, most sectors in all regions would see lower imports.

The distributional impacts of reshoring

Before COVID-19, additional efforts were needed to put the world on track to eradicate poverty by 2030. In the baseline scenario, without the effect of COVID-19, the number of people living in extreme poverty would have fallen to 375 million by 2030, down from 663 million in 2018. This decline is equivalent to halving the poverty headcount ratio from 9.0 percent to 4.5 percent in 12 years. Despite the sustained trend of poverty reduction in the baseline scenario (without the effect of COVID-19), the number of people living in extreme poverty would still be above the global target of 3 percent in the extreme poverty headcount ratio. An additional 125 million people must be lifted from extreme poverty to reach that target, as stated in the World Bank goals of ending poverty and promoting shared prosperity.

Under the COVID-19 L-shape recovery, extreme poverty increased to 738 million in 2020 and, as economic activity resumes, will decline to 405 million by 2030, equivalent to a global poverty headcount ratio of 4.9 percent. Further, 122 million people fell into extreme poverty as a result of the economic and health consequences of the pandemic, and one in four of them will still be living in extreme poverty by 2030 (figure 5.5).[6] Low- and middle-income countries in South Asia constitute the majority of the new COVID-19-induced poor, with 71 million additional people living in

TABLE 5.3 Top-three increases in import sectors for the reshoring leading economies scenario: Change in the value of imports compared with the COVID-19 L-shape scenario, by region
Change in value in (2014 US$, billions)

Region	Sector	Reshoring leading economies	Reshoring all	GVC-friendly liberalization + TF imports
China	Natural resource products	3	−8	−4
	Air transport	0	−2	0
	Electricity	0	0	0
East Asia and Pacific	Computer, electronic, and optical products	8	−74	23
	Metals	7	−19	−13
	Oil extraction	5	−23	−2
Western Europe	Electricity	−1	−2	−3
	Nonmetallic minerals	−5	−6	−7
	Accommodation, food, and service activities	−5	−6	−6
Europe and Central Asia	Metals	6	−6	−10
	Natural resource products	0	−1	−1
	Nonmetallic minerals	0	−2	−2
Latin America and the Caribbean	Computer, electronic, and optical products	7	−30	−20
	Metals	2	−7	−11
	Oil extraction	2	−16	11
Middle East and North Africa	Metals	5	−15	−23
	Natural resource products	0	−2	−4
	Electricity	0	−1	0
Rest of high-income countries	Electricity	0	0	0
	Livestock	−1	−1	−1
	Construction	−1	−2	−2
South Asia	Oil extraction	2	−41	−35
	Gas extraction and distribution	0	−4	−1
	Natural resource products	0	−4	−7
Sub-Saharan Africa	Metals	1	−4	−6
	Nonmetallic minerals	0	−2	−3
	Gas extraction and distribution	0	0	0
United States	Metals	2	−1	−3
	Electricity	0	0	0
	Coal extraction	0	0	0
World	Electricity	−2	−5	−4
	Natural resource products	−8	−31	−39
	Nonmetallic minerals	−11	−29	−30

Source: Original calculations for this publication.
Note: GVC = global value chain; TF = trade facilitation.

FIGURE 5.5 Distributional impacts, by region and scenario, 2010–30

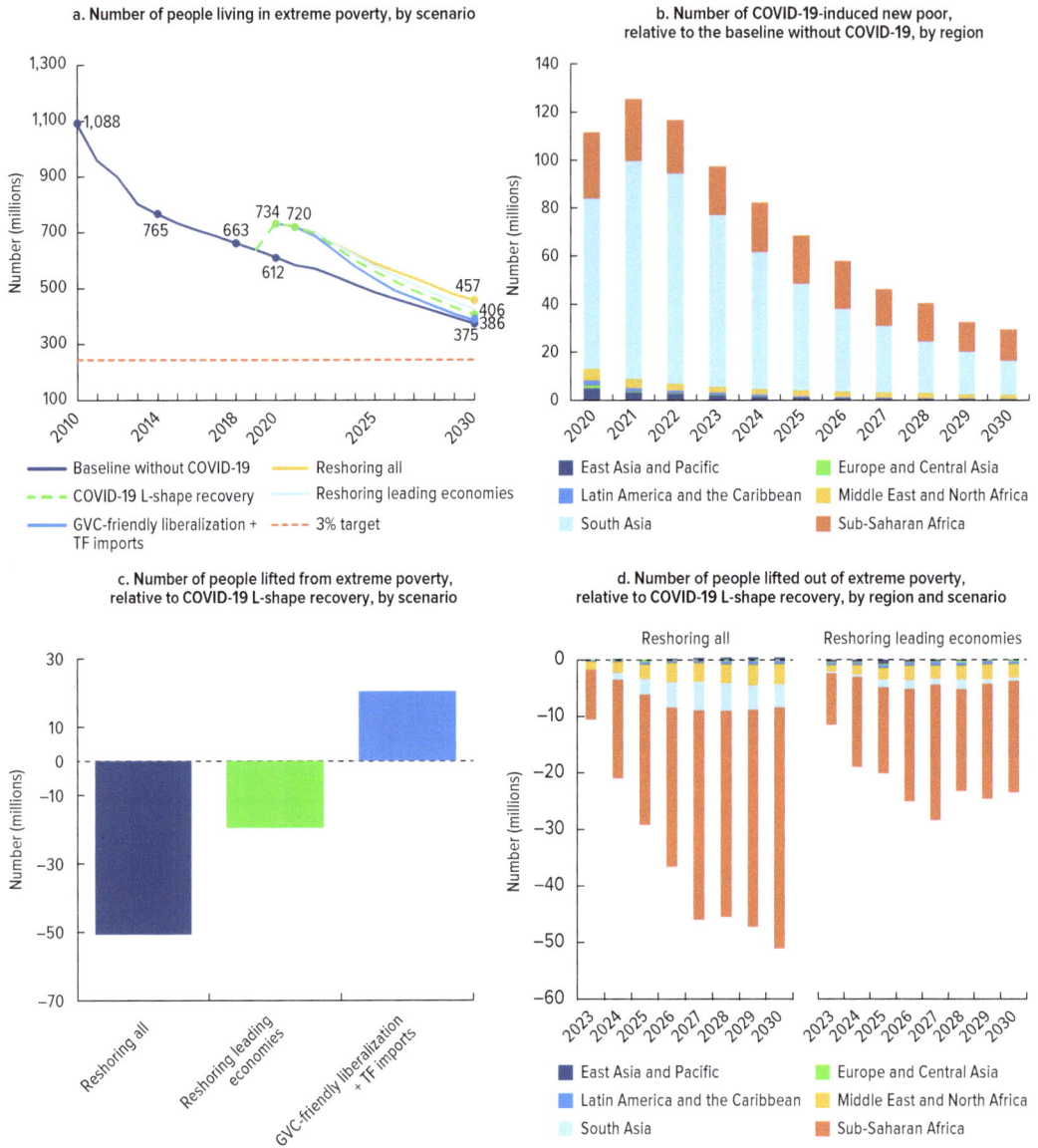

a. Number of people living in extreme poverty, by scenario

b. Number of COVID-19-induced new poor, relative to the baseline without COVID-19, by region

c. Number of people lifted from extreme poverty, relative to COVID-19 L-shape recovery, by scenario

d. Number of people lifted out of extreme poverty, relative to COVID-19 L-shape recovery, by region and scenario

Source: World Bank staff estimates.
Note: GVC = global value chain; TF = trade facilitation.

extreme poverty in 2020, followed by Sub-Saharan Africa, with 27.7 million. By 2030, 14.4 million people in South Asia and 13 million people in Sub-Saharan Africa will still be living in extreme poverty as a result of the pandemic.

Reshoring production could impair the recovery by increasing the number of people living in extreme poverty by 51 million. In the reshoring leading economies scenario, poverty reduction would resume at a lower rate than in the L-shape recovery. By 2030, reshoring efforts by leading economies would increase the number of people living in extreme poverty by 19.6 million. Under the reshoring all scenario, 51.8 million additional people would fall into extreme poverty by 2030, equivalent to an increase of 0.6 percentage point in the global extreme poverty headcount ratio. Figure 5.5 shows that, under either the reshoring leading economies scenario or the reshoring all scenario, Sub-Saharan Africa would be affected the most, with about 80 percent of the new poor caused by reshoring, followed by South Asia and the Middle East and North Africa.

But a GVC-friendly liberalization could lift 21.5 million people from extreme poverty by accelerating poverty reduction and bringing the world close to full recovery from COVID-19; the global poverty headcount ratio would be 4.6 percent or 10.5 million people above the baseline without the effect of COVID-19 (figure 5.6). A GVC-friendly scenario would help to reduce extreme poverty, particularly in South Asia, which was affected very heavily by the effects of COVID-19. Under this scenario, 56.2 million people would graduate into global middle-class status, measured as individuals with per capita consumption of more than US$10.00 a day purchasing power parity. As shown in table 5.4, more than half of the new entrants in the global middle class, or 30.9 million persons, would be in South Asia, and between 6.3 million and 7.2 million would be in each of the following regions: East Asia and Pacific, Latin America and the Caribbean, and Sub-Saharan Africa. High-income countries would see a decline of 500,000 people in middle-class status, with respect to the L-shape recovery. Therefore, high-income countries would be better off not implementing any reshoring efforts at all, but the GVC-friendly scenario would have a less negative impact on high-income countries than reshoring all and reshoring leading economies, in which the middle class (in high-income countries) would be reduced by 760,000 and 960,000, respectively.

In line with the World Bank goal of achieving shared prosperity, trade liberalization helps to raise the income of the bottom 40 percent (figure 5.7). In the reshoring leading economies and reshoring all scenarios, the population in the

FIGURE 5.6 Reduction in extreme poverty in the GVC-friendly liberalization and TF imports scenario relative to pre-COVID-19 conditions, by region

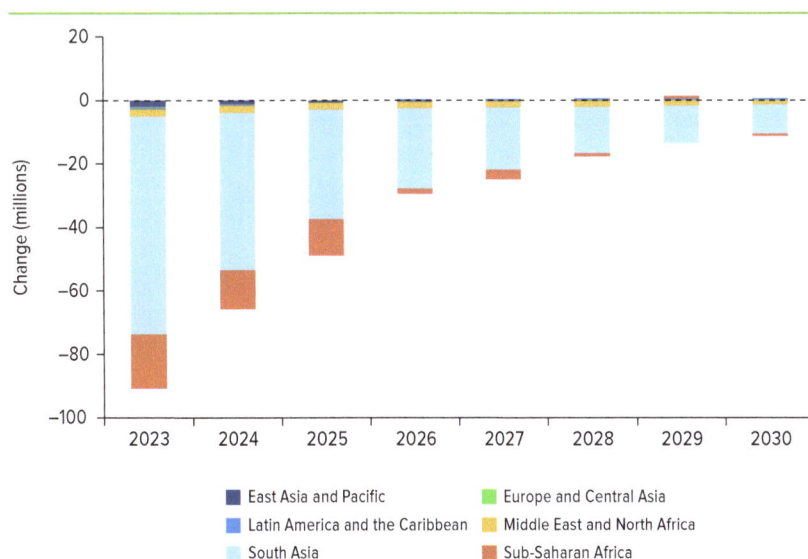

Source: World Bank staff estimates.
Note: GVC = global value chain; TF = trade facilitation.

TABLE 5.4 Number of people lifted from extreme poverty and joining the global middle class, by region and scenario
Change relative to COVID-19 L-shape recovery (millions)

Region	Extreme poverty US$1.90 PPP a day			Global middle class US$10.00 PPP a day		
	Reshoring all	Reshoring leading economies	GVC friendly + TF imports	Reshoring all	Reshoring leading economies	GVC friendly + TF imports
East Asia and Pacific	−0.06	−0.19	0.41	−29.48	−22.65	6.34
Europe and Central Asia	−0.26	−0.22	0.02	−7.21	−5.22	2.66
Latin America and the Caribbean	−0.54	−0.38	0.59	−6.99	−6.99	6.96
Middle East and North Africa	−3.47	−2.06	0.27	−16.90	−10.59	2.11
South Asia	−4.95	−1.04	6.10	−20.54	−5.91	30.90
Sub-Saharan Africa	−42.54	−15.44	14.10	−12.66	−6.38	7.19
Low- and middle-income countries	−51.82	−19.33	21.49	−93.78	−57.73	56.15
High-income countries	−0.02	−0.02	−0.01	−0.76	−0.96	−0.53
World	−51.84	−19.35	21.48	−94.54	−58.69	55.62

Source: World Bank staff estimates.
Note: GVC = global value chain; PPP = purchasing power parity; TF = trade facilitation.

bottom 40 percent of the income distribution (by region) would lose more than the top 60 percent of the population (figure 5.7). In the East Asia and Pacific region, the income of the bottom 40 percent would decline by 4.0 percent under the reshoring leading economies scenario and by 4.8 percent if low- and middle-income countries respond in kind. The top 60 percent would experience a decline, but at a lower rate, by 2.4 and 2.8 percent, respectively. Nevertheless, the GVC-friendly liberalization would increase the welfare gains faster for the bottom 40 percent than for the top 60 percent. By 2030, the welfare of the bottom 40 percent would improve by 3.3 percent with respect to L-shape recovery, 1.6 percentage points above the growth of the top 60 percent. The pattern is the same across regions, with the exception of the Middle East and North Africa.[7] Although GVC-friendly liberalization can lead to sustained poverty reduction and an increase in the income of the bottom 40 percent (by region), it does not guarantee that wages for unskilled females would necessarily grow faster than wages for the rest of the economy. This situation is particularly acute in Sub-Saharan Africa, where even with GVC-friendly liberalization, wages for unskilled females would not keep pace with the growth of wages in the rest of the economy (figure 5.8).

Climate change mitigation policies: Reshaping the comparative advantages of countries

NDCs will have profound impacts on the structure of production and trade. The COVID-19 pandemic reduced global CO_2 emissions but had a limited

FIGURE 5.7 Change in income of the bottom 40 percent and top 60 percent of the income distribution relative to the COVID-19 L-shape recovery, by scenario and region

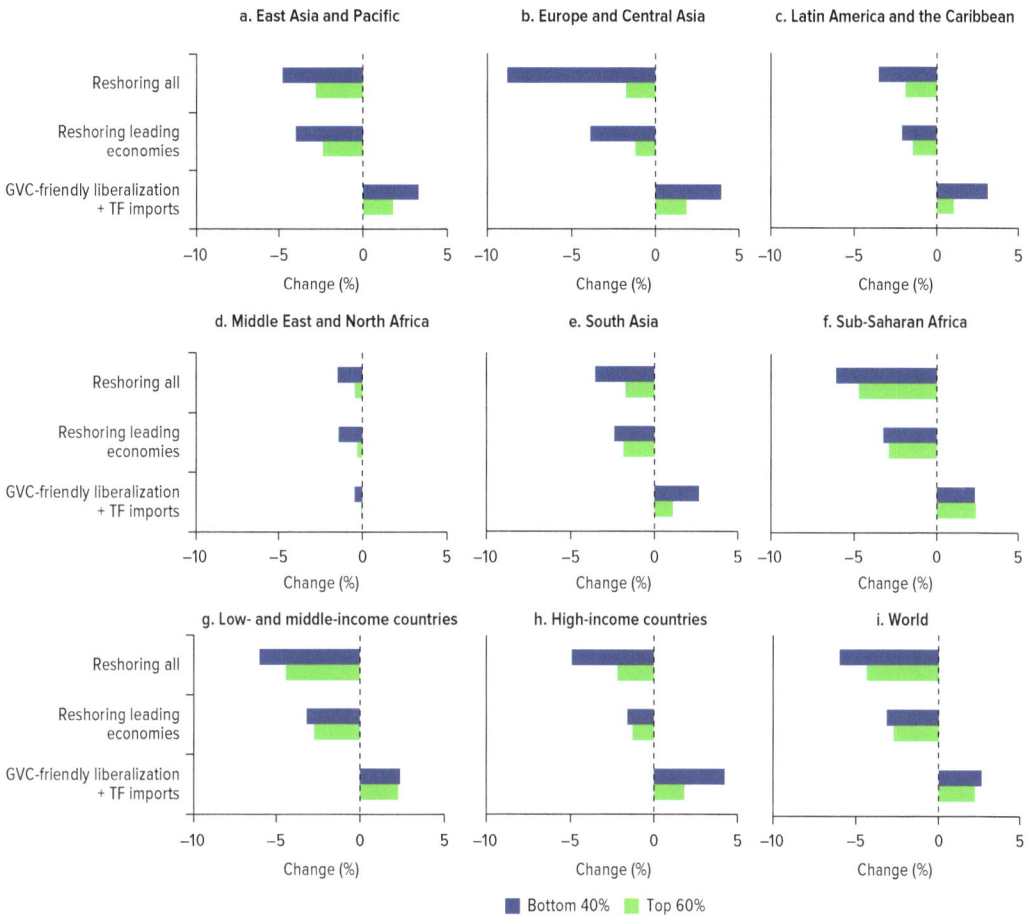

Source: World Bank staff estimates.
Note: GVC = global value chain; TF = trade facilitation.

impact on achieving climate change goals. The pandemic shifted down the emissions trajectory of "current policy" in almost all countries and regions. Global CO_2 emissions decreased by about 7 percent in 2020 relative to 2019 (Friedlingstein et al. 2020). These short-term trends in emissions reduction are expected to have a limited impact on long-term emissions pathways (Forster et al. 2020).

The simulations suggest that by 2030 global CO_2 emissions would fall by about 3.8 percent relative to the pre-COVID-19 baseline if the Paris Accord commitments were fully implemented. The global average unconditional NDC target for emissions reduction[8] is about 10.8 percent relative to the baseline in 2030.[9] In three regions—the Middle East and North Africa, South Asia, and Sub-Saharan Africa—the

FIGURE 5.8 Wages for unskilled females relative to rest of wages, 2030, by scenario and region

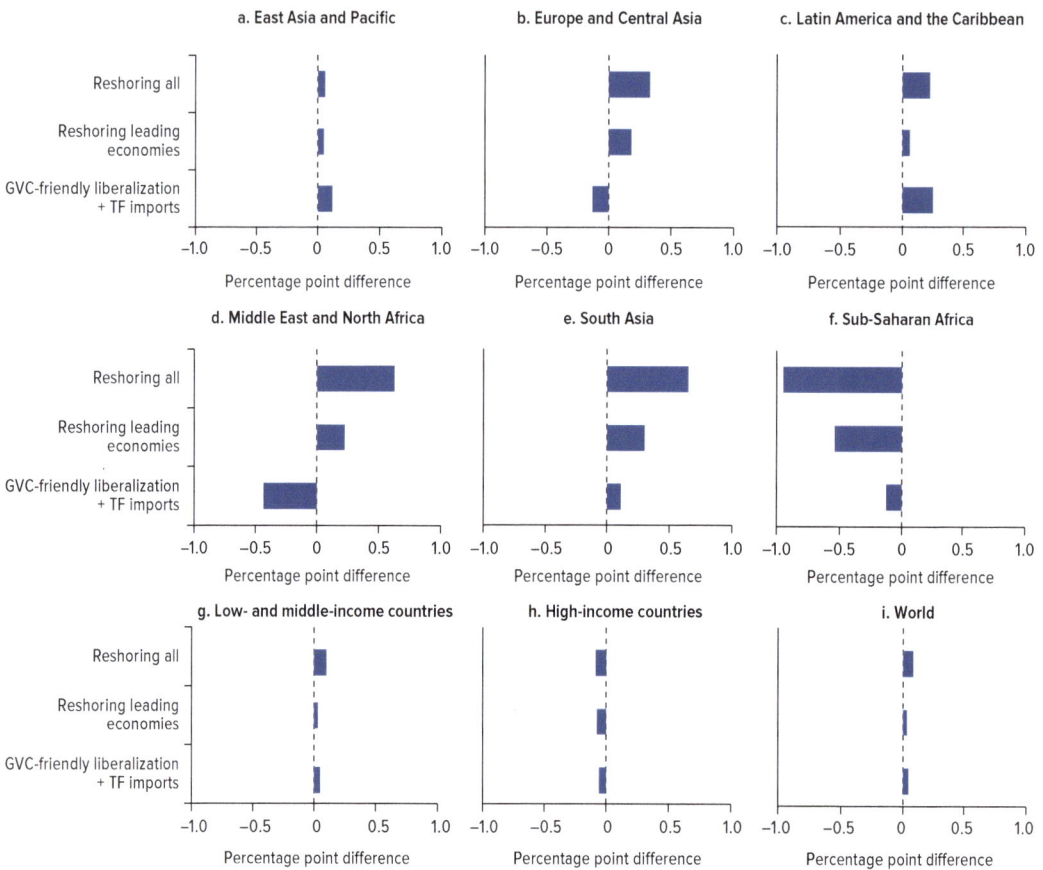

Source: World Bank staff estimates.
Note: GVC = global value chain; TF = trade facilitation.

COVID-19-induced CO_2 emissions reduction would exceed the NDC target (figure 5.9). These regions have the least-ambitious targets and were also among the most adversely affected by the pandemic.

Each region and sector will be affected differently as countries strive to reach their NDC targets. Focusing on the three sectors in each region with the largest reduction in output following the stylized implementation of NDCs, one key outcome is that coal would be the most affected sector in all regions (table 5.5). An increase in carbon prices under the NDC scenario would reduce global demand for coal. Coal production would drop significantly, from between 6 percent and 7 percent in China and the Middle East and North Africa to between more than 20 percent and 30 percent in Europe, Latin America, the United States, and the rest of high-income countries. All other sectors would experience much less significant reductions in output. Natural gas extraction would be the second most affected activity in almost half of the regions analyzed. Because of an increase in fuel prices following the implementation of carbon taxes, transportation, including air, water, and ground transport, would also be hit hard.

FIGURE 5.9 Change in CO_2 emissions in 2030 relative to the pre-COVID-19 baseline: Impact of the COVID-19 pandemic and NDC targets, by region

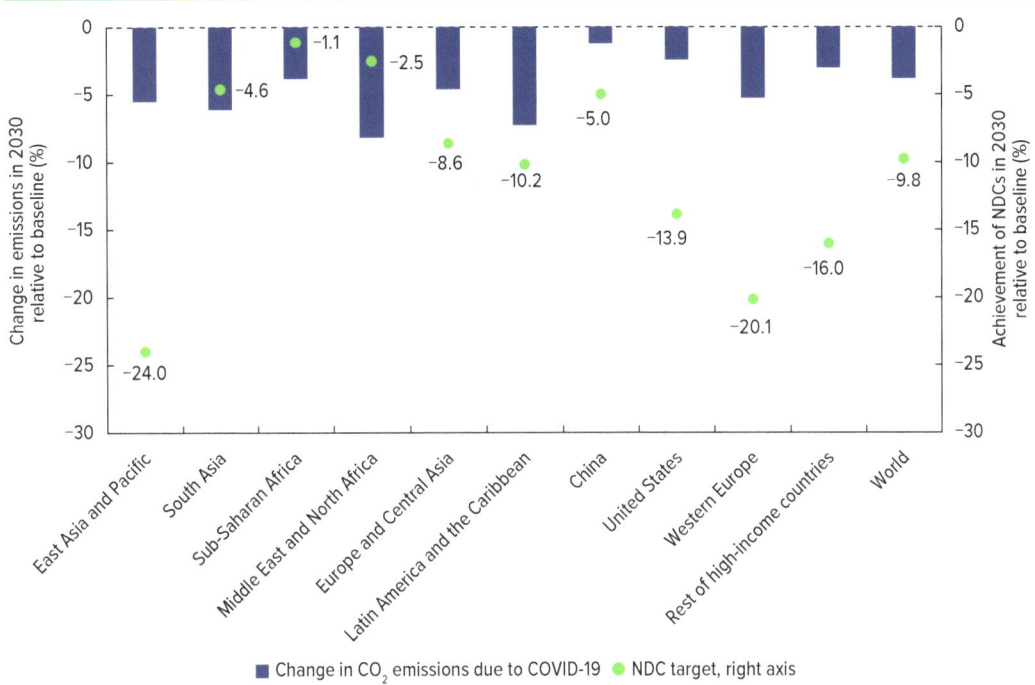

■ Change in CO_2 emissions due to COVID-19 ● NDC target, right axis

Source: Original calculations for this publication.
Note: CO_2 = carbon dioxide; NDC = Nationally Determined Contribution.

Consistent with the observed changes in production patterns, exports and imports of fossil fuels would be affected the most (figure 5.10). With lower global demand for fossil fuels, the volume of trade for these commodities is expected to decline, accompanied by a moderate reallocation of trade to places with less stringent environmental regulations. China, which is the world's largest net importer of fossil fuels and has a relatively low carbon price consistent with its NDC target, would increase its imports of fossil fuel commodities. Both Sub-Saharan Africa and East Asia, being large net energy exporters, would suffer reductions in their exports of fossil fuels. In Sub-Saharan Africa, the reduction in exports of fossil fuels would be compensated for by an increase in exports of other goods and services, including agricultural commodities.

Climate policies and carbon border adjustment mechanisms

Carbon border charges are a force to be reckoned with for carbon-intensive exporters. This section splits the impact of the stylized EU Green Deal into two parts: more ambitious emissions reductions by the EU and implementation of the CBAM, a charge on imports into the EU of carbon-intensive products from "less climate ambitious countries." The impacts of the EU Green Deal are measured relative to the scenario with NDC-consistent climate mitigation. These impacts are driven through two key channels. First, because of the increasing carbon price in the EU (from US$39 per ton of

TABLE 5.5 Changes in output following NDC implementation, by sector and region
Change (% relative to post-COVID-19 baseline)

Region	Top 1 sector		Top 2 sector		Top 3 sector	
	Sector	Change (%)	Sector	Change (%)	Sector	Change (%)
China	Coal extraction	−6.0	Gas extraction and distribution	−3.0	Wearing apparel and leather products	−0.2
Rest of East Asia and Pacific	Air transport	−10.6	Coal extraction	−8.6	Other transport	−5.8
Europe	Coal extraction	−33.2	Air transport	−2.5	Gas extraction and distribution	−2.2
Europe and Central Asia	Coal extraction	−15.7	Gas extraction and distribution	−1.1	Nonmetallic minerals	−0.6
Latin America and the Caribbean	Coal extraction	−18.3	Gas extraction and distribution	−3.3	Refined oil	−1.3
Middle East and North Africa	Coal extraction	−5.7	Gas extraction and distribution	−0.3	Wearing apparel and leather products	−0.2
Rest of high-income countries	Coal extraction	−18.5	Gas extraction and distribution	−3.3	Textiles	−1.2
South Asia	Coal extraction	−6.1	Wearing apparel and leather products	−0.4	Gas extraction and distribution	−0.4
Sub-Saharan Africa	Coal extraction	−8.9	Gas extraction and distribution	−0.2	Meat products (including fisheries) and other food	−0.2
United States	Coal extraction	−25.0	Gas extraction and distribution	−4.9	Other transport	−0.5
World	Coal extraction	−10.9	Gas extraction and distribution	−2.2	Air transport	−0.9

Source: Original calculations for this publication.
Note: The three sectors with the largest reduction in output are reported for each region.

CO_2 equivalent under the NDC target to US$213 per ton of CO_2 equivalent under the EU Green Deal target), demand for fossil fuels would fall within the bloc. This lower demand would have an adverse impact on regions like the Middle East and North Africa and Central Asia, including the Russian Federation, because the EU is a primary destination for their fossil fuel exports. Second, because of the increasing price of carbon in the EU, production would become more expensive, which negatively affects key destinations of EU energy-intensive exports, such as neighboring European countries. Unlike the EU carbon tax, which mainly affects the demand for and prices of fossil fuels, CBAM puts more pressure on energy-intensive goods, such as metals, chemical products, nonmetallic minerals (cement, lime), and electricity. As a result, the main exporters of these commodities to the EU (Europe and Central Asia for chemicals, metals, electricity; China and the Middle East and North Africa for chemicals) are among the regions that experience lower exports following CBAM implementation.

The impact of climate policies on other countries will depend on the degree of their carbon intensity and reliance on related exports (figure 5.11). Separating the macro impacts of the CBAM on EU trading partners from the impacts of domestic EU mitigation policies (within the EU Green Deal) shows that the impacts correlate with the carbon intensity (kilograms per US$1 of exports) and magnitude (share of

FIGURE 5.10 Change in exports and imports due to the implementation of NDC policies, 2030 relative to the post-COVID-19 baseline, by region

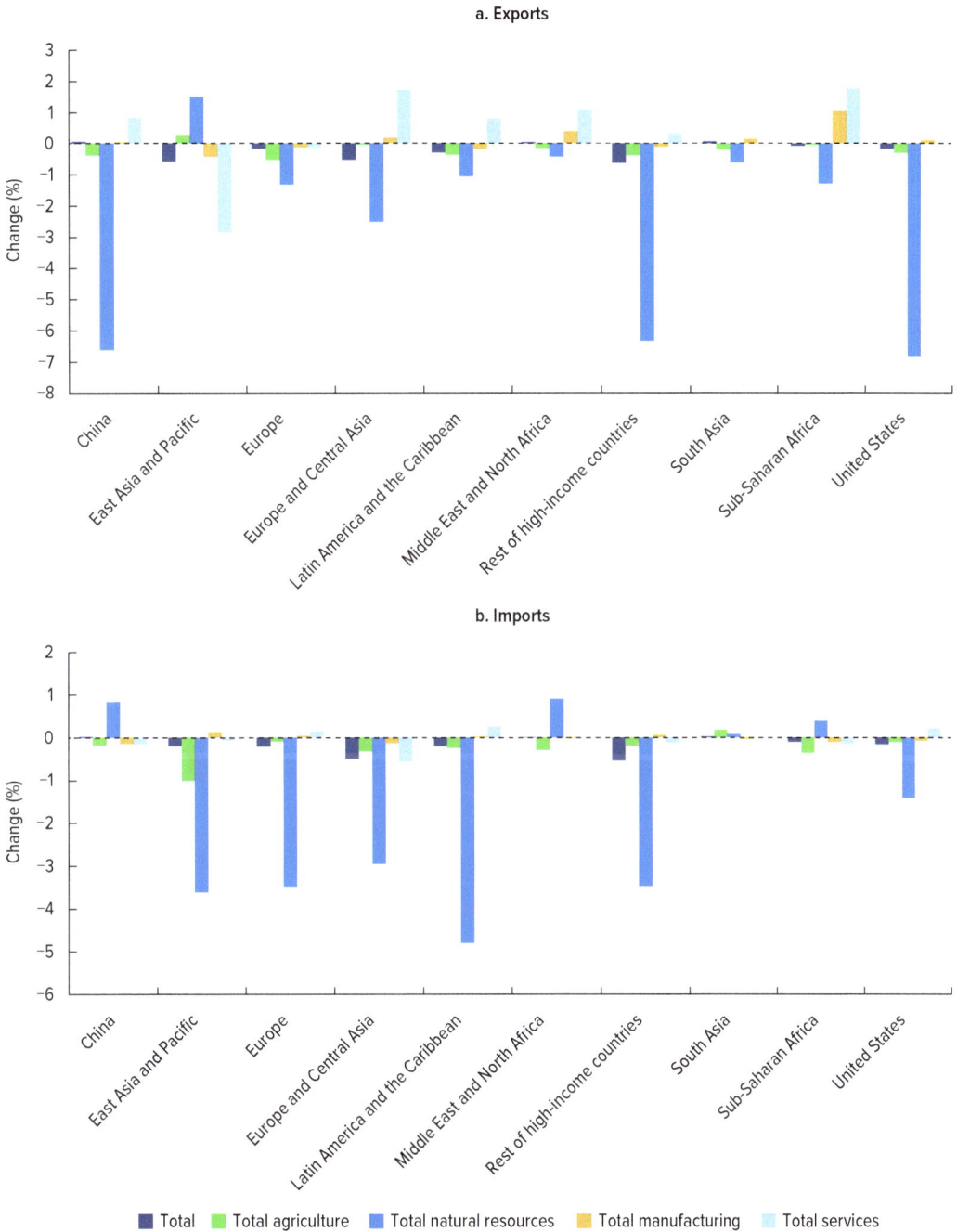

a. Exports

b. Imports

■ Total   ■ Total agriculture   ■ Total natural resources   ■ Total manufacturing   ■ Total services

Source: Original calculations for this publication.
Note: NDC = Nationally Determined Contribution.

FIGURE 5.11 Impacts of the CBAM on total exports by EU trading partners and carbon intensity of exports to the EU: 2030 relative to the EU Green Deal implementation scenario, by region

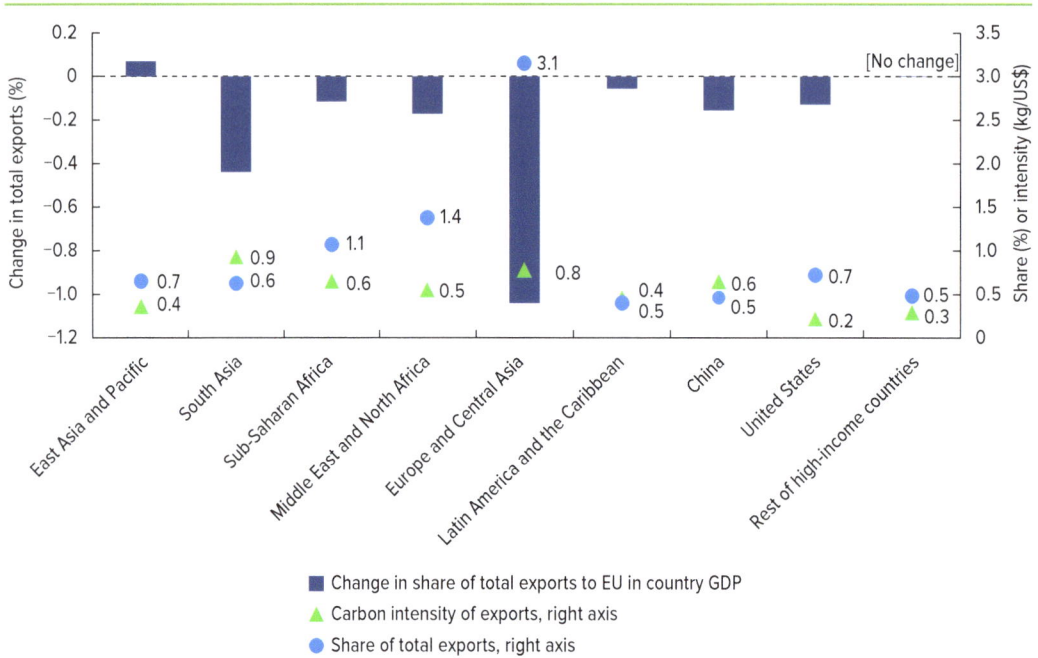

Source: Original calculations for this publication.
Note: CBAM = carbon border adjustment mechanism; EU = European Union.

exports to the EU in a country's GDP) of exports to the EU. The estimate of both carbon intensity and share of exports in a country's GDP focuses on commodities that correspond to the EU ETS sectors and thus face the CBAM in the simulations. The top-three regions most affected by the CBAM—Europe and Central Asia, the Middle East and North Africa, and Sub-Saharan Africa—have high carbon intensity of exports per US$1 and at least 1 percent of the EU-designated export share in the country's GDP. For the most affected region, Europe and Central Asia, the carbon intensity of exports is among the highest at 0.8 kg per US dollar and the share of affected sectors in total exports is the highest at 3.1 percent. At the same time, high-income countries with the lowest carbon intensity of exports to the EU, including the United States, experience negligible impacts from the CBAM.

Imposition of the CBAM could compensate European producers only partially for the potential reduction in output from a more ambitious climate mitigation target under the EU Green Deal (figure 5.12). At the aggregate EU level, CBAM would have virtually no impact on output, whereas implementation of the EU Green Deal itself would reduce total output by about 0.4 percent. Fossil fuels, petroleum products, metals, and transportation would be affected the most. Although most EU energy-intensive sectors (petroleum products, nonmetallic minerals, metals, electricity) would benefit from the CBAM rollout, this is not the case for producers that rely on imported intermediate inputs. The rising costs of carbon-intensive imported intermediate inputs would reduce domestic EU production in several manufacturing sectors: electronic equipment, machinery, and motor vehicles.

FIGURE 5.12 Impacts of the EU Green Deal and CBAM on output in the EU: 2030 relative to the scenario with NDCs, by sector

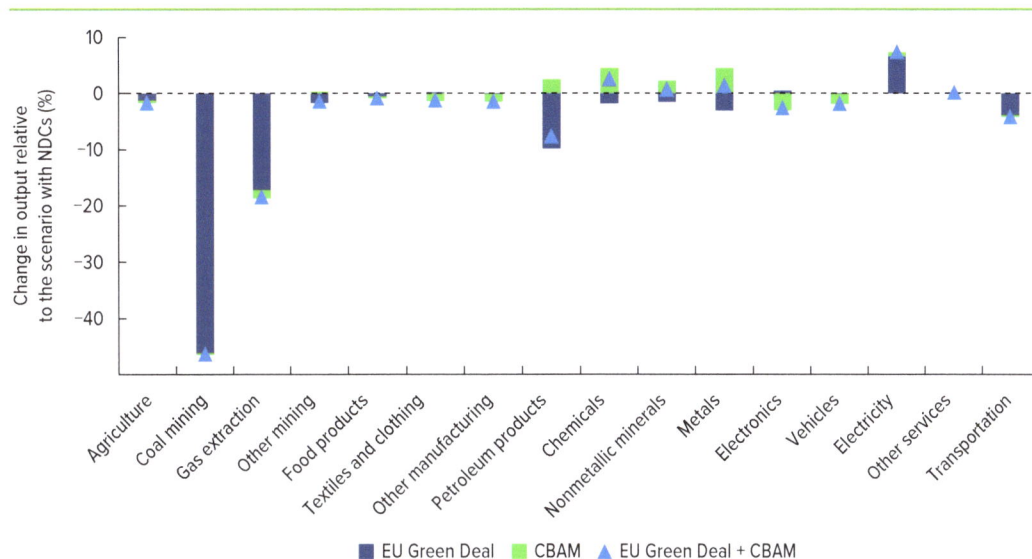

Source: Original calculations for this publication.
Note: CBAM = carbon border adjustment mechanism; EU = European Union; NDCs = Nationally Determined Contributions.

The EU Green Deal would likely reduce imports of fossil fuels and petroleum products because of lower EU-wide demand. It would not have any significant impact on imports of other commodities (figure 5.13). A partial shift would occur toward increased imports of electricity and nonmetallic minerals to the EU, representing a channel for carbon leakage if CBAM is not implemented. Implementation of the CBAM would reverse trade patterns compared to the impacts of the EU Green Deal. Imports of fossil fuels would rise moderately, whereas imports of commodities covered by the EU ETS sectors would fall significantly—anywhere from 11 percent in the case of petroleum products to 40 percent in the case of electricity. The imports-to-output ratio for the latter is only 0.8 percent. CBAM would not have a major impact on the EU's domestic electricity producers, unlike in the case of other EU ETS sectors, for which the imports-to-output ratio varies from 6.6 percent for nonmetallic minerals to 20 percent for petroleum products, chemicals, and metals. These high shares of import dependence explain why CBAM would have a relatively significant impact on EU energy-intensive manufacturing industries as the substitution from imported to domestic production takes place.

When it comes to commodities, imports of coal would be affected the most, with a potential reduction of 65.8 percent under EU Green Deal with CBAM scenario (figure 5.13). This reduction in imports would be due largely to shrinking US exports to the EU (table 5.6). Imports of electricity from Europe and Central Asia would be the second most affected trade flow. But, whereas coal exports from the United States to the EU would decline by 70.8 percent, aggregate coal exports from the United States would decline by only 19.7 percent because of the reallocation of exports to other destinations and toward domestic markets. The pattern of export reallocation, away from

FIGURE 5.13 Impacts of the EU Green Deal and CBAM on EU imports, 2030 relative to scenario with NDCs, by sector

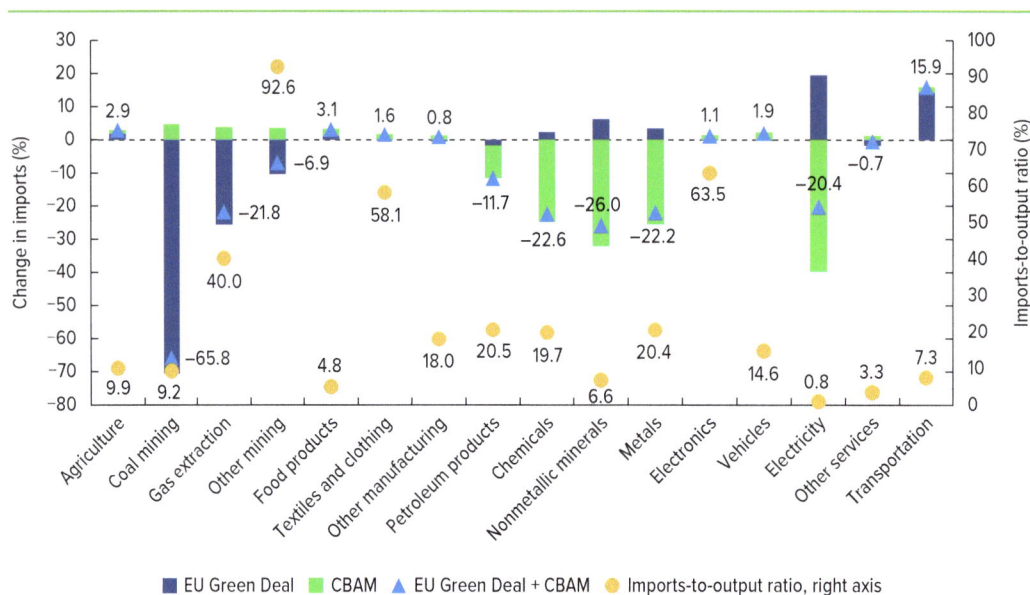

Source: Original calculations for this publication.
Note: Percent change in 2030 relative to the scenario with NDCs. Trade within the EU is excluded from the reporting. The imports-to-output ratio is estimated for 2030 based on the baseline with implemented CBAM = carbon border adjustment mechanism; EU = European Union; NDCs = Nationally Determined Contributions.

TABLE 5.6 Impacts of the EU Green Deal and CBAM on selected sectors of EU trading partners relative to the scenario with NDCs, by region
Change (%)

Sector	Change in EU imports	Key source region	For key source region			
			Share of total imports	Change in exports to EU	Change in total exports	Change in output
Coal	−69.1	United States	38.9	−70.8	−19.7	−5.4
Electricity	−28.2	Europe and Central Asia	58.2	−34.3	−15.6	−1.2
Nonmetallic minerals	−28.0	China	48.7	−33.8	−4.2	−0.2
Wood and paper products	−28.0	China	33.9	−37.5	−7.4	−0.6
Chemicals	−23.2	China	18.4	−38.4	−5.8	−0.7
Metals	−23.0	Europe and Central Asia	26.6	−38.7	−9.2	−3.2
Natural gas	−22.8	Europe and Central Asia	45.9	−20.9	−9.1	−1.5
Petroleum products	−11.5	Europe and Central Asia	47.1	−12.6	−5.4	−1.2
Crude oil	−9.3	Europe and Central Asia	52.5	−5.6	−1.6	−0.4

Source: Original calculations for this publication.
Note: The share of total imports for key source region is estimated for total imports excluding intra-EU trade. For chemical products, the second most important EU trading partner (China) is reported, as is the most important partner (United States); observed changes in flows are not significant. Selected sectors with the largest reduction in EU imports are reported. CBAM = carbon border adjustment mechanism; EU = European Union.

the EU, would compensate for some of the negative impacts of the EU Green Deal and CBAM on EU trading partners. In almost all cases, the reduction in total exports (by commodities and regions) would be much smaller than the reduction in exports to the EU. Additional reallocation toward domestic markets would further smooth out the negative impacts on production in general (table 5.6). Europe and Central Asia as well as China have the largest number of sectors heavily involved in trade with the EU that would be affected adversely by the EU Green Deal and CBAM. The commodities affected would include electricity, gas, oil, and metals for Europe and Central Asia and nonmetallic minerals, wood products, and chemicals for China.

EU trade with the rest of Europe and Central Asia is likely to be hardest hit by the CBAM, with carbon-intensive sectors the most vulnerable. Figure 5.14 reports the most affected sectors in terms of changes in output. The impact of CBAM on changes in the output of the exporting country depends on two key drivers: the carbon intensity of exports and the share of total output that is exported to the EU. ECA commodities that have both high carbon intensity and a large share of production that is exported to the EU (metals and chemicals) would suffer the largest reductions in output. At the same time, output of highly carbon-intensive commodities, like electricity, would not be affected significantly because of the low share of exports to the EU in total output.

The potential negative impacts on the output of selected sectors in low- and middle-income countries can be mitigated by their national policy responses. By pursuing more ambitious climate mitigation policies themselves, countries could transform potential income losses into long-run income gains by supporting the use of more efficient and cleaner technologies, facilitating a green transition, and attracting green investment. In addition, low- and middle-income countries would benefit from the environmental and health co-benefits of taking more stringent climate action. Even energy exporters, a group of countries that would be hit hard by implementation of the EU Green Deal because of lower global prices of fossil fuels, transitioning from a traditional diversification to a proactive diversification of assets (with increasing investments in research and development) could be an important welfare-improving channel, as shown by Peszko et al. (2020).

Impacts of climate mitigation policies on GVC participation

Implementation of climate mitigation policies, including the NDCs, the EU Green Deal, and the CBAM, would reshape GVCs at both the regional and sectoral levels. Decomposing the impact of these stylized climate mitigation measures on the GVC participation rate[10] reveals an overall trend of declining GVC participation by country and region (figure 5.15) relative to the scenario with NDCs. Impacts would be rather moderate, ranging from about −2.5 percent in Western Europe, a region with the most stringent mitigation policies in the scenarios, to essentially no impact in some countries with a high GVC participation rate in low carbon-intensive commodities, such as Malaysia, the Philippines, and Vietnam.

Despite minor impacts of NDC targets on GVC participation, some countries and regions would increase their participation in GVCs—for example, countries benefiting from the changes in trade patterns, such as India, the Philippines, South Africa, and several countries from Latin America (figure 5.15). The impacts on countries such as Brazil, EU member states, Turkey, and the rest of East Asia would be moderately negative.

FIGURE 5.14 Impacts of CBAM on Europe and Central Asia, 2030

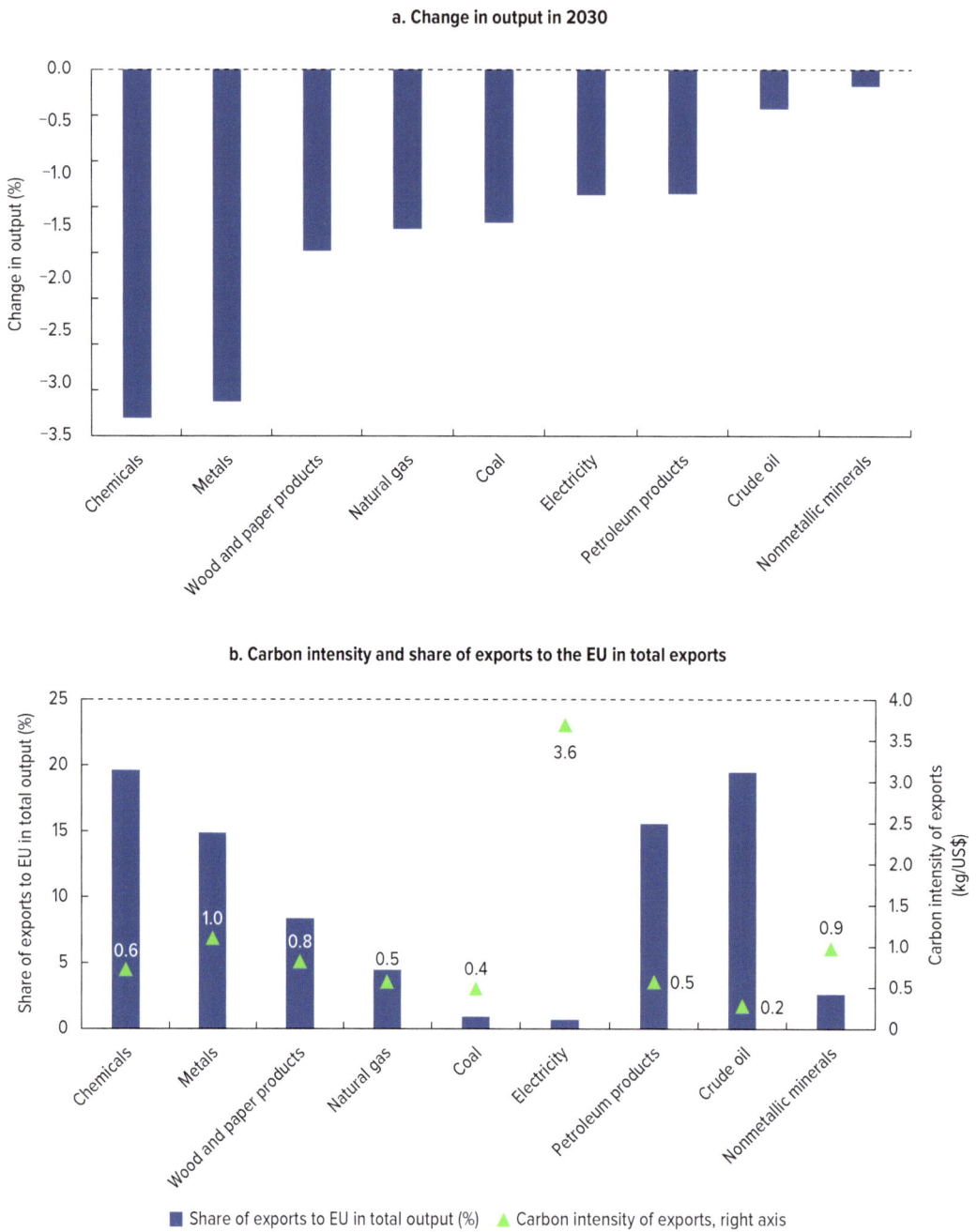

a. Change in output in 2030

b. Carbon intensity and share of exports to the EU in total exports

■ Share of exports to EU in total output (%)   ▲ Carbon intensity of exports, right axis

Source: Original calculations for this publication.
Note: CBAM = carbon border adjustment mechanism; EU = European Union.

FIGURE 5.15 Impacts of climate mitigation policies on GVC participation: 2030 relative to the the post-COVID-19 baseline and GVC participation rate, by country and region

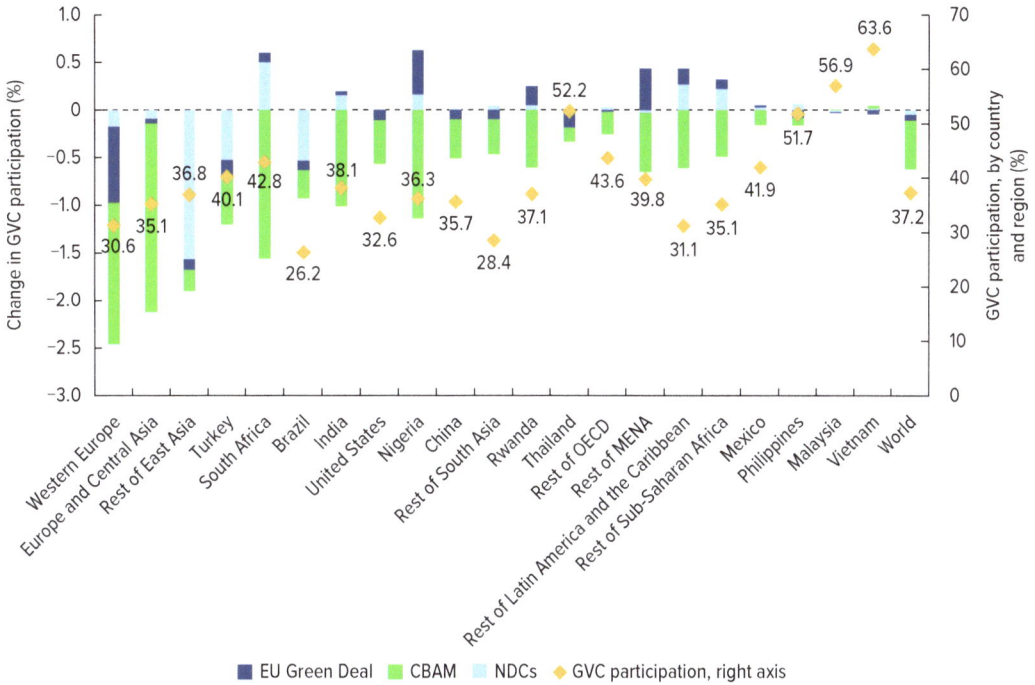

Source: Original calculations for this publication.
Note: Percent change in 2030 relative to the the post-COVID-19 baseline and GVC participation rate in 2030. CBAM = carbon border adjustment mechanism; EU = European Union; GVC = global value chain; MENA = Middle East and North Africa; NDCs = Nationally Determined Contributions; OECD = Organisation for Economic Co-operation and Development.

Implementation of the EU Green Deal would reduce the GVC participation of firms in Western Europe, with integration into GVCs declining by about 0.8 percent. At the same time, with the redirection of trade flows and increasing trade intensity outside of the EU, the GVC participation rate for most other countries and regions would increase. Only the closest EU trading partners would experience minor reductions in GVC participation due to implementation of the EU Green Deal. Among the climate policy measures considered, CBAM would have the most adverse impacts on GVC participation. With higher taxes applied to carbon-intensive EU imports, not only would Western European countries experience a decline in GVC participation (−1.5 percent) but some EU trading partners would experience a more substantial reduction, with Europe and Central Asia seeing a decline of 2 percent.

At the commodity level, it is not surprising that trade in fossil fuels would be affected the most adversely by NDC policies, with coal at the top of the list (figure 5.16). Implementation of the EU Green Deal mitigation efforts would further reduce trade in fossil fuels, commodities that are not involved heavily in forward and backward GVC links. In contrast, CBAM targets selected energy-intensive sectors with relatively higher participation in GVCs, with chemical products topping the list. Under CBAM, participation in GVCs would shrink, with chemicals,

FIGURE 5.16 Impacts of climate mitigation policies on GVC participation: 2030 relative to the the post-COVID-19 baseline, by sector

Global average

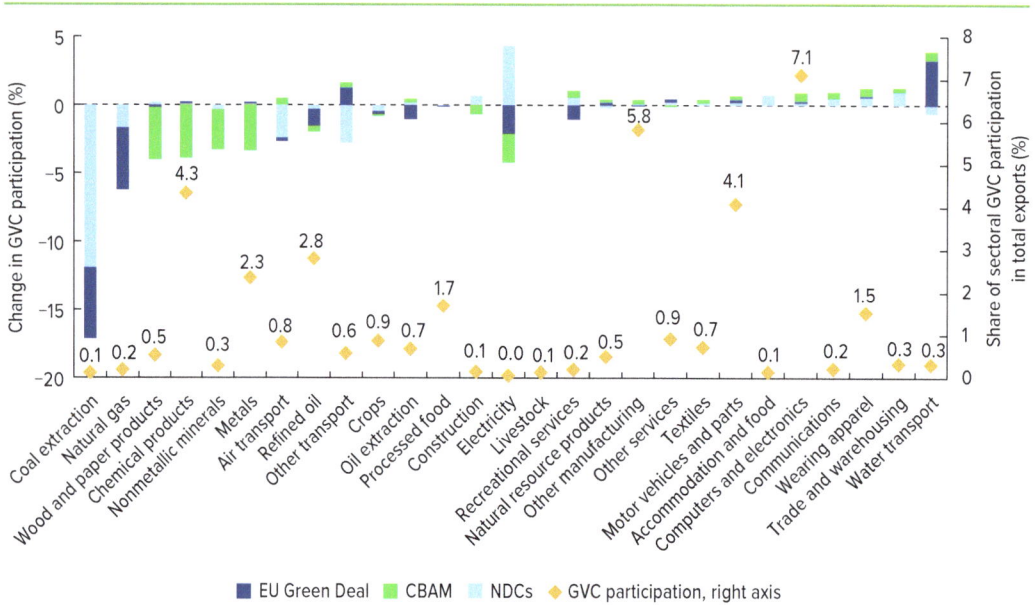

Source: Original calculations for this publication.
Note: Percent change in 2030 relative to the the post-COVID-19 baseline. CBAM = carbon border adjustment mechanism; EU = European Union; GVC = global value chain; NDCs = Nationally Determined Contributions.

wood and paper products, nonmetallic minerals, and metals all experiencing a reduction of 3 percent to 4 percent.

New opportunities will arise for countries that are relatively carbon efficient in key tasks along GVCs. Whereas fossil fuels and energy-intensive sectors would experience a reduction in GVC participation rates, service sectors and light manufacturing activities would experience a moderate increase. These sectors include highly GVC-integrated sectors like computers and electronics, motor vehicles and parts, and other light manufacturing. Climate mitigation policies would stimulate both trade and GVC participation for these commodities, making them even more integrated in GVCs.

Sectors with the strongest backward and forward links in GVCs would become even more integrated. Focusing on the CBAM impacts on computers and electronics—a sector with the highest rate of GVC participation—all EU trading partners would experience an increase in GVC participation (figure 5.17). As the trade barriers for heavy manufacturing increase, demand for electronics would rise worldwide, with a global average increase in GVC participation for producers of electronics of about 0.6 percent. Key exporters of electronics, such as China, Malaysia, and Vietnam, also would strengthen their integration into GVCs because of the carbon border adjustment measures. Thus, the climate mitigation policies not only would lead to decarbonization of the economy but also would stimulate higher integration into GVCs of the low carbon-intensive commodities.

FIGURE 5.17 Impacts of the CBAM on GVC participation for the electronics sector, by country and region

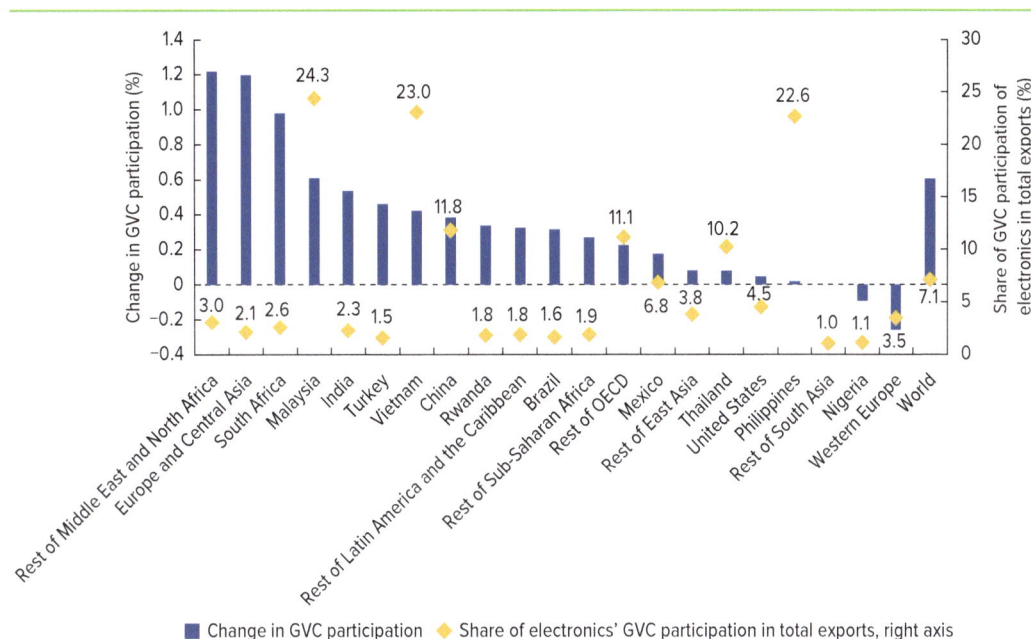

Source: Original calculations for this publication.
Note: Percent change in 2030 relative to the EU Green Deal baseline. CBAM = carbon border adjustment mechanism; GVC = global value chain; EU = European Union; OECD = Organisation for Economic Co-operation and Development.
a. GVC participation rate equals the sum of the backward and forward GVC participations.

Annex 5A Regional and sectoral aggregations in computable general equilibrium analysis

TABLE 5A.1 Regional and sectoral aggressions in computable general equilibrium analysis

Region code	Region description	Global Trade Analysis Project (GTAP) 10 regions
WER	Western Europe	Austria (AUT); Belgium (BEL); Bulgaria (BGR); Croatia (CRO); Cyprus (CYP); Czech Republic (CZE); Denmark (DNK); Estonia (EST); Finland (FIN); France (FRA); Germany (DEU); Greece (GRC); Hungary (HUN); Ireland (IRL); Italy (ITA); Latvia (LVA); Lithuania (LTU); Luxembourg (LUX); Malta (MLT); the Netherlands (NLD); Poland (POL); Portugal (PRT); Romania (ROU); Slovakia (SVK); Slovenia (SVN); Spain (ESP); Sweden (SWE); Switzerland (CHE); United Kingdom (GBR); Norway (NOR); Rest of European Free Trade Association (XEF); Rest of Europe (XER); Rest of the World (XTW)
USA	United States	United States (USA)
CHN	China	China (CHN)
BRA	Brazil	Brazil (BRA)
MEX	Mexico	Mexico (MEX)

Table continues next page

TABLE 5A.1 Regional and sectoral aggressions in computable general equilibrium analysis (*continued*)

Region code	Region description	Global Trade Analysis Project (GTAP) 10 regions
IND	India	India (IND)
TUR	Turkey	Turkey (TUR)
ZAF	South Africa	South Africa (ZAF)
RWA	Rwanda	Rwanda (RWA)
NGA	Nigeria	Nigeria (NGA)
VNM	Vietnam	Vietnam (VNM)
PHL	Philippines	Philippines (PHL)
THA	Thailand	Thailand (THA)
MYS	Malaysia	Malaysia (MYS)
XSS	Rest of Sub-Saharan Africa	Benin (BEN); Burkina Faso (BFA); Cameroon (CMR); Côte d'Ivoire (CIV); Ghana (GHA); Guinea (GIN); Senegal (SEN); Togo (TGO); Rest of Western Africa (XWF); Central Africa (XCF); South-Central Africa (XAC); Ethiopia (ETH); Kenya (KEN); Madagascar (MDG); Malawi (MWI); Mauritius (MUS); Mozambique (MOZ); Tanzania (TZA); Uganda (UGA); Zambia (ZMB); Zimbabwe (ZWE); Rest of Eastern Africa (XEC); Botswana (BWA); Namibia (NAM); Rest of South African Customs Union (XSC)
XHY	Rest of high-income	Australia (AUS); New Zealand (NZL); Canada (CAN); Hong Kong SAR, China (HKG); Japan (JPN); Republic of Korea (KOR); Taiwan, China (TWN); Singapore (SGP)
XLC	Rest of Latin America and Caribbean	Argentina (ARG); Bolivia (BOL); Colombia (COL); Ecuador (ECU); Venezuela, RB (VEN); Chile (CHL); Paraguay (PRY); Peru (PER); Uruguay (URY); Rest of South America (XSM); Costa Rica (CRI); Guatemala (GTM); Honduras (HND); Nicaragua (NIC); Panama (PAN); El Salvador (SLV); Rest of Central America (XCA); Dominican Republic (DOM); Jamaica (JAM); Puerto Rico (PRI); Trinidad and Tobago (TTO); Rest of Caribbean (XCB); Rest of North America (XNA)
XEA	Rest of East Asia	Rest of Oceania (XOC); Mongolia (MNG); Rest of East Asia (XEA); Brunei Darussalam (BRN); Cambodia (KHM); Indonesia (IDN); Lao PDR (LAO); Rest of Southeast Asia (XSE)
XSA	South Asia	Bangladesh (BGD); Nepal (NPL); Pakistan (PAK); Sri Lanka (LKA); Rest of South Asia (XSA)
ECA	Europe and Central Asia	Albania (ALB); Belarus (BLR); Russian Federation (RUS); Ukraine (UKR); Rest of Eastern Europe (XEE); Kyrgyz Republic (KGZ); Tajikistan (TJK); Rest of Former Soviet Union (XSU); Armenia (ARM); Georgia (GEO); Kazakhstan (KAZ); Azerbaijan (AZE)
XMN	Middle East and North Africa	Bahrain (BHR); Iran, Islamic Rep. (IRN); Kuwait (KWT); Oman (OMN); Jordan (JOR); Qatar (QAT); Saudi Arabia (SAU); United Arab Emirates (ARE); Rest of Western Asia (XWS); Israel (ISR); Rest of North Africa (XNF); Egypt, Arab Rep. (EGY); Morocco (MAR); Tunisia (TUN)

Source: Original table for this publication.

Notes

1. Trade costs declined 14 percent in East Asia, Europe and Central Asia, the Middle East and North Africa, and South Asia and 16 percent in Latin America and the Caribbean and Sub-Saharan Africa.

2. CBAM, a policy measure discussed in the EU Green Deal (European Commission 2019), aims to protect domestic industries, create incentives for other countries to adopt carbon taxes, avoid carbon leakage, and limit the reallocation of the EU-based industries to the countries with less stringent climate regulations.

3. Because NDC mitigation targets are included in the baseline scenario, the carbon price level used to determine the CBAM rate is estimated as the difference between the carbon price in the EU and the carbon price in the country or region of origin of the imported commodity.

4. Only CO_2 emissions from fossil fuel combustion are considered here.

5. All percentage changes in this and the following paragraph are stated relative to the 2019 baseline without COVID-19.

6. This finding is in line with the number of COVID-19-induced new poor presented in Lakner et al. (2021).

7. These estimations on the evolution of welfare of the bottom 40 percent and top 60 percent consider the entire population in each region as a single entity. It is entirely possible that this trend follows a different pattern within countries in the same region, especially in small countries located at either end of the region's distribution. Nevertheless, the general trend shows a pattern of regional convergence at the regional level.

8. According to the current assessment, only unconditional NDC targets are considered. If a country has specified only conditional NDC targets in its Paris Agreement contribution, then the unconditional target is assumed to be 0.

9. If the NDC mitigation targets are implemented, median global warming would be about 2.6°C to 3.1°C by 2100 (Rogelj et al. 2016).

10. The GVC participation rate equals the sum of backward and forward GVC participation (Aslam, Nota, and Rodrigues-Bastos 2017).

References

Aguiar, Angel, Maksym Chepeliev, Erwin L. Corong, and Robert McDougall. 2019. "The GTAP Data Base: Version 10." *Journal of Global Economic Analysis* 4 (1): 1–27. https://www.jgea.org/ojs/index.php/jgea/article/view/77.

Aslam, Angel, Natalija Nota, and Fabiano Rodrigues-Bastos. 2017. "Calculating Trade in Value Added." IMF Working Paper WP/17/178, International Monetary Fund, Washington, DC.

Böhringer, Christoph, Sonja Peterson, Jan Schneider, and Malte Winkler. 2020. "Carbon Pricing after Paris: Overview of Results from EMF 36." Paper presented during the 23rd Annual Conference on Global Economic Analysis (virtual conference), Purdue University, West Lafayette, IN, June 17–19, 2020. https://www.gtap.agecon.purdue.edu/resources/res_display.asp?RecordID=6067.

Carrico, Caitlyn, Erwin Corong, and Dominique van der Mensbrugghe. 2020. "The GTAP Version 10A Multi-Region Input Output (MRIO) Data Base." GTAP Memorandum 34, Center for Global Trade Analysis, Purdue University, West Lafayette, IN. https://www.gtap.agecon.purdue.edu/resources/res_display.asp?RecordID=6164.

Chepeliev, Maksym, Israel Osorio-Rodarte, and Dominique van der Mensbrugghe. 2021. "Distributional Impacts of Carbon Pricing Policies under Paris Agreement: Inter and Intra-Regional Perspectives." *Energy Economics* 102 (October): 105530. https://doi.org/10.1016/j.eneco.2021.105530.

Chepeliev, Maksym, Maryla Maliszewska, Israel Osorio-Rodarte, Maria Filipa Seara e Pereira, and Dominique van der Mensbrugghe. 2022. "Pandemics, Climate Mitigation, and Re-Shoring: Impacts of a Changing Global Economy on Trade, Incomes, and Poverty." Policy Research Working Paper 9955, World Bank, Washington, DC.

European Commission. 2019. "The European Green Deal." Communication from the European Commission to the European Parliament, the European Council, the European

Economic and Social Committee, and the Committee of the Regions, European Commission, Brussels. https://ec.europa .eu/info/sites/info/files/european-green-deal-communication_en .pdf.

European Commission. 2021. "Proposal for a Regulation of the European Parliament and of the Council Establishing a Carbon Border Adjustment Mechanism." European Commission, Brussels. https://ec.europa.eu/info/sites/default/files/carbon_border_adjustment_mecha-nism_0.pdf.

Forster, Peter M., Harriet I. Forster, Mat J. Evans, Matthew J. Gidden, Chris D. Jones, Christoph A. Keller, Robin D. Lamboll, Corinne Le Quéré, Joeri Rogelj, Deborah Rosen, et al. 2020. "Current and Future Global Climate Impacts Resulting from COVID-19." *Nature Climate Change* 10: 913–19. https://doi.org/10.1038/s41558-020-0883-0.

Friedlingstein, Pierre, Michael O'Sullivan, Matthew W. Jones, Robbie M. Andrew, Judith Hauck, Are Olsen, Glen P. Peters, Wouter Peters, Julia Pongratz, Stephen Sitch, et al. 2020. "Global Carbon Budget 2020." *Earth Systems Science Data* 12: 3269–340. https://doi .org/10.5194/essd-12-3269-2020.

IIASA (International Institute for Applied Systems Analysis). 2016. SSP Database (Shared Socioeconomic Pathways). Version 1.1. Laxenburg: IAASA. https://tntcat.iiasa.ac.at /SspDb/dsd?Action=htmlpage&page=about.

ITC (International Trade Centre). 2020. "Market Access Map (MACMAP). Trade Agreements." ITC, Geneva. https://www.macmap.org/en/query/trade-agreement.

Lakner, Christoph, Nishant Yonzan, Daniel Gerszon Mahler, R. Andres Castaneda Aguilar, and Haoyu Wu. 2021. "Updated Estimates of the Impact of COVID-19 on Global Poverty: Looking Back at 2020 and the Outlook for 2021." *Data Blog* (blog), January 11, 2021. https://blogs.worldbank.org/opendata/updated-estimates-impact-covid-19-global-poverty -looking-back-2020-and-outlook-2021.

Li, M. 2018. CARD Trade War Tariffs Database. Ames: Iowa State University, Center for Agricultural and Rural Development. https://www.card.iastate.edu/china/trade-war-data/.

Maliszewska, Maryla, Aaditya Mattoo, and Dominique van der Mensbrugghe. 2020. "The Potential Impact of COVID-19 on GDP and Trade: A Preliminary Assessment." Policy Research Working Paper 9211, World Bank, Washington, DC. http://documents1 .worldbank.org/curated/pt/295991586526445673/pdf/The-Potential-Impact-of-COVID -19-on-GDP-and-Trade-A-Preliminary-Assessment.pdf.

Moïsé, Evdokia, and Silvia Sorescu. 2013. "Trade Facilitation Indicators: The Potential Impact of Trade Facilitation on Developing Countries' Trade." OECD Trade Policy Paper 144, OECD Publishing, Paris.

OECD (Organisation for Economic Co-operation and Development). 2020. "Shocks, Risks, and Global Value Chains: Insights from the OECD METRO Mode." OECD, Paris.

Peters, Glen P. 2008. "From Production-Based to Consumption-Based National Emission Inventories." *Ecological Economics* 65 (1): 13–23. https://doi.org/10.1016/j.ecolecon .2007.10.014.

Peszko, Grzegorz, Dominique van der Mensbrugghe, Alexander Golub, John Ward, Dimitri Zenghelis, Cor Marijs, Anne Schopp, John A. Rogers, and Amelia Midgley. 2020. *Diversification and Cooperation in a Decarbonizing World: Climate Strategies for Fossil Fuel–Dependent Countries.* Washington, DC: World Bank.

Rogelj, Joeri, Michel den Elzen, Niklas Höhne, Taryn Fransen, Hanna Fekete, Harald Winkler, Roberto Schaeffer, Fu Sha, Kaywan Riahi, and Malte Meinhausen. 2016. "Paris Agreement Climate Proposals Need a Boost to Keep Warming Well Below 2 °C." *Nature* 534: 631–39. https://doi.org/10.1038/nature18307.

van der Mensbrugghe, Dominique. 2019. "The Environmental Impact and Sustainability Applied General Equilibrium (ENVISAGE) Model. Version 10.01." Center for Global Trade Analysis, Purdue University, West Lafayette, IN. https://mygeohub.org/groups/gtap /envisage-docs.

World Bank. 2019. *Macro and Poverty Outlook: Country-by-Country Analysis and Projections for the Developing World: Annual Meetings 2019.* Washington, DC: World Bank.

World Bank. 2020. *Macro and Poverty Outlook: Country-by-Country Analysis and Projections for the Developing World: Annual Meetings 2020.* Washington, DC: World Bank. https:// thedocs.worldbank.org/en/doc/77351105a334213c64122e44c2efe523-0500072021 /related/mpo-am20.pdf.

WTO (World Trade Organization). 2015. *World Trade Report 2015: Speeding up Trade; Benefits and Challenges of Implementing the WTO Trade Facilitation Agreement.* Geneva: WTO.

6

COVID-19 and the Reshaping of GVCs: Policy Messages for Resilient Trade-Driven Development

Key messages

- Maintaining trade flows in a global crisis is essential. Well-operating global value chains (GVCs) are a source of resilience far more than a source of vulnerability. GVCs provide access to food and medical supplies, inputs for farmers, and employment and income, especially for the poor.

- Improving border procedures and easing impediments to trade flows are an appropriate approach to a supply chain crisis. This approach includes eliminating duties on essential food and medical supplies, facilitating trade, and reducing unnecessary export formalities. A crisis is in general a bad time to increase trade barriers, because the need for imports may spike.

- Nonetheless, during COVID-19 (coronavirus), many countries restricted the movement of food and medical supplies, including vaccines. Thus, there is substantial scope for improved policies.

- Information sharing can play a key role in improved resilience, including information on key stockpiles of medical and food supplies as well as information between logistics providers and the mapping of value chains in general.

- Access to finance is important for the most vulnerable traders. An important lesson of COVID-19 is that some small exporters are not deeply embedded in networks with lead firms and can experience heightened risk if contracts are suddenly canceled. When there is no support from the network, the financial system and government are the remaining backup.

- A global economy facing an increasing prevalence of risks from pandemics, extreme weather events, and other shocks is more dependent on trade, requiring stable and predictable trade policies.

- Trade diversification and integration into a broader set of GVCs is especially important for low-income countries to limit the impact of, and speed the recovery from, more frequent shocks.

Introduction

Is the COVID-19 pandemic a wake-up call for governments and international institutions to reshape the future course of global trade and GVCs? What kind of global integration through GVCs should low- and middle-income countries pursue, and how can they minimize the risks associated with external shocks such as pandemics, extreme climate events, and trade policy conflicts? This chapter discusses the lessons for trade policies during a global crisis, especially those that affect access not only to essential products, such as medicines and vaccines, that were essential during the pandemic, but also to food and strategic products, such as rare earth elements and semiconductors. Building on the analysis in previous chapters, it also examines the implications of the increasing prevalence of risks, from both nature and policy, for global supply chains and for trade and development strategies. Do strategies that have focused on attracting foreign direct investment (FDI) in specific sectors need to be revised to focus on achieving greater diversification across sectors and both backward and forward links? How can governments assist firms to address the risks they face from external shocks as participants in GVCs? How should low- and middle-income countries respond if other countries seek to reshore production aggressively through trade policy restrictions and domestic measures such as subsidies?

Appropriate trade policy responses during a global crisis and in the recovery

Despite the initial inclination of policy makers to close borders, maintaining trade flows during a global crisis is crucial. In general, GVCs have proved to be an important source of resilience. Trade in both goods and services plays a key role in overcoming global shocks and limiting their impact in the following ways:

- Providing access to essential goods (including material inputs for their production) and services. During the COVID-19 pandemic, essential goods included medical goods and supplies to help to contain the pandemic and treat those affected as well as vaccines to prevent serious illness.

- Ensuring access to food throughout the world.

- Providing farmers with necessary inputs (seeds, fertilizers, pesticides, equipment, veterinary products) for the next harvest.

- Supporting jobs and maintaining economic activity in the face of a global recession. GVCs are an important source of employment and income, including for the poor.

Trade policies are an essential instrument for managing a global crisis. Trade policy reforms, such as tariff reductions, contribute to

- Reducing the cost and improving the availability of essential goods and services, such as medical equipment, pharmaceuticals, and food;

- Reducing the tax and administrative burdens on importers and exporters;

- Reducing the cost of products heavily consumed by the poor, who are typically hit hardest by a global crisis and economic downturn; and

- Supporting the eventual economic recovery and building resilience through greater diversification of imports and exports.

Measures to streamline trade procedures and facilitate trade at borders can contribute to the response to a crisis by expediting the movement, release, and clearance of goods, including goods in transit, and enabling the exchange of services. During the pandemic, for example, reforms were designed to reduce the need for close contact between traders, transporters, and border officials so as to protect stakeholders and limit the spread of the virus, while maintaining essential assessments to ensure revenue, health, and security. Interventions to sustain and enhance the efficiency of logistics operations can also be critical in avoiding substantial disruption to distribution networks and hence to regional and global value chains.

Experience from previous global and food crises that provided guidance for dealing with the COVID-19 pandemic will be equally relevant for future shocks and crises. Box 6.1 documents a large number of positive measures that governments could take

---

BOX 6.1 Dos and don'ts of trade policy responses to a global crisis: The COVID-19 pandemic

Do facilitate access to essential medical goods and supplies:
- Reduce to zero import tariffs on COVID-19-related medical goods.
- Exempt from value added tax imports of COVID-19-related medical services and goods.
- Waive withholding taxes (advance income taxes) on imports of COVID-19-related goods.
- Commit to refrain from imposing export bans or taxes on COVID-19-related medical goods or services.

Do support consumption of essential items and limit negative impacts on the poorest:
- Reduce to zero import tariffs on all food products.
- Waive withholding taxes on imports of food products for the duration of the crisis, because enhancing the nutritional intake of the poor will boost immune systems and strengthen their ability to resist the virus.
- Refrain from imposing export bans or taxes on critical food staples.

Do support exporters to maintain jobs and foreign exchange earnings:
- Remove all bans, quantitative restrictions, and taxes on exports.
- Waive withholding taxes on exports.
- Review all export applications, licenses, and permits; and remove those that are not required to maintain market access or to protect health, safety, and security.
- Reimburse exporters that have lost overseas sales for the value added tax paid on inputs in the expectation that it would be refunded on export for the duration of the crisis.

Box continues next page

BOX 6.1 Dos and don'ts of trade policy responses to a global crisis: The COVID-19 pandemic (*continued*)

Do contribute to macroeconomic policy efforts to shield the economy from COVID-related downturn:
- Reduce to zero import tariffs on all goods, and streamline regulations affecting trade in services.
- Waive withholding taxes on imports of all goods and services.
- Allow importers to defer value added tax payments for an initial period of 12 weeks.

Do streamline regulatory and border procedures:
- Remove the need for applications, permits, and licenses for products that pose minimal risk to human health, environmental safety, or consumer protection; streamline the procedures for those that are required, using web-based or automated options for requesting and obtaining documents; prioritize the issuance and regulatory approval of imports of all COVID-19-related medical goods, essential food items, and perishables; and suspend fees and charges associated with the issuance of any licenses, permits, and certificates required for these products.
- Recognize certificates or systems of conformity for medical equipment, essential food items, and farming inputs from accredited agencies in countries with similar or higher standards.
- Implement risk management to allow low-risk critical supplies to pass clearance controls quickly.
- Enhance border management coordination mechanisms, both at the policy level (such as the National Committee on Trade Facilitation) and at the operational level (ports, airports, and border posts); and support increased internal and external collaboration between border agencies—for example, customs and agencies responsible for sanitary and phytosanitary standards should work together to design special regimes for expedited clearance of essential medical goods, food products, and farming inputs.
- Improve business continuity through greater use of information and communication technology, flexible working schedules, longer border opening hours, and expanded access to telephone and online enquiry points, all of which can improve efficiency and limit the physical presence and interaction of logistics workers and officials at facilities and border crossing points.
- Support cooperative arrangements among small-scale cross-border traders to organize their supply chains, reduce the movement and interaction of people, but enable business continuity, particularly in cases where borders are closed to the movement of people.

Do not constrain investment in and access to essential COVID-19-related medical goods and supplies by imposing export taxes or bans on them, the materials used to produce them, or agricultural products. Indeed, commitments from policy makers to keep markets open for these essential products would create greater certainty and help to avoid large price swings.

Do not undermine consumption of essential goods or constrain job-maintaining exports by arbitrarily closing borders. Work with neighbors to implement containment measures, including distancing, while allowing commerce to flow as much as possible.

Do not impose additional trade restrictions to protect domestic industries that may be adversely affected by falling demand. Other measures of support for temporarily affected sectors will be more effective in maintaining output and less damaging to the economy and to the poor.

to ameliorate the impact of the COVID-19 crisis and a relatively smaller number of measures that they should avoid because experience shows they would only worsen outcomes.

Many of the positive measures in box 6.1 involve a short-term fiscal loss to the government; international institutions, such as the World Bank, can support low- and middle-income countries through global crises by providing concessional financing with instruments including development policy loans.[1] Trust funds and other resources could be used to assist countries in reengineering border cross- ings to allow continued operation, effective protection of staff, and maximum con- tainment. The international community can also support the provision of policy advice on how to design effective trade measures to address the crisis and support the economic recovery. During the COVID-19 pandemic, the World Bank and other institutions collected high-frequency data to monitor impacts of the crisis on trade flows and prices to inform policy responses. This essential activity will be required in all future global shocks as well as region-specific extreme weather events.

Reviewing trade policies for better management of future shocks

Risk and uncertainty related to trade are inherent in a world in which future global and regional shocks are inevitable. There is good reason to believe that such shocks will become more prevalent in the coming decades. COVID-19 is unlikely to be the last global health pandemic that the world will see. There is much discussion on what can be done to reduce the likelihood of future outbreaks, including limiting deforestation, closing wet animal markets, and investing more in health research. Nevertheless, the scientific evidence suggests, "It is almost certain that we will see more and more disease outbreaks caused by bat viruses," for example; these risks relate not just to zoonotic spillover to humans but also to livestock (Wang and Anderson 2019, 79).

It is also becoming increasingly apparent that extreme weather events related to climate change are affecting GVCs and that this risk will intensify as global average temperatures continue to rise. Events such as storms, flooding, and droughts are becoming both more frequent and more intense, affecting production, infrastructure, and transport. In addition, extreme events such as plagues of locusts, which are related to the changing weather, are becoming more prevalent.[2] GVCs will face even greater challenges when, as is probable, these types of extreme events occur simultaneously and firms have to deal with a pandemic at the same time as an extreme weather event. Such a situation arose in eastern Africa, which had to deal simultaneously with both COVID-19 and a locust infestation. Attempts to mitigate climate change and meet obligations under the Paris Agreement are leading some countries to formulate domes- tic carbon regulations with accompanying carbon border adjustment mechanisms that will affect trade. An increase in trade tensions and weakening of the influence of the World Trade Organization (WTO) as the custodian of an open global trading regime are exacerbating policy uncertainty.

Avoiding export restrictions

One of the biggest international policy challenges in the COVID-19 crisis has been how to avoid having countries with production capacity in medical products and vaccines apply export restrictions that limit the access of other countries to these essential products. There has also been concern over the application of export restrictions to essential food products. This concern echoes the experience of previous crises, in which producing nations resorted too easily to limiting exports of food at the expense of consumers around the world. Without some form of international agreement, this issue will recur in future crises, despite the clear consensus among economists that export restrictions and precautionary purchases of essential goods by a small number of key countries can lead to rapid rises in global prices and severe shortages in other countries. Hence, greater coordination and stronger discipline are needed on the use of such measures.

Early in the pandemic, it became apparent that the production and export of critical COVID-19 products[3] were highly concentrated (Espitia, Rocha, and Ruta 2020). This concentration is of particular importance for low- and middle-income countries, because most are dependent on imports of these products. Many countries imposed restrictions on exports of certain medical goods and some foodstuffs. Between January and August 2020, at least 67 countries imposed 152 measures to restrict exports of medical goods, including personal protection equipment and sanitation products, while 18 countries imposed 24 measures to limit exports of food (map 6.1).[4] These restrictions occurred at the same time that other countries, including many low- and middle-income countries, were reducing their import barriers on these products to improve access.

Economic analysis over a long period of experience with export restraints shows their detrimental impact:

- Export restrictions, particularly when imposed by large producers, have effects throughout the global economy, limiting overall supply and increasing the volatility of supply and prices. They reduce the availability of the affected products and

MAP 6.1 Implementation status of COVID-19-related export curbs in the medical sector

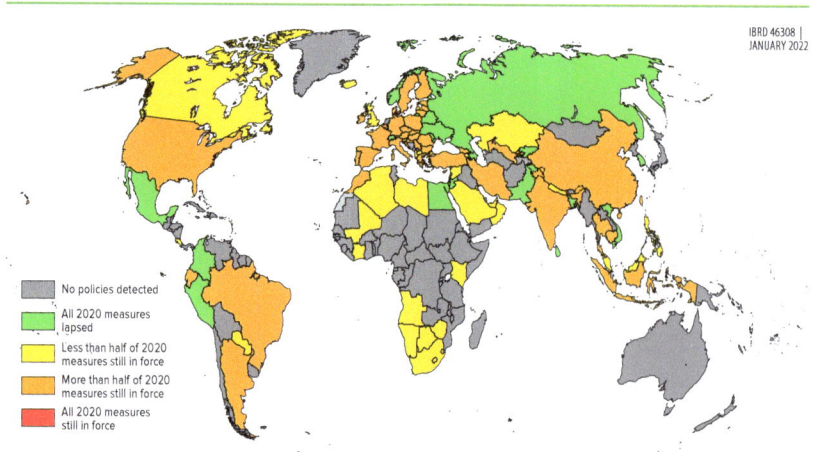

Source: Global Trade Alert.

create price instability in countries that are least able to bear the costs—that is, low-income countries with substantial levels of poverty and weak capacity to increase production when export restrictions in producing countries curtail access through the global market.

- Limits on exports may result in lower domestic prices and increased domestic supply of critical medical and food products in the short run, but such measures reduce the incentives to invest in such activities and can reduce supply in the long run not only globally but also in the countries imposing the restrictions.

- Export restrictions can lead to retaliatory measures that further disrupt global markets and exacerbate problems for low-income countries in accessing essential supplies.

- Export restrictions and countermeasures disrupt global supply chains, create uncertainty, and may even limit access to critical inputs that the country imposing restrictions requires for production.

Models of global food demand and supply, for example, reinforce these conclusions. On the one hand, declines in local production of food in most countries have limited effects on global prices and supply. On the other hand, export restrictions and precautionary purchases by a few large producing countries create rapid increases in global food prices and severe local food shortages. For example, if three major grain-exporting countries imposed complete export bans, the price of wheat could rise by as much as 70 percent, while the price of maize and rice could increase by 40 percent and 60 percent, respectively (Falkendal et al. 2021). Many low- and middle-income countries would not be able to address this disruption to global grain markets through their domestic reserves. Hence, open trade policies are the best approach to ensuring global food security.

In the early months of 2021, this issue came firmly to the fore in the context of COVID-19 vaccines. Vaccine production is concentrated in 13 producing nations, but these countries source almost 90 percent of the key vaccine ingredients from other members of this vaccine-producing "club" (Evenett et al. 2021). These cross-border vaccine value chains impose a degree of discipline on members of the club, with the threat of retaliation discouraging them from imposing export restrictions that affect other members. However, countries that are not part of this vaccine club, especially small and poor countries, have no leverage to prevent such restrictions. Although no explicit export restrictions have been imposed on vaccines, countries in the vaccine club have signed advance purchase agreements for large amounts of vaccines. The effect of some of these contracts likely has been to restrict exports. There also have been signs of less overt but equally restrictive measures, such as delays on foreign shipments.

Countries and the international community can take steps to protect low-income countries in future crises from the use of export restrictions that limit access to critical products, including medical goods, vaccines, food, and other essential products such as seeds and fertilizers, rare earth elements, semiconductors, and steel.

Increase information, transparency, and monitoring

To an extent, policy makers resort to export restrictions based on the perceived risks and fears of domestic shortages during a crisis. They may also be influenced by well-connected domestic actors who will benefit from export restrictions, such as food processors seeking to make larger profits when the domestic prices of basic food products decline. The decisions by policy makers are, in turn, influenced by data and information that can shed light on the extent of these risks and the capacity to mitigate them both domestically and through coordination with other countries. Market instability, reflected in substantial price volatility, can be intensified by lack of accurate and timely information on international supply and demand. Better information on global markets and more transparency can help to avoid panic-driven policy measures and contribute to more informed and coordinated responses that avoid price surges.

Information on global stocks of food, for example, is crucial in informing policy makers of the risks of impending food shortages. Indeed, lack of reliable data on stocks of grains and oilseeds and deficiencies in the monitoring of food prices contributed to export restrictions that destabilized global food markets during the global financial crisis of 2008–09. Subsequent investments by the G-20 (Group of Twenty) countries in food information systems improved the quality of information available to policy makers and may have tempered the use of export restrictions on food during the COVID-19 pandemic.

In particular, an agricultural market information system (AMIS) was created in 2011 under which (a) G-20 governments would instruct their statistical and other relevant agencies to provide timely and accurate data on food production, consumption, and stocks and to invest in necessary mechanisms and institutions if they did not exist; (b) international organizations would enhance global food security by monitoring, reporting, and analyzing market conditions and policies and by introducing a global early warning system; (c) a rapid response forum would be formed to promote policy coherence and coordination during crisis periods; and (d) international organizations would support the improvement of national or regional monitoring systems in vulnerable low- and middle-income countries and regions (Sharma 2011).

Throughout the COVID-19 crisis, the AMIS regularly provided timely information on food stocks and production levels, contributing to greater awareness and dialogue between countries. Despite the imposition of measures on food early in the crisis, many of which were subsequently removed, overall countries adopted "a restrained and reasonable approach to trade restrictions on food during the crisis" (Torero and Javorcik 2020). Support for additional investments in food monitoring systems in low-income regions such as Sub-Saharan Africa could further enhance regional and global food security.

The experience with critical medical supplies and now vaccines has shown how lack of credible information sharing between governments, manufacturers, and their suppliers can lead governments and officials to make panic-driven decisions that have adverse consequences for trade and for the global response to the pandemic. For example, better information on available vaccine production capacity throughout the world would have facilitated matches between vaccine developers, potential vaccine producers, and funding agencies (Evenett et al. 2021). Similarly, for essential protective medical equipment, there appears to have been little effective information on global stocks and production capacities and little sharing of information as production facilities were repurposed for the production of sanitizers, masks, and other protective equipment, for example.

Information sharing needs to be backed up by effective monitoring of policy responses by governments. In situations where the government needs to implement emergency business closures, the definition of an "essential business" that can stay open is key. In 2020 some governments implemented a "positive list" approach, identifying businesses that were allowed to operate. A common mistake is that the providers of goods, services, and inputs necessary to keep essential businesses open are not listed as essential, so essential businesses may end up closing and waivers may be issued in a haphazard way (for example, in Malaysia). A more efficient approach is to compile a "negative list" in which the government identifies those businesses that must close, ideally consulting with key lead firms that are expected to map and identify their network of suppliers (for example, in Singapore). As the situation in Malaysia developed, private sector efforts at mapping their own supply chains aided government in identifying which firms needed to be open for business. This was particularly important for tier 2 and tier 3 suppliers that otherwise would have escaped the notice of policy makers.

Increase cooperation on trade issues that are critical for health and food security

Although better information and effective monitoring are important steps in underpinning confidence, effective coordination is necessary. In an open trade regime in essential products and with geographically concentrated production, the perceived risk that producing countries will restrict exports in times of crisis may be sufficient to dissuade importing countries from fully liberalizing tariffs on such products. In fact, the use of export restrictions by a small number of countries has encouraged some observers to decry trade, arguing against making temporary tariff cuts permanent and for imposing higher tariff protection in the future to develop what would be more costly domestic capacities for production. Export restrictions undermine the incentives of importing countries to liberalize. This situation, in turn, limits the market and therefore investment and employment in firms in large producing countries. Ideally, an agreement among producing countries not to use export restrictions in return for tariff liberalization in importing countries would reduce policy uncertainty and lower the risks associated with global markets in essential products.

Some countries have taken steps to deepen cooperation within existing regional agreements. New Zealand and Singapore, for example, committed to remove customs duties and to refrain from imposing export restrictions on 124 essential goods, including food and health care products.[5] In April 2020, 22 WTO members[6] committed "not to impose agriculture export restrictions" and agreed that "emergency measures related to agriculture and agri-food products designed to tackle COVID-19 must be targeted, proportionate, transparent, and temporary." They also committed to "engage in a dialogue to improve our preparedness and responsiveness to regional or international pandemics, including multilateral coordination to limit unjustified agriculture export restrictions, in particular at the WTO."[7]

Enforceable commitments at the global level may be required to ensure better responses to future crises than happened for medical products and vaccines in the COVID-19 crisis, given the small number of producing countries and the large number of importing countries. Although not banning export restrictions outright, which some major producing countries perceived to be unacceptable, proposals have been made to enhance discipline on the use of export restrictions (Evenett and Winters 2020):

- All countries would eliminate tariffs on an agreed list of essential goods and remove all export limits on these goods.

- Export limits may be introduced if (a) the triggering event and a clear rationale for the change is provided; (b) the products covered and the extent of the limit are consistent with tackling the triggering event; (c) in the first instance, the export limit is in place for no longer than six months (renewable for up to a further six months subject to notification and a clear rationale); and (d) the limit is publicly stated as a percentage reduction in exports from a customary value that would not exceed 50 percent.

These principles could also be applied to other essential goods.

Enhancing the resilience of global supply chains

Low rates of trade flow survival, already an important challenge for low-income countries, were exacerbated during the crisis. The analysis in chapter 3 shows that, although much of global trade remained resilient through the crisis, with adjustments taking place through reductions in volume rather than reductions in the number of trade flows, the trade flows of low-income countries were hit hard, with a substantial decline in firm survival rates.

Although there is evidence that some multinational firms provided assistance to their suppliers during the pandemic, in certain sectors of particular importance to low-income countries, such as apparel, exporters experienced strong negative impacts. Major apparel brands and retailers based in the European Union (EU) and the United States canceled or postponed orders, including orders for products already produced by suppliers in low- and middle-income countries. Because brands typically do not pay for products until after they are shipped, when orders are put on hold or canceled, so are payments. Canceled orders thus left firms in clothing-producing low- and middle-income countries, such as Bangladesh, Myanmar, and Vietnam, without revenue and unable to pay the wages of their workers. The closing of factories pushed already precarious workers toward more economic vulnerability.

Despite these vulnerabilities, a retrenchment from trade by low-income countries would likely reduce, not increase, their resilience to future shocks. Within an economy, exporting firms tend to be larger than nonexporting firms, and firm size is important in weathering shocks. Over time, trade is associated with declining informal employment, even if the evidence is mixed in the short term, with impacts being determined by the nature of trade reforms and underlying institutions and economic policy activities. Economies with higher rates of informality tend to be locked into the lowest-value-added activities, which increases their vulnerability to shocks. Hence, the challenge is to increase trade integration while addressing the factors that increase the vulnerability of low-income countries to global shocks.

Addressing information failures can help trade to become more resilient. Larger firms and larger trade flows tend to survive longer. One of the challenges for low-income countries is that their trade flows tend to start small and are therefore more vulnerable. Lack of information and uncertainty are one factor: buyers in high-income countries are likely to start with small transactions while they obtain an understanding of the suppliers' capacities. Similarly, firms in low- and middle-income countries are unlikely to invest significantly in large-scale export volumes if they lack information about the buyer. Increasing information can ensure better matches between firms in low- and middle-income countries and buyers and suppliers overseas and allow transactions to occur at a larger scale.

Information challenges are more acute when contracts are poorly specified and contract enforcement is weak. In a weak institutional environment, some buyers with little concern for the future behave opportunistically and default. Forward-looking distributors, in contrast, try to build a reputation over time. Export flows start small but increase over time as the exporter develops a better understanding of the trustworthi-ness of the buyer and the likelihood that the firm will default on the contract in the future. Therefore, the probability of exit from exporting declines, the longer the part-nership continues. Strengthening the institutions for contract enforcement can reduce uncertainty and increase the expected return of the exporter, with a direct and positive effect on exports. Development partners can contribute by promoting corporate social responsibility among buyers and lead firms in GVCs and increasing awareness among exporters in low- and middle-income countries about buyers in high-income countries that are implementing such commitments and honoring contracts during periods of crisis.

Information costs may be lower and contract enforcement easier in nearby mar-kets with similar legal systems and institutions. Such information is also likely to be easier to obtain, the greater the presence of other exporters to the particular overseas market and the greater the overall experience in exporting the specific product. Pasquali and Godfrey (2020) find initial evidence from the apparel sector in Eswatini that regional production networks connecting buyers and suppliers in low- and middle-income countries were more robust following the COVID-19 shock than GVCs governed by buyers based in Europe and the United States. In particular, smaller indirect suppliers with arm's length relationships with design houses were hit harder than direct suppliers to South African retailers.

Access to trade finance is another factor that impinges heavily on the ability of small firms in low- and middle-income countries to enter and survive exporting activi-ties. The evidence suggests that improving access to trade finance is associated not only with higher exports but also with job creation in export sectors. Even in periods of normality, there is an enormous shortfall between the demand for and the supply of trade finance, which is exacerbated during a global crisis.[8] This shortfall especially affects small firms, which report that the main cause of rejection is the inability to meet the standard requirements of the financial institution, such as collateral, necessary documentation, and valid company records. In low- and middle-income countries, these issues create particular challenges for women-led firms.

The costs and availability of trade finance are likely to become more restrictive, especially for firms in low- and middle-income countries. This restriction will make trade riskier in the coming years because of rising uncertainty over shocks related to climate change and increasing doubts about the commitment of major countries to an open global trading regime. Together with the increased regulatory requirements fol-lowing the global financial crisis of 2008–09, these factors are likely to increase compli-ance costs further. A key issue then is what governments in low- and middle-income countries and development institutions should do to address this important constraint on exports in general and on the resilience of smaller exporting firms during a crisis. Strengthening the domestic financial sector, improving firms' knowledge of bank requirements and the capacity to satisfy them, and enhancing the availability of credit information are among the main measures that have been proposed traditionally. However, new financial technology (fintech) is offering an opportunity to support innovative, nonbank solutions based on paperless transactions, online management of trade documents, and use of distributed ledger technology (blockchain).

Low- and middle-income countries would also benefit from understanding where their critical inputs are being sourced and what the vulnerabilities are in the main des-tinations for their exported outputs. Just as large firms in high-income countries are increasingly investing in supply chain mapping to understand vulnerabilities to shocks, exporters and importers in low- and middle-income countries could be supported to do the same. This mapping could contribute to a dialogue with policy makers on identifying weak network links and how they might be addressed—for example, through investments in trade facilitation and trade logistics as well as policy reforms that promote greater diversification of input sources and export markets. Nontariff barriers, especially those related to standards, testing, inspection, and certification, are likely to be of particular importance.

Governments could develop stress tests for specific supply chains that are critical for their country, akin to those developed for financial institutions after the 2008–09 crisis (Simchi-Levi and Simchi-Levi 2020). These tests could inform the need for policies such as those related to the creation of strategic stockpiles and buffer stocks to prevent shortages in the future; investments in and policies regarding the capacity and use of warehousing (customs control, value added tax); approaches to the provision of private insurance for firms and workers; and the nature of employment protection and social safety nets.

Could analysis of trade flows from a network perspective contribute to these discussions? Efforts to analyze trade flow data to identify and rank the fragility of individual traded goods and a country's overall vulnerability offer a promising avenue. Initial efforts faced some data challenges—in particular, with regard to identifying the availability of close substitutes for products traded internationally (Korniyenko, Pinat, and Dew 2017). There is little consensus on the values of estimated elasticities of substitution, and simple proxies, such as the distribution of human capital across exporting countries, may not be representative, especially for low- and middle-income countries. Further refinement of this approach is required.

Trade and development in a more uncertain world

Responses to reshoring in rich countries

As the analysis in chapter 5 shows, low- and middle-income countries are more resilient to shocks when they participate in GVCs, reducing their own trade costs through trade facilitation and lowering duties on intermediate inputs. If the world's larger trading nations choose to use strategic trade policy and subsidies to pursue reshoring and near-shoring, there is no advantage for low- and middle-income countries to play the same game. A reshoring of production by the leading economies and China would have a noticeably negative impact in most regions, particularly in developing regions, leaving them more vulnerable. Global income and trade would contract substantially, pushing millions of people into poverty. To counter this sharp negative impact on regions that are highly dependent on and integrated in GVCs, countries may be tempted to respond in kind by pursuing their own reshoring policies. However, as the analysis indicates, having all economies reshore would compound the damage, and developing regions would be the most negatively affected.

Closer integration in the global economy would pay dividends for low- and middle-income countries. Eliminating input tariffs and implementing trade facilitation measures would strengthen the integration of low- and middle-income countries in regional and global value chains and make them more resilient to supply chain shocks. The gains would be evident in all developing regions. In other words, GVC-friendly policies could reverse the real income losses inflicted by the reshoring efforts of the leading economies. A GVC-friendly environment would boost resilience to future supply shocks, widening access to raw materials, goods, and services.

In fact, high-income economies are also likely to be more resilient when they lower trade costs and participate in GVCs. But because such countries can afford subsidy schemes and, if large enough, may have some influence on global prices, they are more likely to be tempted to engage in strategic trade policy. Subsidy schemes large enough to make a difference in global markets are likely to be out of the range of most low- and middle-income countries.

Technology, e-commerce, and home working

New technologies provided much resilience during pandemic-related shutdowns. The share of people working from home rose markedly. The share of e-commerce in retailing increased. Firms that had implemented flexible automation were able to monitor factories from a distance and adapt more quickly to requirements for less onsite labor. Information technology services were among the few categories of services trade that expanded, rather than contracted, during 2020.

The events related to COVID-19 highlighted more than ever the need to foster healthy ecosystems for the digital economy in low- and middle-income countries. The methods by which this ecosystem can be fostered are clear and remain the same as before 2020:[9]

- Expand the availability of broadband internet at affordable prices.
- Install workable payments systems for online transactions.
- Expand digital skills both for online entrepreneurs and for workers who may work remotely.
- Improve logistics for the small parcels used in e-commerce, including postal services.
- Ensure that regulatory systems can address digital transactions, data protection and privacy, consumer protection, and cybercrime in a manner that does not put excess burdens on cross-border transactions.
- Provide financing for digital entrepreneurs.

The digital economy does not stand by itself; rather, it is intertwined with the rest of the economy. For example, information technology outsourcing or business process outsourcing could fail in a crisis because of a lack of electricity, lack of internet connectivity, or restrictions on the movement of people. This failure could escalate quickly into the failure of government or major manufacturers to meet payroll or the loss of key government or business records. Thus, planning for emergencies should seek to ensure the continuity of modern business processes.

Trade strategies for low- and middle-income countries in a world with more frequent shocks and greater risks

Trade will be more important in a world of greater volatility, which requires greater stability and certainty of trade policy. For example, restrictions on trade undermine disaster response and recovery and limit the ability of affected firms to reengage with GVCs. When increasing trade barriers intertwine with disasters such as flooding, overall economic losses increase. Numerical modeling shows that, whereas all regions suffer from export restrictions, regions that depend more on regional trade are more vulnerable to export restrictions if they are hit by an extreme weather event (for example, see World Bank 2021). Specialization that leads to the concentration of key sectors in particular regions and limits the possibilities for substitution raises the vulnerability of the economic network to such risks. Export restrictions imposed on highly specialized and strategic sectors can trigger devastating impacts on the global economy in the aftermath of extreme weather events. The operation of trade value chains is an essential element of resilience to disasters and the recovery. Trade becomes more important, not less, with climate change. Hence, there is a need for investments in climate-resilient transport and logistics infrastructure; continuing efforts to streamline border procedures to minimize delays in accessing inputs, machinery, and exports during a crisis; and further steps to reduce tariff and nontariff barriers to facilitate access to new technologies that strengthen climate resilience.

A riskier environment for trade puts even more emphasis on the need for export diversification, especially in low-income countries. Export diversification has long been advocated as a policy objective to reduce vulnerability to sector-specific shocks and to drive economic diversification. It is becoming increasingly apparent that diversification of imports is also important. But diversification is not just about more products; rather, it is about contributing to economic transformation more broadly and moving from lower- to higher-productivity activities by shifting into manufacturing, services, and also high-value agriculture. Hence, trade diversification should be seen as comprising (a) the export (and import) of new products (goods or services), (b) the export (and import) of existing products to new markets, and (c) the quality upgrading of exported (and imported) products. Are the opportunities for trade diversification radically different in a post-COVID-19 world?

Export diversification is driven by the entry of new firms into exporting and into new markets, but survival often is the main challenge. Recent analyses find that, rather than initiating new trade flows, sustaining new exports is particularly difficult for low-income countries (see, for example, Besedeš and Prusa 2006; Brenton, Saborowski, and von Uexkull 2009; Cadot et al. 2013). The experience of low-income countries during the pandemic confirms this view. As discussed here, issues relating to the information and market knowledge needed for successful entry into exporting are likely to be important in explaining high exit rates. Improved access to imported inputs may also contribute to stronger export survival rates (Boehe, Campos, and Menezes-Filho 2019).

The shift of China away from labor-intensive segments of manufacturing is providing new, but uncertain, opportunities for low-income countries to diversify into manufactured exports. China's relative decline in the global market for products such as apparel and footwear is, in principle, leaving room for low-income countries to increase their manufactured exports.[10] Much of the space left by China has been taken by exports from countries in South and East Asia, with some signs of a shift to Africa, where countries such as Ethiopia are developing export capacities in these sectors. Nevertheless, the durability of some of the shift to low-income countries in East Asia may be uncertain because of the coup in Myanmar and political issues in Cambodia. In addition, low-income countries in the region together with Bangladesh are moving toward graduating from low-income-country status, which will entail loss of preferential access, especially to the EU market. A further development is the recently ratified EU-Vietnam Free Trade Agreement, which will remove virtually all customs duties between the two parties over the next 10 years.

The opportunities generated in labor-intensive segments of manufacturing are unlikely to be eroded quickly by robots and automation. Among manufacturing sectors, apparel and footwear are the most resistant to the use of robotics and advanced automation. Operations such as sewing depend on the detailed movements of the human hand, which are difficult at present for robots to replicate, making human labor competitive (Hallward-Driemeier and Nayyar 2017). Automation so far has been restricted to high-end operations such as embroidery rather than assembly. However, the future of automation is uncertain, and breakthroughs applicable to these sectors may emerge.

At the same time, capturing these opportunities will require a focus on the business climate and general competitiveness. Apparel and footwear are among the most footloose of manufacturing sectors, moving easily from country to country in response to small differences in wages, business conditions, or market access arising from preferential trade agreements. Global middlemen in these sectors, operating on behalf of lead firms, are quick to respond to changes in incentives. Thus, the gains from any medium-run geographic pivot will not accrue equally to all countries with an abundant supply of less-skilled labor; rather they will accrue to countries with a strong climate for business and investment generally.

There is increasing emphasis in higher-income markets on the labor and environmental standards of trading partners. The EU, for example, has introduced the Generalized System of Preferences Plus (GSP+) scheme whereby GSP beneficiaries can receive enhanced zero tariff preferences subject to the implementation of 27 international conventions related to human rights, labor rights, protection of the environment, and good governance. Several countries in Asia that export products such as apparel and footwear, including Pakistan, the Philippines, and Sri Lanka, are current beneficiaries of this scheme. Bangladesh, for example, has recognized the importance of gaining access to the GSP+ scheme for its export-oriented ready-made garments sector and is planning to satisfy the requirements of the scheme following graduation from the category of least developed country. Other low-income countries seeking to develop exports in these sectors would do well to design and implement policies that will support compliance with international human and labor rights and environmental standards. There also is increased emphasis on compliance and the capacity of the domestic regulatory structure to monitor and address violations of these conventions. This effort, in turn, may reduce the risks to workers in these countries from participation in GVCs if it encourages upgrading in GVCs. This issue requires further empirical analysis.[11]

A further source of uncertainty is whether the COVID-19 pandemic will lead to shifts in consumer demand that have long-term implications for trade. Prior to COVID-19, relatively stagnant consumer demand in Europe and North America had led to some shift of GVCs toward supplying new markets in emerging economies and the regionalization of what were previously global supply chains. Global firms interviewed as part of this research said that they expect China to be a major growth market in the future and FDI and trade to continue to be attracted to China. But will the growth of Chinese demand drive exports of manufactured exports from low-income countries? The answer will depend on policies toward manufacturing in China and the extent to which they seek to support domestic manufacturing production relative to the transition to higher technology- and services-related activities that would normally be expected as incomes rise and development continues.

At the same time, COVID-19 may lead to long-lasting impacts on aggregate consumer demand in Europe and especially the United States, if (a) consumption shifts toward older and richer groups as a result of the ongoing rise in the share of population over 65 and a bigger hit and slower postpandemic recovery for low-income groups; (b) changes in consumer behavior during the pandemic (to an extent related to the first point) persist, including the increase in e-commerce and the shift toward "home nesting" (that is, the increase in demand for products that result from spending more time in the home for both work and leisure); and (c) the accumulated savings that have been built up are spent (McKinsey Global Institute 2021). These changes may materialize, for example, in the form of lower spending in the long run on office wear.

Nevertheless, there is nothing to suggest that the essential policy frameworks required to support effective trade diversification and to reduce risks from trade have changed. There is no magic recipe for diversification. Investments in skills, infrastructure, institutions, and quality of governance (that is, enhancing the transparency, accountability, and predictability of government decision-making) increase the likelihood that diversification will succeed. In addition to these essential horizontal investments (see, for example, Salinas 2020; World Bank 2017), the following actions support trade diversification:

- *Appropriate trade policies to remove bias against exporting, ensure access to imported inputs and technology, and promote effective competition* in product markets and in key backbone services such as transportation, energy, and communications.

- *Investments and policy reforms to lower trade costs and improve connectivity,* because declining trade costs and efficient trade logistics are at the heart of integration of low-income countries into the global economy.

- *Effective policies to support adjustment and the reallocation of resources to new activities*—from declining sectors but also from the informal sector and new entrants to the job market.

- *Government interventions targeting specific market, policy, and institutional failures.* Once these priorities are in place, governments can seek to identify shortcomings in the marketplace and tailor interventions to target those problems.

Notes

1. For example, in Sub-Saharan Africa alone, the World Bank delivered 27 development policy operations in 23 countries amounting to US$3.6 billion between October 2019 and the end of February 2021. Some of these operations included measures related to the taxation of imports of medical products and food and measures to facilitate trade in such goods.

2. Rising temperatures and changing patterns of precipitation will also affect countries' endowments, with consequences for the structure of global production and the location of activity within GVCs.

3. These products included essential items for diagnosis and treatment processes, such as enzymes; hygiene products, such as liquid soap and hand sanitizers; personal protection equipment, including gloves and medical masks; and case management products, such as oxygen, concentrators, and respirators.

4. See Congressional Research Service, https://crsreports.congress.gov/product/pdf/IF/IF11551.

5. Declaration on Trade in Essential Goods for Combating the COVID-19 Pandemic, April 15, 2020, https://www.beehive.govt.nz/release/covid-19-response-new-zealand-and -singapore-launch-initiative-ensure-free-flow-essential.

6. These economies included Australia; Brazil; Canada; Chile; Colombia; Costa Rica; the European Union; Hong Kong SAR, China; Japan; the Republic of Korea; Malawi; Mexico; New Zealand; Paraguay; Peru; Qatar; Singapore; Switzerland; Taiwan, China; Ukraine; Uruguay; and the United States.

7. Declaration on Trade in Essential Goods for Combating the COVID-19 Pandemic.

8. ADB (2016) estimates that the global trade finance gap in 2015 was US$1.6 trillion relative to the global market for trade finance of between US$6.5 trillion and US$8 trillion.

9. See https://etrade4all.org for further resources on this topic.

10. This opportunity may be accelerated by the sourcing decisions of global brands related to the issue of cotton from the Xinjiang region of China.

11. Upgrading at the firm and sector levels is seen to be associated with reducing the risks to workers in those firms or sectors (Gereffi and Luo 2015).

References

ADB (Asian Development Bank). 2016. "2016 Trade Finance Gaps, Growth, and Jobs Survey." ADB Brief 64, Asian Development Bank, Metro Manila.

Besedeš, Tibor, and Thomas J. Prusa. 2006. "Ins, Outs, and the Duration of Trade." *Canadian Journal of Economics* 39 (1): 266–95.

Boehe, Dirk, Camila F. S. Campos, and Naercio Menezes-Filho. 2019. "Imports and the Survival of New Exporters in Colombia." INSPER Working Paper WPE: 386/2019, INSPER, São Paulo.

Brenton, Paul, Christian Saborowski, and Erik von Uexkull. 2009. "What Explains the Low Survival Rate of Developing Country Export Flows?" *The World Bank Economic Review* 24 (3): 474–99.

Cadot, Olivier, Leonardo Iacovone, Martha Pierola, and Ferdinand Rauch. 2013. "Success and Failure of African Exporters." *Journal of Development Economics* 101 (March): 284–96.

Espitia, Alvaro, Nadia Rocha, and Michele Ruta. 2020. "Trade in Critical COVID-19 Products." Trade and COVID-19 Guidance Note, World Bank, Washington, DC.

Evenett, Simon, and L. Alan Winters. 2020. "Preparing for a Second Wave of COVID-19: A Trade Bargain to Secure Supplies of Medical Goods." UKTPO Briefing Paper 40, UK Trade Policy Observatory, University of Sussex and Chatham House.

Evenett, Simon J., Bernard Hoekman, Nadia Rocha, and Michele Ruta. 2021. "The COVID-19 Vaccine Production Club: Will Value Chains Temper Nationalism?" Policy Research Working Paper 9565, World Bank, Washington, DC.

Falkendal, Theresa, Christian Otto, Jacob Schewe, Jonas Jägermeyr, Megan Konar, Matti Kummu, Ben Watkins, and Michael J. Puma. 2021. "Grain Export Restrictions during COVID-19 Risk Food Insecurity in Many Low- and Middle-Income Countries." *Nature Food* 2: 11–14.

Gereffi, Gary, and Xubei Luo. 2015. "Risks and Opportunities of Participation in Global Value Chains." *Journal of Banking and Financial Economics* 2 (4): 51–63.

Hallward-Driemeier, Mary, and Gaurav Nayyar. 2017. *Trouble in the Making? The Future of Manufacturing-Led Development.* Washington, DC: World Bank.

Korniyenko, Yevgeniya, Magali Pinat, and Brian Dew. 2017. "Assessing the Fragility of Global Trade: The Impact of Localized Supply Shocks Using Network Analysis." IMF Working Paper WP/17/30, International Monetary Fund, Washington, DC.

McKinsey Global Institute. 2021. "The Consumer Demand Recovery and Lasting Effects of COVID-19." McKinsey Global Institute, March 17, 2021. https://www.mckinsey.com /industries/consumer-packaged-goods/our-insights/the-consumer-demand-recovery-and -lasting-effects-of-covid-19.

Pasquali, Giovanni, and Shane Godfrey. 2020. "Apparel Regional Value Chains and COVID-19: Insights from Eswatini." Research Briefing, Global Development Institute, University of Manchester. https://hummedia.manchester.ac.uk/institutes/gdi/research /Research-Briefing-Eswatini-Regional-value-chains-Covid19.pdf.

Salinas, Gonzalo. 2020. "Proximity and Horizontal Policies: The Backbone of Export Diversification and Complexity." IMF Working Paper WP/21/64, International Monetary Fund, Washington, DC.

Sharma, Ramesh. 2011. "AMIS: Enhancing Market Transparency." AMIS Secretariat, Food and Agriculture Organization, Rome, November 2011. http://www.amis-outlook.org /fileadmin/user_upload/amis/docs/reports/Improving_global_governance_for_food _security.pdf.

Simchi-Levi, David, and Edith Simchi-Levi. 2020. "We Need a Stress Test for Critical Supply Chains." *Harvard Business Review,* April 28, 2020.

Torero, Máximo, and Beata Javorcik. 2020. "To Counter the COVID-19 Recession, We Need to Invest in Food Systems." *World Economic Forum* (blog), July 31, 2020. https://www .weforum.org/agenda/2020/07/how-we-can-build-more-resilient-and-sustainable -food-systems/.

Wang, Lin-Fa, and Danielle Anderson. 2019. "Viruses in Bats and Potential Spillover to Animals and Humans." *Current Opinion in Virology* 34 (February): 79–89.

World Bank. 2017. "Economic Diversification Guidance Note." World Bank, Washington, DC.

World Bank. 2021. *The Nexus between Trade and Climate Change: Impacts and Issues for Developing Countries.* Washington, DC: World Bank.